The Iconoclastic Mind

The Iconoclastic Mind

The Recombinant Process of Creativity and Innovation

Thom R. Nichols

Write My Wrongs, LLC, P.O. Box 80781 Lansing, MI 48908
United States
www.writemywrongsediting.com

ISBN: 978-1-956932-04-1

Dedication

To Cheryl, who makes it all possible

Contents

Preface

Albert Einstein claimed he never came upon any discovery through the rational process of thinking; rather, it was through his imagination. Richard Feynman claimed it was his curiosity that led to his success. This was true of Leonardo da Vinci and Steve Jobs as well. Jeff Bezos credits the ability to fail for the success of Amazon. Failure also loomed large in the success of Thomas Edison. Henry Ford understood the requirements of the customer were sometimes limited and would not necessarily lead to progress. Blockbuster Video appears to have believed the requirements of the customer would not change, and this may have led to its downfall. Nikola Tesla seemingly preferred to remain in the world of novelty while keeping usefulness at a future distance. For all his success, this may have been his greatest failing.

What those mentioned above—and others who will be discussed in this text—have in common is creativity, or in some cases, the lack thereof. The thing about creativity is it cannot be taught. It is not rote learning or formulary, not the methods learned in art schools, and not the exacting replications of the draftsman. Rather, it is the unleashing of the mind's potential, the generation of ideas and possibilities; it can be channeled, controlled, and exploited.

These same figures also share the idea of innovation, or the absence of it in the case of industries such as Blockbuster Video. Innovation is the methodologic application of creativity toward unarticulated needs. Innovation is a heavy hand building the new and tearing down the old as it evolves.

In the world of creativity and innovation, curiosity is essential. Daydreaming is not considered inattentiveness. Metaphors are a requisite for effective communication. Challenging the status quo is championed. Multiple perspectives are a necessity. Focus, the mantra of schoolteachers everywhere, can be a negative attribute. The non-consumer has greater potential than the current customer. Unlearning leads to learning. There is value in disparity. Inefficiency breeds opportunity. Crisis is a requirement for novelty. It is good to be abrasive and dissenting. Like minds can be a danger. Logic is confining, and can erringly define a problem. Discovery of the problem is more crucial than the discovery of the solution. The irrefutability of an unsolvable problem is not established by solutions not being known. Variance is to be embraced. Social and contextual factors are not to be forgotten.

What is also true of those mentioned above, and others to be discussed in this text, is the ability to network. This does not imply one must be engaged in actual one-on-one collaboration. While this does happen, networks are more often channels bringing the knowledge of others and potential for the exploitation of that knowledge. Networks allow for the bridging of distant worlds and the taking apart and reassembling of the ideas, a recombinant process so vital to the exploitation of creativity and innovation.

Innovation exploits the non-consumer of existing technologies, or more precisely, the reasons they are non-consumers of existing technology. In this, it is disruptive being the action and process of change. We see this in the art of Paul Cézanne, as well as the marketing strategies of Amazon.com. Fortune 500 companies can fail in the face of disruptive technologies, while others rise to the challenge and develop new skill sets. It can strike fear in the hearts of those who champion in-the-box thinking while providing hope, optimism, and wealth for those embracing it.

This is not a "how-to" book of creativity and innovation. In writing this text, it's not my intention to present the reader with step-by-step instructions, as I do not believe such things exist for these variables. This is, however, a book about iconoclastic people and the iconoclastic process involved with creativity and innovation that leads to the necessary changes that allow societies and industries to evolve. There are processes, methods, and philosophies to be learned and applied that move creativity and innovation forward. It's my intention to bring to the reader—the student of the potentials of creativity and innovation, whether they be an individual contributor, manager, active participant of teams, or just curious—the underlying and central themes to the creative and innovative processes, particularly how they have played out over the centuries, with an emphasis on the last two.

In the discussion of the innovative process, it will be made clear innovation is not an independent or spontaneous event, but an evolving, continuous process, sometimes disorganized, complex, and not always easily recognized. This text will present the concept, grounded in fact, that the innovative process is not a random series of unrelated events. Rather, it is a dynamic waiting, a sorting and ordering by time, with new ideas being pieced together from what is known and exploring what is not known. In this, it is a recombinant process requiring other perspectives linked in time to past events and discoveries, often with no apparent relevance or economic value.

While innovation is the pragmatic and visionary application of creativity, creativity is a function of the preparedness of the individual, or group, to respond to the appropriate insight or information. Creativity occurs when there is an interest in discovery, when there is motivation, and when there is a sense of exploration. Where creativity is about the generation of ideas, alternatives, and possibilities, innovation, on many levels, is the measurable construct of those factors.

In the discussion presented here, I will challenge those who champion traditional perspectives and the uniformity of perception. I will explain why predictable destinies are obstacles and why irrationality not only directs the world, but also evolves the world.

I will explain why those who lack knowledge can be as important a contributor to the innovative process as those with knowledge, as well as why language in the form of metaphor is as important as scientific or engineering skills.

The process of thinking is a central theme of this text. I will discuss how to look at problems, convergent as well as divergent thinking, slow thinking and fast thinking, and their contributions or lack thereof in problem-solving. It is understood algebraic formulary, or their analogs, will result in sufficient solutions, but iconoclastic solutions require considerably more. Iconoclastic solutions require multiple perspectives, and discoveries of why the problem exists and what a world would look like without it. I will discuss how to turn an issue inside out, and why its presentation may, in fact, be the reason innovative solutions are not found.

It's important in a text such as this to understand the historic process of innovation. To present this to the reader, I will step back in time to the early Greeks, to Galen and Vesalius, to Newton and Descartes, to the Renaissance, and to the discoveries of the eighteenth, nineteenth, and twentieth centuries. Chapters will be devoted to understanding the process of knowledge and networking, how inefficiency breeds opportunity, and how credit is not necessarily given to the discoverer, but rather to those who find the customer. Adding to this, we will explore the consumer and why knowledge of wants and needs without understanding the perspective of the customer or the value of a product to the customer's lifestyle can be a fatal flaw.

It must be said that I owe much of this book to those I have referenced within this text, to those who did the research and took the time to publish their efforts. To them, I am most grateful and say thank you. I have made every attempt to give credit where credit is due, and I urge the curious reader to review the references I have cited and read the original works by these authors. This will add immensely to the understanding of this text.

—Thom Nichols

Section 1: A Multiplicity of Perspective

Chapter 1: Mindscape, an Introduction

It is a myth that creativity and innovation are spontaneous events, that they are the serendipitous products of genius and the subconscious mind. Even regarding the works of Mozart [1], [2], to some, the product of genius is more the product of commission, meaning order on-demand. But such a statement says little of the creative quality of his work; that's something entirely different. What is true of Mozart, and for others of iconic stature, is creativity and innovation favor the prepared mind. To understand this, one must understand creativity and innovation are not formulated, but are rather adaptable and unprincipled forces derived from dissatisfaction and inefficiency. They do not exist in the averages, and both deny predictable destinies. So, it does not come as a revelation that a mind prepared for such is able to take advantage of this. But what does it mean to have a prepared mind?

When one gathers information from the world around them, it isn't necessarily of immediate use. Rather, it's more likely to be stored alongside past experiences and existing knowledge. But "stored" is perhaps a misnomer, as it presents the idea of static bins and dusty antiquities. Instead, the information becomes part of our internal dynamic mindscape, a landscape providing a probabilistic view of the future based upon a similar experience or repeatable sequence of past events. But can a future based upon similar experience or the repetition of past events be a landscape for creativity and innovation?

To answer this, we must contemplate, from a personal perspective, what a landscape of creativity and innovation looks like in our mind. How would we visualize it? If you, the reader, were to describe this as a landscape, how would you do it? Consider the knowledge, ideas, talents, and skills you have accumulated throughout your life. Would you describe your basis for creativity as mountains with peaks of insight and synthesis, and valleys where ideas erode and wash away? Or perhaps as a vast desert, little more than the status quo of maintaining what is without change but punctuated with verdant oases of learning and experiencing? Would your description be similar to that of another person, say a person from another culture?

Now, if mountains or deserts be the case, consider how these mountains with peaks and valleys or vast deserts punctuated with verdant oases were formed. Were they formed through the fixed and focused processes of repetition? Through formalized academic learning, visits to art galleries, or idle thoughts, daydreams, and the imagination that accompanies early morning walks through parks or city streets? Perhaps it's a combination of all of these, or maybe something entirely different.

No matter the answer, the next question is: What is being done with this information? Is it simply stored, a memory that is little more than a function of rote learning, to be dredged up at the appropriate time to provide an answer or an interesting tidbit to embellish a conversation? This would depend on what type of information is being processed, for what reason, and by what operation.

Consider two people having access to the same stored information. One may only retrieve component parts from memory for answering a question, while the other may retrieve arrays of information forming embryonic but not-yet-sophisticated wholes for the generation of new ideas. One may use it intuitively, and the other systematically. One may be a rote thinker, leveraging memory to extract pigeonholed information on cue or a prompted stimulus; the other, an analytic thinker.

The ability to think analytically, to see arrays and the patterns within, is a component of critical thinking, and is necessary for the creative process. Combining the components and arrays into more complex forms—where the whole is greater than the sum of its parts—is the process of synthesis. It is integrative thinking that provides unique insights—a wash of ideas, of concepts, and of dreams, moving with non-random fluidity. This is the genesis for innovation—currents of thought often colliding in turmoil, sometimes running parallel without meeting, sometimes washing over metaphoric reefs and rocky cliffs designed to do little more than diminish their energy or reject their force—their purpose. But at other times, it is moving forward with lightning bursts of speed, connecting, building, and flourishing. This is the evolving infinite landscape, a mindscape of ideas, creativity, and innovation with the potential to break the mold of what is, to bring about what can be.

This is a peculiar landscape. It's a landscape of the mind that can be limited by singlemindedness and a lack of perspective and restricted to dogma and convention. It's a charged landscape of conflict between those who would fly in the face of convention and those who would benefit from its control. It's a landscape of harsh reality coexisting with pockets of dreams and fantasies. It's a constructive landscape and a destructive landscape. It's a landscape open to untold wealth for the intrepid. It's the landscape of creativity and innovation we shall explore in this text. At this point, it may be worth noting even the rote thinker becomes a synthetic thinker when necessitated by the need to adapt to life's many everyday challenges, but this is a survival process.

Creativity and innovation are not for the faint of heart. Both are forces of immeasurable energy. Creativity unleashes the potential of the mind. It's about the generation of ideas and alternatives. It's about possibilities. It's about the multiplicity of perspective. It's both a disassembly and a recombinant process. It requires elasticity, i.e., the ability to respond to change—flexibility. It will not exist without a tolerance for ambiguity. It will not exist without motivation. Creativity is subjective. Creativity is opportunistic. Creativity favors the prepared mind.

Innovation is a measurable construct of ideas. It's the application of ideas. It's the action and process of change. It's disruptive. It's destructive. It's groundbreaking and revolutionary, but at the same time, it can be simple and patently obvious. Innovation abhors sufficiency. It's the creation of new markets and values through the catastrophic replacement of established technologies. It's about successfully challenging the incumbent. It drives the iconoclastic solution. In the face of globalization, it's a survival skill. In the face of competition, it's a customer expectation. It's the differentiator between organizations that lead and organizations that chase.

Creativity and innovation deny predictable destinies. They do not allow us to wager the averages, the predictive probability of the continuous. Rather, they direct our attention to the tails of the distribution, and into the realm of remote possibilities.

Creativity and innovation are strict in their requirements. They require the ability to examine and understand—to set aside conventional wisdom, to think from a multiplicity of perspective, to be able to effectively communicate. They are the nature of the iconoclastic person.

This is what we shall explore in this text.

Chapter 2: Iconoclasts

Iconoclast: a person who attacks settled beliefs or institutions.

—Merriam-Webster [1]

A problem cannot be solved by the same consciousness that created it. We must look at the world anew.

—Albert Einstein [2]

A shared vision is not an idea…it is, rather, a force in people's hearts…at its simplest level, a shared vision is the answer to the question: What do we want to create?

—Peter Senge [3]

To the above quotes, I will add one of my own defining iconoclastic momentum; *an evolutionary and often revolutionary force required to change convention or create anew.*

There are numerous interesting and entertaining quotes to be had if one wants insight into the minds of creative or innovative people.

However, consider someone who does not usually come to mind when thinking of creative or innovative people. Consider George Patton, the intemperate but highly successful field commander of World Wars I and II. He is often credited with the following quote: "*If everybody is thinking alike, then somebody isn't thinking*" [4].

It's a good quote, and an admonishment of group thinking, but while Patton is credited with it, he may not be the originator. Patton may not even be the name that first comes to mind when thinking of creative or innovative people. We tend to think of names such as Edison, Hawking, or Jobs. But Patton, the consummate warrior, did not have his success or reputation come from military rigidity or lack of vision, nor did he steadfastly defend the status quo of warfare. Rather, his success came from the foresight to champion a virtually unknown and unproven technology—mobile armored warfare—to include the development of new and innovative strategies to successfully command this machinery.

During World War I, he initiated the first tank school—quite an accomplishment given he did not have tanks at the time. But Patton, despite his accomplishments, does not necessarily get credit for being creative or innovative. Accolades to the creative or innovative are generally bestowed on scientists, inventors, artists, and experimentalists, not military commanders. Even the above quote is in question when it comes to him. He may or may not have said this; there seems to be doubt in the minds of those who chronicle such things. It doesn't matter, though. The reference dates back to the early twentieth century; this is important because this was a time of creative awakenings.

At a similar time in history, the Cubist artist Georges Braque said very much the same thing as Patton's questionable quote, but from a different perspective (literally): "*I felt dissatisfied with traditional perspective. Merely a mechanical process, this perspective never conveys things in full. It starts from one viewpoint and never gets away from it*" [5].

Both Patton and Braque were expressing the same things—a dissatisfaction with the body of knowledge at hand, which is little more than an agreement and acceptance of what is, and the tendency to believe "what is" is what it should be. The problem with the acceptance of what is, is the fundamental belief in a predictable destiny. This was also the basis—the foundation—for the philosopher Karl Popper's paper, "The Poverty of Historicism," first introduced in 1936. Popper, ever critical of acceptance and the search for confirmation of what is, stated, "*If we are uncritical, we shall always find what we want: we shall look for, and find, confirmations, and we shall look away from, and not see, whatever might be*" [6].

As you will soon discover, this text is not about predictable destinies. Rather, it is in part about the consequences of being fooled by the singular perspective, by the lack of vision required to move forward in the world around us. It's about decisive transformations. It's about successive increments, increases, and obstacles. It's about how to overcome.

Suffice it to say the creative and innovative forces that arm the world against a predictable destiny are fortunately in abundance, but unfortunately, they are not well understood and easily dismissed. As a result, the belief in a predictable destiny is still manifested in boardrooms, insisted upon by investors, encouraged by industry analysts, and practiced by mid-level managers.

The belief is pervasive and championed by notorious in-the-box thinkers everywhere. If we are to believe the singular perspective and its resultant predictable destiny are obstacles to creativity and innovation, then how does one counter these? Or more appropriately, how are these overturned? What are the forces, the thoughts, the technologies that disrupt these? Is it through rational plans and smooth transitions, or is it a cultural or scientific revolutionary act that tears down what exists, to build what can be? To paraphrase, Popper's revolution is not brought about by rational plans, but by conflicts of interests [7]. Popper was referring to social revolutions, and the folly of those believing revolutionary changes can be thought out so they do not conflict with known facts or laws. In his words, "*a utopian dream.*" When he stated revolution is not brought about by rational plans, he could have just as easily been talking about the adoption of disruptive technologies that require the creation of new markets and values through the often-catastrophic replacement of established technologies.

The political economist Joseph Schumpeter echoed these sentiments when he compared business cycles to revolution, stating those who would believe in a perennial lull do not understand the perennial gale of creative destruction [8]. This was a warning to those who would believe spans of comparative quiet in business cycles sponsor predictable events; they do so at an inevitable risk. The basis for Schumpeter's work is his belief capitalism is an evolutionary process of continuous innovation and creative destruction.

In the advancement of science, as well as societies, and the businesses that profit from it, there are the iconoclasts and the iconoclastic thinkers who know a simple truth—irrationality directs the world. It is a force that moves society and all its connotations and identities forward.

Chapter 3: Fooled by Perspective

To begin a discussion of perspective—that is, our ability to view the world—consider the artist Paul Cézanne [1]–[3] (1839–1906). Early on in his life, he studied drawing at the Free Municipal School of Drawing in Aix; however, complying with his banker father's wishes, he attended law school from 1858 to 1861. Finding he had no taste for law, he left his studies at the University of Aix-en-Provence, deciding he would rather pursue a career in the arts.

Encouraged through his friendship with the young Émile Zola, but against his father's wishes, he persuaded his parents that this was to be his future and left for Paris in 1861. But Paris was not kind, nor was his technical proficiency adequate to keep him at Académie Suisse, where he began his instruction. After five months, he went home, but with a new resolve.

He returned to Paris a year later, this time not to study the classical approach to art, but to entrench himself in a revolution in artistic interpretation sponsored by the likes of Manet, Pissarro, Degas, and others. However, success was long in coming. He was repeatedly criticized for his art. He was rejected by the Salon in 1870, 1873, 1875, and again in 1885. One critic published an article in 1903, titled "Love for the Ugly," criticizing his art. Yet despite this, a major retrospective of his work went on display in 1907, shortly after his death.

Paul Cézanne, now considered the founding father of modern art, is often associated with the Impressionist movement, but this is more an association in time and personal relationships than in artistic identity. Although he exhibited (unsuccessfully) with the Impressionists, he cannot be truly defined as an Impressionist. In fact, many of the Impressionist painters of the day were dismissive of Cézanne's style, which displayed his intrigue with the perception of form.

His art vividly demonstrated his belief that form was more important than the subject matter he was painting; he often revisited the same subject matter over and over with seemingly little regard for the integrity of an object in the painting in relation to other objects. Driven to find what he believed to be the truth of perception, he explored simultaneous visual perceptions of the same image from slightly different perspectives, an example being his numerous paintings of Mont Sainte-Victoire, a limestone mountain ridge in the south of France. Other paintings, such as his *Still Life with Fruit Basket* (1888–1890), exhibit objects that lean and tip in balance but are out of perspective with each other, bringing the viewer to the conclusion that on a single canvas, Cézanne altered his perspective many times. The result was perceptual contradictions in which the interactivity of the elements of the painting provided an animation to the perspective. The intent was to provide the viewer with an experience of depth different from a single-point perspective. Cézanne took the familiar and made it strange by examining the form and the space it existed in instead of the object. As we shall see, this is a hallmark of creativity and innovation.

Many critics of the day considered Cézanne's art a perversion of the object, of the subject matter at hand. This is interesting because modern critics now use the negative terms of those critics, such as "diminish" and "destroy," to describe the positive influence of Cézanne's contribution to the arts, and his great influence. And what of his great influence? What was it he gave not only to the arts, but also to the world, that one would consider including him in this book? The answer may be simple. He taught the world that to truly see something, one must have a multiplicity of perspective, that the solitary view is insufficient for understanding. Was he an iconoclast? Yes! Did he put into play an iconoclastic momentum?[A] Without a doubt!

Cézanne championed multiple perspectives and successive perceptions. He brought out the importance of the space around the object as being equal to the object; he taught us the value in searching past the single answer, and that importance exists on different planes at different depths. Seeking truth, he eliminated many artistic factors from his canvasses and through this, diminished the influence of tradition. Cézanne was not alone.

Cézanne died in 1906, a year before a large-scale retrospective of his work took place at the Salon d'Automne in Paris. It was here Georges Braque [4] (1882–1963) came under the influence of Cézanne's disruptive and innovative methods.

Braque, adding his own interpretations of geometry and simultaneous perspective enhanced by shading, is credited—along with Pablo Picasso—with the creation of Cubism, presenting multiple perspectives, often fragmented, on the same canvas. Early examples of Cubism are Braque's *Port en Normandie*, 1909, depicting the *Little Harbor in Normandy* as a series of triangles and cubes viewed from multiple vantage points; and Picasso's *Les Demoiselles d'Avignon*, 1907, depicting the human form from multiple viewpoints. With both artists the result was not just a representation of the subject matter in a greater context. It was the challenge to fully appreciate form through its simultaneous disassembly from varying vantage points; for the viewer to reconstruct it from the original vantage points.

Cubism can depict form from not only multiple points in space, but also time. There is a sense of visual fluidity brought to the viewer that does not exist in the frozen-in-time effect of single-point perspective. The viewer is, from a metaphorically visual perspective, provided with not only literal and metaphysical interpretations, but geometric as well. The early twentieth-century school of thought called Imagism mirrored much of Cubism, in that it attempted to take the single image and, by separating it from its environment, reveal its essence. Ezra Pound [5],

---

[A] Note to the reader regarding the phrase iconoclastic momentum. I define it as an evolutionary and often revolutionary force required to change convention or create anew. It is a creative, innovative, and destructive force necessary to push aside accepted dogma and in-the-box-thinking.

the often maligned and expatriate twentieth-century American poet, used rhetorical devices to synthesize multiple perspectives into a single image, stating, "*The image is more than an idea. It is a vortex or cluster of fused ideas and is endowed with energy.*"

Cézanne's contribution to Cubism and modern art did not stop at the visual arts, but had a major influence in the literary arts also. Ernest Hemingway and those following in Hemingway's footsteps owe much to Cézanne. Hemingway admitted it was from Cézanne he learned to fabricate verbal terrains [6]. Frequent visits to the Musée du Luxembourg to study the works of Cézanne, by Hemingway's admission, taught him to compare and juxtapose his characters, to link content through the repetition of words. Hemingway's writings, like Cézanne's complex visual language, challenged and transcended traditional single-point perspective. Much like Cubism portraying a fluid context of subject matter, Hemingway offers a holistic view through nontraditional perspectives.

A good example is "The Three-Day Blow" [7] (1925), a short story of seclusion, alcohol-fueled conversation, and an autumn storm. Hemingway purposely departs from color in portions of his narrative to strengthen perception, rather than to objectively describe and differentiate. The reader, as a result, is drawn into a personal assessment of the scenario instead of being told what it is from a single-minded view. Hemingway referred to this as his "iceberg theory," focusing on what is visible at the surface while implying deeper meanings, which to the reader was the discovery of deeper meanings. This is similar to the viewer of a Cézanne painting discovering the importance of the space around the object being equal to that of the object [8], [9].

Somewhere in the period between the latter days of Cézanne and the early writings of Hemingway came the evolution of that giant of American architecture, Frank Lloyd Wright [10]. Wright, in a fashion similar to Cézanne and Hemingway, removed traditional elements. He bravely stated, "*Get rid of the attic,*" the "*dormer,*" the "*unwholesome basement,*" that walls were little more than boxes in which holes had to be punched. He spoke of the expressive flow of continuous surface and was an advocate of houses scaled to fit a normal human being. Wright also embraced the philosophy that the space around the object was equal to the object itself. I will explore this philosophy later in this book, where it will be understood that as a concept, this is the root of disruptive technology.

It is not certain whether Wright was influenced by Cézanne or even particularly aware of him, but one thing was certain; all three men embodied an ability to think beyond the single point of traditional perspective, to view the world holistically, to depart from traditional frames of reference, and to provide others with the ability to see the world as they envisioned it. All three were iconoclasts.

More recent champions of the creative process have discovered, or perhaps rediscovered, what Cézanne articulated so well on canvas, Hemingway on the written page, and Wright on the draftsman's desk—creativity can be a conscious process of achieving a new look at a familiar world. These three, by inverting or transposing the familiar, that is, making the familiar strange, and disrupting and dismissing convention, by integration of diversity into the problem at hand, moved beyond what was sufficient to what was not only creative, but also innovative.

Chapter 4: Challenges to Traditional Perspective

Challenges to traditional perspectives—our ways of seeing the world—can be contrary to who we are. We have a predilection to put things in places suitable and appropriate. We assign like and unlike things to their own place according to some cumulative exposure to them. We push in chairs that are set out from tables; we remind small children to color within the lines; we dutifully take our place in the queue. In other words, we actively engage in maintaining order, semblance, and normalcy, often without thought.

The consequence of this is a uniformity of perception that pervades both our persona and our professional being. This uniformity of perception has become almost an etiquette de rigor, paying respect to conventional wisdoms, traditional views, and accepted bodies of knowledge through the confirmation of their reason for being. The result of this is a probabilistic view of the future based upon a similar or repeatable sequence of past events, providing a semblance of order and the luxury of a sense of certainty.

But this could be a false narrative. The problem with order, as Bernhard Waldenfels [1], the German philosopher and highly regarded student of experience, strangeness, and corporeality, explains is that order, while making experiences possible, also prevents experience, excluding as it includes. A strict adherence to a probabilistic view of the future based upon past events, and its accompanying semblance of order, would mean rules allowing for little or no deviation from predictable outcomes. The consequence is the further one deviates from the path of order, the less probable it is the path will exist—not a good thing for risk-averse people.

For those who are risk-averse, the paths of order do not allow for flying in the face of conventional wisdom or criticizing traditional views and accepted bodies of knowledge, because this would mean the demise of order. But what if the paths of order were widened, where rules allowed for the variability of predictable events with the certainty of one event no more important than the lesser certainty of another? We may not develop such paths purposely in our everyday professional lives, but we do attempt to do this when challenged with difficult problems to resolve. We put together teams in the hope they will develop a broader path, champion events of lesser certainty, and advance an iconoclastic momentum that can both refute convention and create anew.

Whether this can be accomplished first requires an ability to view the world differently from what we originally perceived it to be. But this is the problem. In our predisposition for a normed environment, we find it very difficult to overcome or even be aware of constraints designed to do little more than maintain the path of order, to hold us back.

***

My usual habit is to rise in the predawn morning—to drive south toward Chicago, to my office, which up until a few years ago was in the research and development wing of a large medical device manufacturer. Lake Michigan is on my left, to the east. The late winter season over the lake brings spectacular early-morning bursts of sunlight to punctuate the drive. Hues of brilliant color streak through holes in the clouds and scatter an artist's pallet across the horizon.

I find myself mesmerized by the beauty of the sunrise, distracted from the road…but this is not a sunrise. As much as I know it is not a sunrise, I will always think of it as such. It is instead the Earth turning toward the sun. From my small vantage point on Mother Earth, I can force myself to be heliocentric, to applaud Copernicus for his contributions [2], but I can also acknowledge his contemporary's (Philip

Melanchthon, German Lutheran Reformer and Humanist: 1497–1560) [3] derision of he who "moves the earth and fixes the sun."[B] From my perspective, it's much easier to view a geocentric world—such is the deceit of perspective. Georges Braque once cautioned against the single perspective when he said, "*Traditional perspective does not satisfy me...It is as if someone who all his life drew profiles would come to believe that man has only one eye*" [4].

Recognizing the limitations of a single perspective can be difficult, and getting people to think from a different perspective can be difficult at best. If you have ever led or sat in on a brainstorming session, you have realized a common difficulty to overcome in such activities is the promotion of multiple perspectives. Why? Because multiple perspectives are abrasive and contrary to what is generally referred to as groupthink, the tendency to make decisions everyone can agree on. In fact, even though there is considerable evidence in the published literature about the dangers of groupthink, it is often a stated outcome for success in meetings, perhaps under the false belief that the pooling of intellect is quantitatively additive.

Groupthink almost always begins with the creation of an attitude. Once two or more people agree to the attitude, this begins a process of creating and reinforcing relationships to the extent that other perspectives are dropped from the discourse. But Alvin Toffler, writer and futurist, says, "*We need a multiplicity of visions, dreams, and prophecies—images of potential tomorrows*" [5].

While Toffler was speaking more to societies and the conflict of possible versus preferable futures, his words apply here. It is easy to substitute the word "perspective" for his use of the word "vision." Without multiple visions, or multiple perspectives, we tend to fixate on a solution within the constraints of the dilemma. Fixation, which may be thought of as convergent thinking, is a part of ordinary problem-solving. We learn it very early in our lives. Concentrate, we are told. We

---

[B] The German theologian and reformer Philip Melanchthon (1497–1560) derisively referred to Copernicus as "that Sarmatian astronomer who is trying to stop the sun and move the Earth," calling it an absurd notion. Of note: Philolaus (Greek 470–385 BCE) is credited with the development of the first non-geocentric view of the universe. However, the first known model placing the sun at the center of the known universe with the Earth revolving around it was presented by Aristarchus of Samos (310–230 BCE).

then draw upon our experience with similar problems to solve or find unsolvable. We make use of stored knowledge and algorithms. But is this the best way to approach a problem? If not, how do we overcome, and why?

Most of us fixate without even realizing it. Many of us believe the ability to fixate on a problem is a good thing, that it helps in finding solutions. But it can be a hindrance. Davidson [6], [7] presents the following example of fixating on a solution:

I have brown socks and black socks in a drawer at a ratio of 4:5. How many socks do I have to remove to ensure finding a matched pair? Take a minute and think about this. Did you focus on the ratio of 4:5? Did you concentrate on a mathematical formula to derive the solution? Many reading this will have done just that.

Daniel Kahneman, who earned the 2002 Nobel Prize in Economic Sciences, calls this slow thinking [8]—a procedural activity involving the retrieval, from memory, of some algorithmic process, a computation, and then deciding the value of the effort. Now, consider rewording the problem as, *I have brown socks and black socks in a drawer. How many do I have to pull out to ensure finding a matched pair?* The answer is an intuitive *no more than three*; if the first two don't match, pull out a third. No matter what the ratio, the answer is immediate and never more than three. Better yet, suppose you were given a photo of a drawer full of brown socks and black socks. If your vision is not impaired, the correct answer is immediate and absolute—two. No matter the ratio, all the information to solve the problem is visually in front of you. You see brown. You see black. You do not see numbers or ratios. No need to think about it.

Kahneman calls this fast thinking—automatic and effortless, no need for voluntary control. More on Kahneman later. The lesson here is not that fixation is a bad thing; many problems require fixation. But what is often overlooked is that fixation may be the unnecessary result of the method in which the problem is presented or perceived—a matter of perspective.

Consider the simple description of a rectangle with sides of twelve inches and twenty-four inches. How many of you immediately tried to determine the area of the triangle by multiplying twelve by twenty-four and then quickly determined one by two feet was a simpler method of getting an answer?

Some of you did. But here is the thing: there was no question asked, just a description. Yet many of us are hardwired to provide answers when no question has been asked. We do this without thinking. An authority figure presents a problem—or in our minds, something resembling a problem—and we go into task mode. We fixate on answers based on our belief of what the question would be. In doing so, we begin to build parameters and limit our perspective. So, having said this, if a question was asked regarding the rectangle, what would it be? Would it be the area of the rectangle in inches or square feet? The length of a side? The width of a side? The number of rectangles that could be formed given the information stated? Each of these presents a different perspective of the rectangle. Take the time to think about this. What was your perspective and why?

Michael Michalko [9] suggests the following method to get people to take a different perspective. He suggests a game where the alphabet (A through Z) is written down, and then players are asked to provide the names of famous people (real or fictional) whose last name begins with the letters—e.g., D=da Vinci, F=Fred Flintstone. He then asks each player to pick a name that has the same letter as the first letter of their last name before presenting a problem to the group, such as, "How do you encourage people to submit more ideas?" Each player must think how their famous person would provide an answer to the problem. The responses are then shared and combined, the result being a synthesis. In other words, the whole becomes greater than the sum of its parts. Note this is different from Genrich Altshuller's Law of Completeness (credited with the creation of TRIZ) [10] where systems are derived from the synthesis of separate parts into a functional system.

In Altshuller's law, the sum of the parts equals the whole. As an example, getting better gas mileage from an automobile would be the result of decreased weight of the auto, increased internal combustion engine efficiency, or a combination of the two. In this example, Altshuller's law requires access to stored knowledge and the implementation of algorithmic procedures. In other words, Altshuller's law is fundamentally linear and requires constraints on the problem, i.e., better gas mileage from an automobile. A solution can then be derived by recognizing the minimum components of a system that can maximally provide this.

Michalko's game is not linear. In Michalko's game, a viable solution may be to offer an alternative form of transportation rather than increasing the efficiency of the current form. Consider the problem of a parking structure without enough spaces for the cars requiring it. If we think in terms of parking spaces, we find a sufficient solution in adding more parking spaces to accommodate excess cars, but if we think in terms of idle cars, we find one or more creative and alternative solutions in making use of idle cars.[C] If solutions rest on the statement of the problem, it may be fair to say the discovery of the problem is more crucial than the discovery of the solution. In the example above, the question in the discovery of the problem is whether the problem is excess cars (finite space) or idle cars.

To this end, it is generally well recognized that creative process generates alternative solutions, whereas routine problem-solving—generally an algorithmic deductive process—creates solutions that tend to suffice [14].

[C] In August 2013, the business section of many newspapers reported car-sharing services are beginning at some large national airports. Car owners drive to the services' parking lots and leave their cars free of charge. The car service then rents the car to other travelers and returns a portion of the fee to the owner. The fee returned is based on the age and luxury status of the vehicle. As of 2017, car2go, a car-sharing service, estimated 2,500,000 registered members with approximately 14,000 vehicles throughout North America, Europe, and Asia. Navigant Consulting estimates this will be a 6.2-billion-dollar business by 2020 [11]–[13].

Chapter 5: Fooled by Perspective—Confines and Constraints

Our view of the world, be it in our professional lives or personal endeavors, is highly dependent on the basic assumptions we have of the world around us, i.e., our environment and what we perceive to have meaning. We may find meaning to be obscure, perhaps mysterious—or simply a matter of connecting the dots to move through the day. No matter what our personal view, it's fair to say it is limiting.

As an example, consider the nine-dot problem shown below (Figure 1). To people who like puzzles, this is one of the more common ones, and no doubt, most reading this book will have come across this at some point in their experience. This is little more than a simple exercise to stimulate the mind into displaying its potential for problem-solving. The challenge is to link all nine dots in as few moves as possible without lifting the pencil off the paper. The problem is easily solved in five moves, which may be sufficient in that it does not require one to think beyond self-imposed constraints.

Let me explain. In the nine-dot problem, the constraint is the perception of a box the dots define. The recognition of this is important. Most people will self-impose a constraint that keeps the solution within the confines of the dots, as if the dots make up a border; hence, a sufficient solution. But if the challenge is to solve the problem in four moves, then a sufficient solution will not work. One must think outside the box (cliché intended). An even more creative solution is required to solve the problem in three moves, which requires removing not only the constraint of the box, but also the self-imposed constraint of centering the links (the requirement is to only link the dots).

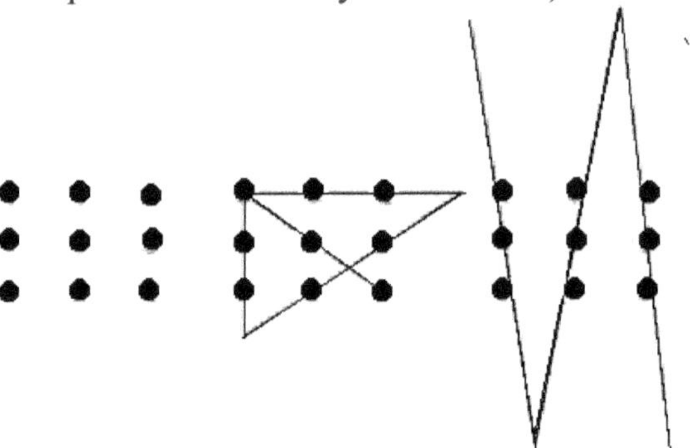

Figure 1.

For the nine-dot problem to be solved in three moves, the problem-solver must move from sufficient solutions to creative ones, which requires looking at the problem from a new perspective—that is, revisiting the solution requirement of linking the dots to find the self-imposed constraints. To emphasize this, consider the top diagram (rectangle) shown in Figure 2. The objective is to draw a continuous line that crosses each line segment of the diagram only once.

The problem, often referred to as the five-room problem or the cross the network problem [1], is considered unsolvable, and reasons for the non-solvability have been put forward in the literature and are well accepted (a mix of two-corner and three-corner vertices). The problem may have its basis in the Seven Bridges of Konigsberg problem (Figure 3), in which one must cross each bridge once and only once in a walk about the city. Konigsberg, a former German city, is now Kaliningrad, Russia. Leonhard Euler [2] laid the foundations for graph theory in his reasoning of why the bridge problem is unsolvable.

One can go on the Internet to review the rules of traversing figures with a mixture of vertices to understand why these problems are considered unsolvable. However, the problem with this is the rules were devised to understand why the problem is unsolvable. They have little or nothing to do with solvability.

The difficulty we have when we try to solve these problems is we see the diagrams as two-dimensional with constraints, little more than a diagram on the planar surface of a page. In this, we impose our own constraints, and in that is the difficulty with its solution. Here's the thing: if I am asked to provide a solution to a problem that is considered unsolvable, then I must think beyond the real and self-imposed constraints. I am, in fact, invited to think outside the box (outside the dimensions given) and have the freedom to change my perspective. In the case of the diagram, if I simply transcribe it onto the surface of a cylinder as shown in in the bottom diagram of Figure 2 (maintaining its two-dimensionality), where the width of the diagram equals the circumference of the cylinder, I find the two-corner vertices are now three-corner vertices, and a solution is readily available.[D]

> Rule 1: An unsolvable problem will remain unsolvable when the solution is sought within the constraints of the problem.
>
> Rule 2: If asked to solve an unsolvable problem, the constraints of the problem are no longer valid.

Incidentally, viewing the nine-dot problem in this manner makes a one-line solution possible. The same would hold true if the city of Königsberg was perched on the side of a hill, or the image was transcribed on a cylinder. All one would have to do to cross each bridge only once would be to walk around to the other side of the hill, or move their pencil around the cylinder, to realize the solution.

[D] There is another solution to this problem. Hint: use a wide brush and cross only three of the three-corner vertices and one of the two-corner vertices. See http://www.archimedes-lab.org.

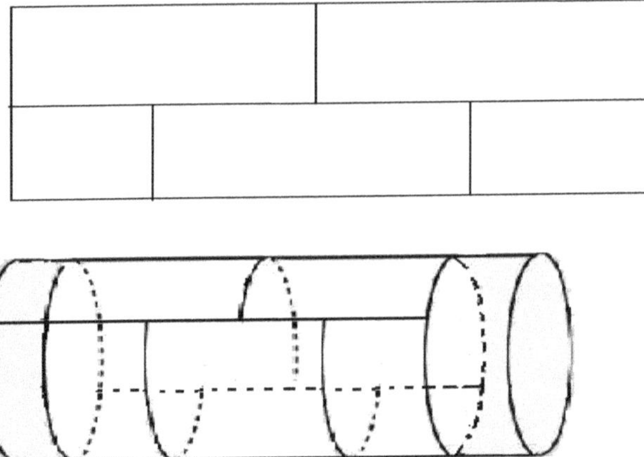

Figure 2

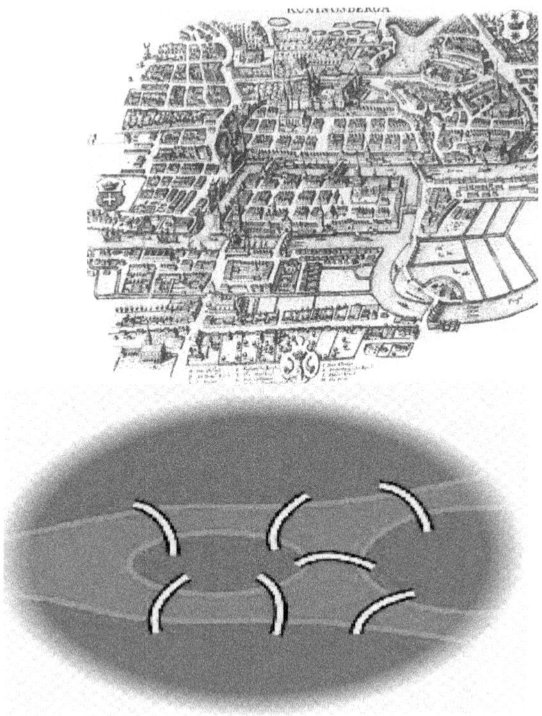

Figure 3

Viewed from this perspective, the centuries-old problem is not a problem at all. Yes, I have taken liberties with this problem, but as the problem is always presented as a two dimensional image on a page with the page being the limiter I believe I am justified. The point is that the irrefutability of an unsolvable problem is not established by solutions not being known. Also, there is no faster method of walking away from a problem than to listen to an "expert" state it is unsolvable.

Euler's contribution was a reason why the problem could not be solved, and in this, many credit him with a solution. But there is a fundamental difference between devising a method to solve problems and stating they can't be done. Euler was an exceptional mathematician, and his logic in devising the reason for the non-solvability of the problem was impeccable. But it was not the unsolvable we were interested in, and that is the point.

Logic, within the constraints of a problem, can be a difficult thing to overcome because it is confining. It can erringly define the problem, establish boundaries, and allow us to accept its conclusions. If our understanding of a problem is erringly defined, it can lead to a limitation in intellectual acuity, a blind spot in a normal field of perception. But to solve the difficult—the seemingly unsolvable—we must move past this. It goes without saying one must be careful when devising their logic.

Consider the paradoxes devised by Zeno of Elea [3] (490–430 BC) described in the next few paragraphs. Zeno, about whom history knows little except from the writings of Plato and a few other Greek scholars, offers logical arguments that lead to conclusions contradicting what we know from our physical experience. If we accept his logic, would we consider our knowledge or his logic invalid?

Zeno developed "logical" steps to demonstrate motion is an illusion. One of his first arguments centered on the well-known tortoise and the hare story; however, he used the Greek hero Achilles as the more rapid of the two contestants. Zeno argued if the tortoise is given a head start—say it starts a hundred meters ahead of Achilles—then Achilles must first run to the point the tortoise is no longer occupying. Rather, in the time it took Achilles to reach the point, the tortoise has moved to some point ahead. Achilles must then reach the second point the tortoise occupied, but is no longer there, having again moved to some point ahead during the time interval. Achilles must then reach the next point, and so on. While the successive intervals become increasingly small, they are infinite. Hence, his conclusion: Achilles can never pass the tortoise.

Zeno furthers his argument by what is called the dichotomy paradox. In this, a person standing at point A must reach point B, but in order to do this, he must first traverse half the distance between A and B. In order to do this, he must first traverse half this distance, that is, one-fourth the distance between A and B. In order to do this, he must first traverse half this distance, and so on. This results in an infinite number of points that must be traversed, making the task impossible.

There is a second problem in this. Any first distance to travel could be halved, resulting in a new first distance, but this could also be halved, and so on, resulting in no first distance to travel. Therefore, the journey cannot even begin. But there is more. Zeno then argues that for motion to occur, an object must change position, but if there is any instance in time where no duration of time occurs, the object must be motionless. If time is composed of infinite instants, then motion must therefore be impossible.

I will assume the reader understands the absurdity of the arguments. To be fair, Zeno did as well, and he created the arguments to demonstrate the absurdity of the singularity of perspective. Zeno's arguments are referred to as *reduction ad absurdum* or *argumentum ad absurdum*—that is, arguments that inevitably lead to an absurd conclusion.

As a personal observation, if there is a difficulty to be encountered with the logic or arguments of reason, it's that it often presents itself with an arrogant air of obviousness and certainty. This comes from being soundly grounded in cumulative past experience and the accompanying probabilistic view of the future. For example, restricting our perspective from other than it "ought to be." We should remember reason often comes with caveats.

One of the biggest difficulties to overcome is not in thinking beyond the confines of the problem, but rather in recognizing the confines alone may be the problem. In fact, the confines may be self-imposed. Some of the earliest and best examples of the recognition of this problem are found in the art of Pablo Picasso. His *Still Life with Fruit and Glass* (1908) [4], *Still Life with Fish and Bottles* (1909) [5], and *Fruit Dish* (1908–1909) [6], housed in the Museum of Modern Art in New York City, offer evidence that he was clearly aware the framing of the canvas was a constraint enclosing the picture. To overcome this, he portrayed objects touching and being cut off by the framing edge, thus contesting, if not detesting, the edge's ability to confine the picture. Other Cubists, particularly early in the development of the movement, painted as if the flatness of the canvas (a constraint) would overwhelm the composition. To overcome this, they pulled their compositions away from the edges and concentrated them toward the middle to provide a three-dimensional effect (to overcome the flatness of the canvas).

Indeed, Picasso and Braque went as far as leaving many of their paintings unsigned. The reason for this could be interpreted as the result of an impersonal style. It is also easily argued that the corners of the painting—that is, the intersection of two sides, being the greatest distance from the center—were those areas the artist wanted the least attention directed toward. To direct attention to this would be to direct attention to the plane of the canvas. Braque and Picasso, in an attempt to overcome this, introduced the oval format [7]. What's interesting with this is many of Braque's works depict a round table in the oval format. Art critics often discuss the "equation" between the oval of the canvas and the shape of the table. Art critic Karen Wilkin writes, "*When the canvas is made to assume the oval shape of the tabletop, then the canvas is neither a background nor even a necessary support, but a confronting plane that presents the image, just as the real tabletop presents the still life*" [8].

Ask yourself when confronted with a problem: Are the confines little more than artificial constraints imposed by the presenter of the problem, or did I subconsciously impose confines that were not part of the problem, as demonstrated by the nine-dot problem or the example given below?

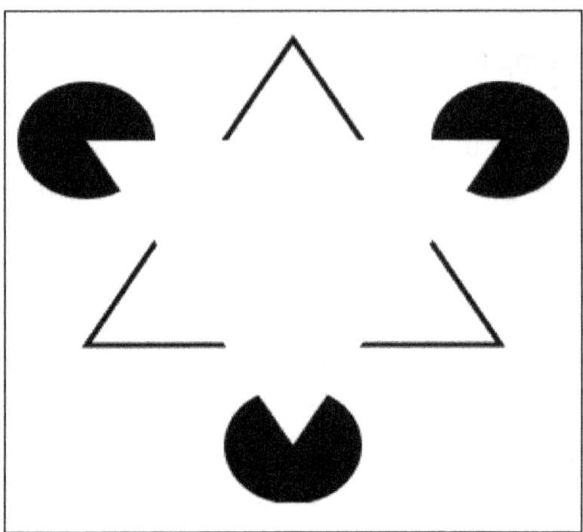

Figure 4

Notice the white equilateral triangle in the center of the diagram in Figure 4. The triangle, known as a Kanizsa triangle [9], [10] after the Italian psychologist and artist Gaetano Kanizsa [11], is an imposed image. We see a triangle because of what Kanizsa called illusory contours—that is, visual illusions that suggest the perception of an edge. Hence, we see a triangle. It does not exist in that it is not drawn. Rather, it is a perception. It's little more than an illusion created by the separation of black and white, but even black and white becomes difficult, if not impossible, to resolve when viewed from the perspective of Adelson's checker shadow illusion (Figure 5) [12], [13].

Figure 5

In the checker shadow illusion shown above, square A and square B are exactly the same shade of gray (interpreted as black and white, or light and dark). However, when viewed in reference to the other squares, we do not see this similarity. Rather, we see black and white (distinct shades of gray). Why? Because of the visual references and the fact that one of the primary functions of our visual system is to assist in breaking down information into meaningful components. As Dale Purves (Duke Institute for Brain Sciences) and R. Beau Lotto (University of London) explain, breaking down into the most likely explanation of what your eyes are transmitting, "*What observers actually experience in response to any visual stimulus is its accumulated statistical meaning, i.e., what the stimulus has turned out to signify in the past*" [14]. The sameness cannot be determined until the visual references are removed. Superimposing B onto A allows for sameness to be seen (Figure 6).

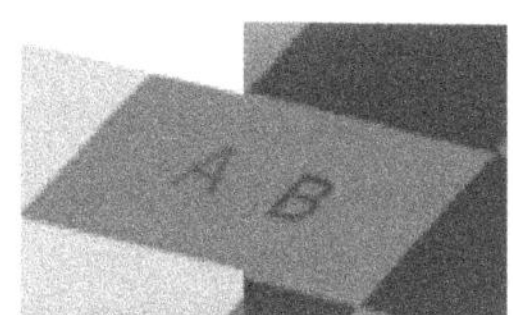

Figure 6

To the reader who still does not believe perception is a function of context, you may Google Adelson's checker shadow illusion and use your computer's cut and paste features to prove this to yourself.

***

Had the Pac-Man-shaped visual references in the Kanizsa triangle been removed, all that would be seen are three angled lines; but even in this, many would have imposed a connection between the angles and viewed a triangle. The same is true for removing the angled lines and keeping the Pac-Man shapes as references. The same is also true for listening and reading. We do not listen with a full understanding of the impact of each word in a conversation to form an opinion about the direction, intent, or content of the conversation. This is particularly true if we are overhearing a conversation we are not part of. Instead, we listen to inflections, phrasings, and keywords and then draw from stored knowledge to form an opinion about the content or context of the conversation. This is comprehension—that is, our ability to understand. Comprehension comes from the Latin term for "a seizing." When we comprehend, we have seized information and integrated it into our body of knowledge. This, in turn, is incorporated into our personal internal and interactive working model of the world around us [15], which in turn allows us to realize far more than we have been taught.

How interactive is our internal working model? Consider our discussion of Cézanne. If we know of Cézanne, then we know somewhat of his contributions. We no doubt know of his contemporaries, of his controversies. We know about painting, canvases, easels, brushes, and frames. We know of colors. We know there are people who like his work, who like modern art, and we know there are people who do not. We know of Europe, France, Paris, and in turn, the Seine and Eiffel Tower. We know the French have a different word for "yes," and we can or cannot speak the language; French cuisine differs from a cheeseburger and a beer; and to travel to Paris from the United States, the shortest distance means we must cross the Atlantic. This brings up knowledge of airlines, departure times, cost, and so on, seemingly without end. This is our interactive working model—seizing information, comprehending, and integrating to provide a personal model of the world around us, allowing us to realize far more than we have been taught.

An extreme example of comprehension is "Jabberwocky," found in *Through the Looking-Glass* by Lewis Carroll [16], [17]. If you have not read it, or have not read it recently, take the time to read the opening stanza shown below.

'Twas brillig, and the slithy toves Did gyre and gimble in the wabe: All mimsy were the borogoves, And the mome raths outgrabe.

It's pure nonsense, and as numerous linguistic experts have remarked, makes no sense at all; or does it [18], [19]? I would wager somewhere in the back of your mind, in some deep recess, there was a semblance of meaning, perhaps a sense of description keyed by the use of the word "*'Twas.*" Did the phrase "*and the,*" a conjunction and article, transform "*slithy*" into an adjective and "*toves*" into a noun? It may be nonsense, but it has a sentence structure.

If English is your first language, you no doubt immediately see two sentences joined by the conjunction "*and.*" Sentence one is "*'Twas brillig,*" which is translated as *It was* (subject and verb) and *brillig* (the adjective). So, "*'Twas brillig*" is a complete sentence in which brillig expresses some sort of quality, and we recognize it as such. The second sentence would be "*The slithy toves*" (article and subject) *did "gyre and gimble"* (verbs) *"in the wabe"* (prepositional phrase). In this sentence, "*toves*" appear to be animated (*did gyre and gimble*), and this takes place in something or somewhere called "*the wabe.*" As nonsense as "*slithy toves*" is, it tends to make sense. It could be inserted just about anywhere and would still make sense. Consider the Chuck Berry song "Brown Eyed Handsome Man" [20]. Insert "*slithy toves*" into the opening lyrics and it still has a recognizable meaning. "*The judge's wife called up the district attorney. She said, 'Free that brown-eyed man.'*" Substitute "*slithy toves*" for "*brown-eyed man*" and you will see what I mean.

What other grammar clues do we have that provide some meaning to the nonsense? The rules of grammar allow us to understand much, particularly about the sounds of the words. The sounds of words in the lines from "Jabberwocky" allow us to accept them as potentially English in origin. As an example, I determine "*slithy*" to be an adjective because the "y" ending implies it is a state of being of the root "*slith.*" Similarly, the "*s*" ending gives a plural connotation to "*borogoves.*" Thus, there is a perceived similarity of nonsense words to actual words. Consider the context of the next stanza, which also contains nonsense words.

> *"Beware the Jabberwock, my son! The jaws that bite, the claws that catch! Beware the Jubjub bird, and shun The frumious Bandersnatch!"*

"*Frumious*" is a nonsense word, but the use (and sound) of "*-ious*" tells us it's an adjective.

But there is more, and perhaps it has to do with the sound of the flowing rhyming style it is written in, somewhat akin to the poem "The Night Before Christmas," which also begins with "*'Twas.*" "*'Twas the night before Christmas and all through the house...*"—"*'Twas briliig,*" and the "*slithy toves.*"

The remarkable thing about all of this is we do not consciously examine each word. We don't consciously diagram the sentences according to their structure, nor puzzle over the subtle or not-so-subtle clues that provide us with insight or meaning to the nonsense. Rather, this is brought about automatically. Kahneman [21] refers to this as System 1 thinking—fast thinking. The "*effortlessly originating impressions and feelings that are the main source of the explicit beliefs and deliberate choices of System 2 thinking*"—slow thinking. System 2 thinking is derived from the conscious reasoning self—a slower process. System 1 and System 2 thinking are terms widely used in psychology, having their origins in the works of Keith Stanovich and Richard West, published as Individual Differences in Reasoning: Implications for the Rationality Debate [22].

Interestingly, each word, phrase, or inflection could, in fact, be a random selection, one from a possible set of utterances limited only by the language and culture. But in the sequencing of random events, there is always the perception of non-random regularity that directs our perspective. We find by removing original references, we can change perspective. Was this what the early twentieth-century Cubist school of painting had in mind when reducing and fragmenting form into discrete planes?

***

Conventional problem-solving requires using the information given with the problem—the reference—but this may, in fact, be the root of the problem. Consider my earlier statement: "*There is no faster method of walking away from a problem than to listen to an 'expert' state it is unsolvable,*" as it applies to the late George Dantzig [23], PhD, Professor of Operations Research at Stanford University. Reflecting on his achievement, while a student, of solving two previously known-to-be unsolvable statistical problems, he said, "If I had known the problems were not homework, but were, in fact, two famous unsolved problems in statistics, I probably would not have thought positively, would have become discouraged, and would never have solved them."[E]

Similarly, and nearly a century earlier, there was Henry Bessemer, 1813–1898, the English inventor of the first inexpensive process for the mass production of steel. Bessemer, recounting his invention, said, "*I had an immense advantage over many others dealing with the problem in as much as I had no fixed ideas derived from long-established practice to control and bias my mind, and did not suffer from the general belief that whatever is, is right*" [24]. He used oxygen in air blown through molten pig iron to burn off impurities to create a high-quality steel. This is considered one of the most significant innovations of the second industrial revolution.

While many, if not most, problems can be solved through conventional methodologies such as accessing stored knowledge or implementing algorithmic procedures, this does not preclude the necessity of creative solutions. As Einstein said, "*We must look at the world anew*"[25], which may lead us to the need for irrational thought. No, not the need for mood-altering negative reinforcing irrationality the evening news offers up as examples of the world around us. Rather, the need to break away from the norming cues that are part of our internal working model of the world that led us to accept the "accepted

[E] As a student, Dantzig was late for class on the day his professor (Jerzy Neyman) was discussing famous unsolved statistical problems. Viewing the problems on the blackboard but not hearing the discussion, he assumed this was homework.

constraints" as solution limiters. To take the iconoclastic position to discount tradition and popular ideas.

But the iconoclastic position is not without its detractors, and in fact, may be ridiculed. The International Exhibition of Modern Art, aka the Armory Show [26] of 1913, billed as the first large-scale exhibit of twentieth-century modern art in America, included the works of many important artists. Important by current standards, but in 1913, Duchamp's cubist and very fluid *Nude Descending a Staircase* was attacked as inept and little more than an explosion of shingles. Matisse's *Blue Nude* was considered to be primitive and childlike by an audience used to seeing anatomically proportioned figures, and at least one critic labeled it hideous and a monstrosity. A likeness of Matisse's work was burned in effigy by Chicago students. An iconoclastic position may take courage.

Interestingly, the Armory Show is now considered by many art historians as one of the more important, if not the most important, exhibitions in modern art. Perhaps it was the times. Stravinsky's *Le Sacre du printemps*, or *The Rite of Spring*, also debuting in 1913, prompted catcalls, spitting, and even fistfights [27]. In a theatre full of Parisian sophisticates, a melee broke out—some say a riot—over the music and dance of a ballet historians would later refer to as a gateway to modernism.

We could say the norming cues that make up our internal model of the world are at times barely more than acceptance cues. Many early astronomers favored circular orbits for planets for little reason other than the Greek supposition of ideal perfection. But as Eric Temple Bell, mathematician and number theorist (1883–1960), bluntly put it, "*One look at an ellipse should have convinced even the most mystical of astronomers that the perfect simplicity of the circle is akin to the vacant smile of complete idiocy*" [28].[F]

While I think the word "complacency" would have been a better choice than the phrase "complete idiocy," the point is made; the early sciences, particularly that of the Greeks, would have benefitted greatly

[F] Aristotle and Hipparchus were inclined to believe the Earth was a sphere; however, Ptolemy expanded on this, introducing a revolutionary geocentrism. His model of the sun, stars, and planets tracking the heavens in large and small circles was wrong, but his concept was fact for over thirteen hundred years.

from a willingness to adopt an iconoclastic philosophy. The Greek obsession with perfection kept them from reaching their full potential. It is fair to say mysticism intertwined with perfection played an important role in the Greek sciences, particularly math. As a result, they were less than enthusiastic about irrational numbers, never developed a basic algebra, and considered zero of such inconsequence they would not assign it so much as its own symbol to recognize it. To the Greeks, their reasoning was simple—why acknowledge a void?

Bell's bluntness toward the Greeks' supposition of perfection can also be taken as a metaphor contrary to rational thought. Those who communicate in rational thought present closed-loop ideas, much like a circle or sphere, in which the arguments have been worked out and logically presented and are contained in the *thought* sphere, which is labeled either "accept" or "reject." Nonrational thought, on the other hand, is much less "worked out." Having its strength in metaphor, it evokes imagination in its incompleteness (more on metaphoric expression later). In that it is incomplete, it welcomes others to fill in gaps, bridge voids, and build on existing idea structures, each according to how they perceive the problem. This then brings us to an interesting premise: solutions are rational while the process of moving to the solution is irrational.

We are all agreed that your theory is crazy. The question which divides us is whether it is crazy enough to have a chance of being correct [29], [30].

—Niels Bohr to Wolfgang Pauli on his presentation of a theory of elementary particles.

The American humorist Artemus Ward [31] (1834–1867), considered America's first stand-up comedian, said, "*It ain't so much the things we don't know that get us into trouble. It's the things we know that just ain't so.*" This quote is sometimes attributed to Mark Twain and others, but in deference to whoever said it first, the words remind me of the decades-old (1930s), often-stated myth that bumblebees cannot fly, which commonly is phrased as *according to the theory of aerodynamics, the bumblebee is unable to fly.*

Consider the 2007 movie *Bee Movie*, directed by Simon J. Smith and Steve Hickner, and this quote, "*According to all known laws of aviation, there is no way that a bee should be able to fly. Its wings are too small to get its fat little body off the ground. The bee, of course, flies anyways. Because bees don't care what humans think is impossible* [32]." As one might imagine, this is an expression of the belief that even in the face of impossibilities, the possible can happen.

Mary Kay Ash, the makeup magnate, often used a similar phrasing to motivate her sales forces [33], as did Mike Huckabee during his 2007 presidential campaign [34], and most recently in the Wendy's 2017 commercial UnBEElievable [35].

While it is not remarkable there are those who would believe this, those who would deny their own observations, what is worth a comment is the individual (there are at least three scientists linked to this) who did the original calculation did not immediately recognize the error in his estimate of bumblebee aerodynamics. Did he, for a brief period of time, believe bumblebees were held up by an unknown force, perhaps a cosmic puppeteer? In deference to this scientist, a correction to the estimate was made within days, but no one was listening; proving bumblebees can fly is simply not interesting.

Chapter 6: Fixation

Karl Duncker [1], the renowned Gestalt psychologist of the early twentieth century, argued we tend to fixate on an object's normal function. In a well-known experiment, he gave his subjects candles, matches, and small cardboard boxes containing thumbtacks [2], [3]. The task presented to them was to mount a candle vertically on a screen to function as a reading lamp. The solution, after the fact, would appear to be simple: light a candle, melt wax onto the top of a box, stick the candle into the wax, and tack the box to the screen. But study subjects who were given boxes of thumbtacks, matches, and candles had great difficulty solving this problem.

Why? Because the accepted perspective was the box was there to contain the thumbtacks, not act as a platform. Viewing the box as a platform was outside the normed perspective. People who received the same supplies with the tacks outside the box did not view the box as a container, but rather as a component of the solution to the problem. This phenomenon became known as functional fixedness.

Functional fixedness is the difficulty we have in visual perception—and in problem-solving—when one component of the situation at hand has a fixed function. The fixed function must be changed to correctly perceive the situation in order to find a correct solution. In this, we find how a problem is presented affects the solution.

In scientific and business environments, problems arise on a daily basis. Some are simple enough that prior knowledge readily resolves issues, but some are more difficult, often requiring the knowledge of one or more experts to resolve. Managers faced with difficult problems must consider not only who they select to help with the problem, but also how they present the problem to those selected to solve it. Problem solvers must think flexibly in the process of solving a problem, that is, they must first find why the problem exists, and then ask what the problem is really demanding. However, this comes with a caveat. A manager selecting a team to resolve a difficult issue may, in fact, give cues as to why the problem exists, and in doing so, offer the team variables to focus on, thus compromising alternate solutions by ignoring the holistic environment of the problem.

Consider this scenario: two managers are tasked with solving the same problem. Manager A provides Team A with all requisite knowledge at the outset of finding a solution. Manager B provides Team B with only the context of the problem in which team members must make assumptions. Here is the question: which team asks more questions? Hint 1: Team A has been deprived of asking questions that may lead to insight and understanding. Hint 2: the generation of questions is part of the problem-solving process.

It may be that both the manager and the problem solver need to become irrational thinkers—to view the problem from different perspectives—which may be all that is needed to solve the problem, or at least bring forth opportunities. By not doing so, they run the risk of erringly confirming the problem is unsolvable, or at least not finding a satisfactory solution. From what we discussed so far, it seems an easy argument that the task of finding a solution is not the sole responsibility of those assigned to the task, but of equal responsibility to those presenting the challenge.

An example of this is found in the basketball dilemma [4], where two groups of people are asked to view a video in which young people wearing either black or white T-shirts are passing a basketball around. One group is simply asked to view the video and report what they see. The other group is asked to count how many times the people wearing the white shirts pass the basketball.

During the video, a person dressed as a gorilla walks through the scene. Those asked to simply report what they see will report a gorilla walking through the scene. However, almost half of those asked to count the number of times the basketball is passed by people wearing white T-shirts will be so focused on the problem presented to them they will not see the gorilla. Even when viewing the video for a second time, but under the same constraints, there are those who still will not see the gorilla. This is known as sustained inattentional blindness [5], or selective attention—that is, when engaged in an attention-demanding task, there is a failure to notice the unexpected. Managers need to be aware of this when posing problems and avoid cues that so accurately describe the problem that the unexpected is overlooked.

The Austrian-born British philosopher Karl Popper (1902–1994) made the point that focusing on falsification rather than verification may be a better way to understand a phenomenon. Popper explains this by stating, "*It is easy to obtain confirmations, or verifications…if we look for confirmations*" [6].

In other words, we need to be diligent in guarding against the tendency to form a hypothesis about what is happening and then search for evidence to support that hypothesis, rather than testing the hypothesis. This is known as confirmation bias, and it is why scientists and statisticians incorporate two hypotheses into their thinking about relationships: a null hypothesis—that is, one of no difference or no change—and an alternative hypothesis of change. Hypothesis testing guards against looking only for confirmation and denying alternatives exist.

But what of alternatives? Consider this. When we have no basis for choosing between alternatives—that is, the non-rejection of the null hypothesis—we assume them to be equal. This, however, is not a declaration, nor is it a statement of the actual composition of things. Rather, it is a formal method of expressing ignorance—that is, a lack of evidence. But, informally, if we tend to seek verification, is our natural tendency to reaffirm what is already believed? If it is, we have to ask ourselves what the value is in doing this. The answer, as you may suspect, is no value at all.

Nassim Taleb, the essayist, statistician, and former stock trader, in the *Black Swan,* describes this as the error of confirmation: "*We focus on preselected segments of the seen and generalize from it to the unseen.*" Those forecasting market futures would be well-advised to take note. To emphasize this, Taleb [7] Americanizes an example provided by the twentieth-century philosopher Bertrand Russell [8] (1872–1970). It goes like this: a turkey is fed generously every day of its life by humans who take great care of it. On any given day, would the turkey expect anything else but to be fed generously by humans on the morrow? From the turkey's perspective, the answer is no. But from the human's perspective, a different view is given, that of the turkey generously feeding humans if the next day is Thanksgiving. To quote Russell, "*The oftener things are found together, the more probable becomes they will be found together another time*," but Russell goes on to state, "*In spite of frequent repetitions, there is sometimes failure.*" Russell was doing little more than stating the basis of frequentist statistics. Note: Russell's "sometimes failure" is better defined as a low probability event.

Wagering the averages in a system with extreme outcomes is a lot like Russian roulette. Wagering the predictive probability of a happy tomorrow based upon past outcomes, for the turkey, would be disastrous. As it was for those buying into financier and investment advisor Bernie Madoff's Ponzi scheme [9], or the free borrowing "banks were too big to fail" philosophy of Iceland [10]. Prior to the economic collapse in 2008, it was estimated that 213 percent of disposable household income in Iceland was held in debt.

The most impactful effects come from the tails of the distribution, away from the average and into the realm of remote probabilities, or as Taleb states, "*Big events don't come from big parents.*" But why do we have an aversion to thinking about the improbable, or at least infrequent, events?

Dennis Mileti, professor emeritus of behavioral sciences at the University of Colorado in Boulder, explains this by saying, "*Humans are hardwired to deny low-probability, high-impact events*" [11]. In other words, we are hardwired for an accumulated statistical meaning and its accompanying semblance of order. Mileti goes on to say, "*If you want to sell earthquake preparation in a way that it affects human behavior, you have to sell it like Coca-Cola.*" In other words, make the strange familiar.

***

No, we can't do that!

If our tendency is to seek confirmation, then perhaps the best way to start a brainstorming session, and to guard against confirmation, is to have everyone in the room stand up and shout, *no!* Say it over and over again, get it out in the open. Have it understood and recognized by all in the room that they are not present to confirm. Rather, to push aside confirmation and the perspective that makes it possible. Instead, focus on the falsification—that is, the perspective that makes *no* a refutable position.

Innovation and creativity do not come from the affirmation of "no," but rather from the discovery of problems or gaps within our knowledge base. Conscious problem finding is integral to iconoclastic momentum, but brainstorming teams must be careful they do not stop with the first "right" discovery and subsequent "right" answer. Iconoclastic momentum does not necessarily recognize right discoveries and answers, but its nemesis, sufficiency, does. Sufficiency places a priority on objective importance over subjective importance. The difference is in the questions asked: what do I need to know to drive toward a solution (sufficiency) versus what can I learn about things that drive toward a solution even if they are not immediately objectively warranted (iconoclastic momentum)?

One sometimes finds, what one is not looking for. When I woke up just after dawn on September 28, 1928, I certainly didn't plan to revolutionize all medicine by discovering the world's first antibiotic, or bacteria killer. But I suppose that was exactly what I did.

— Alexander Fleming [12]

Brainstorming sessions should, in part, be sessions of inquisitiveness, i.e., curiosity, in which it is understood single solution efforts can stifle curiosity and promote sufficiency at the expense of innovativeness. Note: there will be more on brainstorming and why they may be futile in their assignment later in this text.

Marty Sklar, a Disney Imagineering legend, points out Walt Disney had a keen aversion to the word "no." In dealing with Walt, one could use the phrase "yes, if…" and explain options, but never "no." To Walt, "yes, if" was an enabler; "no" was a deal-breaker [13].

"No" is a very strong word and should not be used carelessly, particularly in a creative or innovative environment. The dictionary defines it as opposed to "yes," but this is too simple. The word "no" has the ability to confine a problem or the search for a solution to a single perspective. It is a word designed to save time, to avoid discussion, to eliminate alternate pathways. It is a word used to move toward sufficiency and to support in-the-box thinking. It ignores the dangers of banking one's resources on current business models. But the word "no" is not alone in this. There are many other words similar in nature. Words that dismiss and words that disenable. The use of the word "but"—as in "I really like your idea, but…"—is one such word. In this context, the positive phrase and the pat on the back one receives when told "I really like your idea" is all but forgotten when one hears it qualified by the word "but."

Consider this simple statement: *I really like your idea, but we do not have the technology*. What is happening? The idea is being dismissed. The "but" is a call for removal of the idea. In other words, it is not worthy of discussion. The person voicing this has given a reason; however, this is little more than a verbal gesture to placate the originator of the idea—to have the originator of the idea believe the reason given is sufficient to not move forward with it.

Some authors have pointed out reasons may not necessarily be based on the authority of the speaker [14], and the use of the word "but" does not shelve or park the idea for later discussion. Rather, its sole intent is to dismiss. How many times have you witnessed this in brainstorming sessions? Perhaps you have done this yourself. Now, reframe the statement and including the word "and." *I really like your idea, and the challenge will be to find the technology*. In this, the idea is not dismissed. Its difficulty is recognized and challenged in a positive manner—it is kept alive.

Now, extend this to *I really like your idea, and the challenge is to both find the technology and implement a solution.* This is now a very positive statement with forward momentum and future vision. The idea is recognized and championed, but even though the idea may have momentum, in the long run, it may not move forward. However, this is not brought into focus. In the grand scheme of creating and listing ideas, better ideas may be put forward; however, this simple method of being non-dismissal is a confidence builder that generates ideas. Even if the idea is not moved forward, the very fact it has been put on display acts as a generator for other ideas, something not gained with the dismissive use of "but."

Words that dismiss, such as "but" and "except," and to a lesser degree, phrases like "yet" or "nevertheless," are often negative; they are little more than rhetorical devices to introduce statements in opposition to what precedes it. And what of the statements in opposition? These generally contain the disenabling words such as "delay," "refuse," "reject," "disapprove," "cannot," "prevent," and "inhibit." There are more.

Consider the statement mentioned above: *I really like your idea, and the challenge is to both find the technology and implement a solution.* Now rewrite it as *I really like your idea, but current technologies prevent solutions.* Both statements recognize known technologies are insufficient. The difference is the first puts out a challenge—to come up with something. As stated, it is a very positive statement with forward momentum and future vision, while the second has been restated to be dismissive ("but") and disenabling ("prevent").

The idea has been dismissed and the reason given. It implies any search for a solution will be futile. The message is clear. No need to go forward, there is nothing to be gained following this path. Dismissive and disenabling words are little more than rhetorical tools designed to control or maintain a limited perspective by establishing boundaries, producing a lack of confidence, and maintaining a risk-averse environment, i.e., moving to sufficiency.

***

The challenge becomes how we remove our internal biases—our self-imposed constraints—and change our perspective. Recognizing the constraints of the problem and why the problem exists within the constraints is the first step. It means we recognize and understand the perspective of the presenter of the problem. In other words, we recognize his or her point of view and the evidence for its existence. We then guard against challenging the problem from this perspective, as it may only lead to confirmation of non-solvability, or at best, answers that suffice.

Albert Einstein stated, "*A problem cannot be solved by the same consciousness that created it*[15]." In other words, little is gained, perhaps no more than what is already known. We must guard against embracing the "nonsolution" as irrefutable, or else we will not be able to question it. If we accept it as true, we deny the existence of other perspectives and walk away. In the example of the two-corner versus three-corner vertex problem, one has to ask, what is the perspective of the problem presenter, and what are the constraints? The perspective is easy; it is planar. The constraints are that the problem is presented on the surface of a page as a two-dimensional figure, and as such, there is no way to overcome the two- versus three-corner vertex dilemma.

Changing perspective is not a simple matter of willing oneself to do so. The neuroscientist Gregory Berns [16] makes the point that seeing things differently from others requires "*bombarding the brain with things it has never encountered before*."

According to Berns, "*Novelty releases the perceptual process*," and he advocates breaking out of what he refers to as experience-dependent categories through the continual exposure to new experiences, or, as statisticians have advocated for decades, *embracing the variance*. Note: this is why having R&D, or product development personnel, closeted away in a laboratory without any exposure to the world in which they apply their science results in a lack of innovation and an unfortunate sufficiency of me-too products.

There is ample evidence to support what Berns is saying. Donald Campbell, the American social scientist and psychologist (1916–1996), concludes that those exposed to multiple cultures benefit from a range of hypotheses for consideration over their single-culture counterparts. The reason, he states, is the ability to have multiple perspectives of a situation [17]. Campbell may be best known for his focus on false knowledge and work in convergent and discriminant validation. He effectively argues while one could point out distinct and measurable flaws in any sophisticated method to problem-solving, it is the use of multiple approaches that is required to get at the truth in research [18].

A most notable modern figure to point toward as an example of novelty releasing the perceptual process is Steve Jobs, the late founder of Apple and a true iconoclast. Jobs placed great value on diverse experiences, and this is reflected in his personal and professional life (often difficult to separate).

Carmine Gallo's online biographical essay about Jobs, subtitled "The 7 insanely different principles of Jobs' breakthrough success with Apple," reveals insights into his character. Jobs is said to have created new ideas precisely because he spent a lifetime exploring "new and unrelated things"—hiring from outside the computer/IT profession as well as studying calligraphy and the fine details of European-made washer-dryers [19]. In short, he embraced diversity, and as Berns advocates, he bombarded the brain with things it had never encountered before. But Jobs was just following a widely adopted method of success—the pursuit of curiosity, a long tradition with iconoclasts.

Consider Leonardo da Vinci [20], [21]. As a painter, sculptor, architect, engineer, and musician, it would be a vast understatement to say he was well-known for his curiosity. A glance at his many notebooks reveals much about how his mind worked. Notes are found reminding himself to find a text on mechanics (de Ponderibus) and to ask about the manner people traveled on ice in Flanders. He contemplated the repair of locks and canals, the vitality of a frog, and how to "construct glasses to see the moon large"—a reference, no doubt, to magnifying glasses, as the telescope would have to wait until the next century…or would it? Maybe he just got sidetracked and forgot to work on this invention.

Then there is Benjamin Franklin [22], who debated morals, politics, and natural philosophy. Throughout his career, he involved himself in such pursuits as a scientist, musician, civic activist, diplomat, inventor, and postmaster. He charted ocean currents, helped establish the University of Pennsylvania, and became a wealthy publisher, all while helping forge America into what it is today.

Nobelist and physicist, Richard Feynman [23] kept a notebook he called *Things I don't know about*. Feynman would often remind people his IQ did not fall in the genius range. He would not accept he was smarter than others, but rather said his success came from his habit of solving problems in his head in multiple ways—exploring options. However, in his own words, Feynman would often dismiss himself, saying, "*I'm really a one-sided person and I don't know a lot. I have limited intelligence and I use it in a particular direction.*" That direction apparently was an innate inquisitiveness.

Interestingly, the innate curiosity exhibited by iconoclasts is not limited to them, but can be put forth as a method of practice for all—a method enabling the fruition of ideas through the active pursuit of knowledge-gaining activities.

Chapter 7: Curiosity

I have no special talents. I am only passionately curious.

—Albert Einstein to his biographer, 1952 [1]

We keep moving forward, opening new doors, and doing new things, because we're curious and curiosity leading us down new paths.

—Walt Disney [2]

To foster curiosity is to first recognize it's an attitude of wanting to know. It is an attribute, and as an attribute, the question is, can it be heightened? Yes. But, if we were to ask if curiosity can be taught, I suspect the answer is no, because curiosity is a quality characteristic inherent to human beings.

Infants are innately curious. Preschoolers ask a never-ending tide of questions. Yet studies have shown as children age, their curiosity begins to diminish. Some studies have suggested this is an unfortunate product of the educational process. This is indeed unfortunate because highly curious preschoolers have been shown to have greater academic achievements, regardless of socioeconomic status [3]. Curiosity is said to help us maintain intelligence. It is said to turn on our need to learn. Curiosity is essential to creativity and innovativeness.

Acting on curiosity (to explore) leads to discovery—that is, new knowledge—which, in turn, leads to the freedom to adapt, create, and innovate. But having said this and recognizing it can be encouraged, it likewise can be discouraged, though perhaps poorly managed is a more appropriate phrasing.

Curiosity is about dynamics. Elementary school students are encouraged to explore the properties of light on plants, to visit other cultures via the web, to question what they see and understand the dynamics of why, but within a structured curriculum. It must fit into a discipline as rigid, conforming, and non-imaginative as learning to color within the lines.

Robert E. Kay points out curiosity and, subsequently, creativity are often suppressed in the educational process of children through the use of "telling and testing" [4]. In other words, with the test little more than a method of affirmation, it is a regurgitation of fact devoid of any discovery process.

In the prelude to "Book One: Family" of his autobiography, Frank Lloyd Wright tells of his youth on his uncle's farm near Spring Green, Wisconsin [5]. When not in school, his days were filled with chores, "adding tired to tired," in Wright's words. He recalls a day when a light blanket of snow had fallen, and he was walking with his uncle across a field. His uncle reminded him to walk straight, neither to the right nor to the left. Not to wander from the path, but to remain focused on the destination. This would get him to where he needed to be as quickly as possible.

But Wright did wander. Clusters of weeds silhouetted against the snow, common and uninteresting to the casual observer, caught his attention—they were worth examining, worth cataloging in his mind. Weeds he would later reflect on as sprays of straight lines were patterned to the eye, woven of bronze, and sprinkled here and there. His footprints in the snow, wandering right and left, far from the straight and narrow path to his destination, betrayed his curiosity.

Finally arriving at the point where his uncle stood waiting, he was admonished. The uncle pointed out his own tracks, straight and true, and then his nephew's tracks, a seemingly purposeless meandering trace. His uncle seized the opportunity to impart a lesson. "*Neither to the right nor to the left, but straight is the way,*" recalled Wright. But the lesson was lost on the young Frank Lloyd Wright, for he was rarely content with arriving at a destination. His future architectural achievements demonstrated a man whose vision exhibited great curiosity of the journey, the world around him, and this was encompassed in all he designed.

As to his curiosity of weeds in the snow, we can only speculate as to how this was used, but Wright is quoted as saying, "*I follow in building the principles which nature has used in its domain*" [6]. In this, Wright believed buildings should not be on things, but of things. For instance, it is easy to think of a tree on a hill, but the reality is nature made the tree of the hill. It is in harmony with the hill, and not an add-on; rather, an integration of the elements.

Wright would later use the tree as a visual metaphor. He described the nature of any organic building as to "come out of the ground into the light…the ground itself held always as a component basic part of the building…A building dignified as a tree in the midst of nature" [7]. He believed architecture was not just the design of buildings, but rather a record of life, the soul of a civilization, and architects should approach their profession as poets and prophets.

To add some dimension to this, in June 1943, Wright received a letter from Baroness Hilla Rebay, a German aristocrat and artist who had immigrated to the United States in 1927. She asked him to come to New York to discuss plans for a building that would house a collection of nonobjective art. The art, in her words, "express order and are sensitive to space." As Wright, also in her words, had the "experience of an originator" and could "feel the ground, the sky, and the in-between," perhaps he could feel the paintings too [8]. The result of this letter was the Solomon R. Guggenheim Museum, located on Fifth Avenue, New York, and completed in 1959.

Wright's uncle may not have had an innate curiosity, or perhaps the realities of his world discouraged such in favor of the pragmatic. To this end, we do not know, but what are we to make of the lesson givers, specifically the educators who must champion curiosity within the confines of an academic program far more rote than thesis? There are rules; not just rules on what and how to learn, but rules on when to ask a question. There is no such thing as a stupid question, but as any student who has ever been chastised for asking a question out of turn knows, there certainly is a stupid time to ask a question. Curiosity in the classroom must wait its turn while putting the question at risk of not being asked at all.

Building an environment that promotes curiosity—say a team environment—is to build an environment of inquiry. And there are benefits to this. Author Diane Cole [9] finds curious employees are proactive employees. An environment that allows employees to ask questions, propose solutions, and identify problems will produce motivated employees. Other authors and researchers such as Day, et al., and Garrison offer that curiosity underlies the willingness of an individual to expose himself or herself to information leading to improvements in decision-making. They have found curiosity is a critical component in the discovery and early adoption of disruptive technologies [10], [11].

But how is this done? How does one promote an environment of curiosity? We can take some cues by stepping back in time a bit to examine curiosity more closely.

Curiosity is often divided into two categories: perceptual curiosity, which leads to an increased perception of stimuli, and epistemic curiosity, which leads to knowledge. It is epistemic curiosity that draws our attention. In 1954, D. E. Berlyne (1924–1976), a British and Canadian psychologist and philosopher, developed a theory of curiosity [12] that stated curiosity is most aroused when familiarity is at an intermediate stage. In other words, some level of familiarity must be in place for one to develop a sense of curiosity about the "thing."

This does not mean curiosity does not exist at less familiar states; rather, at less familiar states, the response tendencies necessary to spur curiosity will be too few and too limited in intensity to provide sufficient arousal. The response tendencies, or arousal stimuli in Berlyne's theory, are predicated on the interjection of novel or imaginative questions and complex ideas into the intermediate level of familiarity. Add in an unsolved problem and an environment of curiosity is created. On the other hand, too much familiarity and one will have an expectation of the thing that diminishes any sense of reward that comes from increased knowledge. In other words, too much clarity early on can deprive the individual, or the team, of serious thought on the matter. Clarity, such as at the onset of posing a problem, is not necessarily a good thing.

Berlyne, in later work [13], argued curiosity is a motivational prerequisite for exploratory behavior. George Loewenstein, of Carnegie Mellon University, hypothesized that individuals experiencing a feeling of knowing are more likely to engage in exploratory behavior than those with a feeling of not knowing—or those believing no discrepancies in knowledge exist [14].

In 2005, Litman et al. reported on their study of epistemic curiosity. They found curiosity and exploration were most associated with feelings of being close to the resolution of the problem, referred to as tip of the tongue (TOT). "*Don't know*" states were associated with lower levels of curiosity and exploration, and "*I know*" states provided the least in terms of curiosity and exploration [15]. Metcalfe et al., from a series of experiments, concluded people in a TOT state wanted to see a correct answer more than when they were not in a TOT state [16]. They conclude that most people are not necessarily aware of this. If there is a takeaway lesson in this, it's that in a corporate environment where innovation is to be fostered, curiosity must be managed.

Perhaps a better phrasing would be gaps in knowledge must be managed. If curiosity increases as the desire for knowledge increases, then gaps in knowledge are curiosity stimulators. According to Loewenstein, the gaps must be manageable [17]. Too little and there is minimal challenge. Too much and why bother? Researchers have found the exploitation of existing knowledge reduces the incentive to explore new knowledge and, to an extent, even the ability to do so [18], [19]. Additionally, the evidence suggests too little exploration or exploitation reduces performance [20].

Perhaps managers with a need to foster a curious environment would be advised to take a cue from David Koranda, and colleagues, who developed a university-level course designed to sponsor curiosity [21]. Their course, Curiosity for Strategists, was based on the observation that students struggling with problems often sought sufficiency in problem-solving with little initiative to go beyond trite solutions, or to challenge their own thinking.

I suspect all managers recognize this is not a problem confined to students, but is fairly common throughout academic and industry environments. The question managers must put to themselves is: what is the value of a solution when it is positioned as little more than trite or sufficient? In a business environment, struggling with the possibility of failure, coupled with deadlines and performance expectations, can and does lead to trite solutions. More importantly, perhaps this question should be asked: what is the value of a solution when the possibility of failure, deadlines, and performance reviews are removed from the equation?

The curriculum Koranda designed was to help students challenge traditional notions, to read outside the field of interest and then relate that information to the topic at hand to make connections that otherwise would not be seen. According to the authors, making unusual connections and combinations leads to the development of alternate strategies. By their account, the students in their class moved beyond viewing curiosity as a process to fill knowledge gaps to thinking of it as a collection of various tools to both fill in the gaps and provide a personal challenge. In a business environment, how many managers can say they do this—that is, bring their people to the point of making connections that would otherwise not be seen, to develop alternate strategies?

To this end, successful managers may be advised to place their innovation teams in an environment where sufficient cursory information is given, which provides fundamental knowledge of the situation. Those gaps in knowledge are pointed out, novel questions are put forth, imagination is promoted, and unsolved problems are discussed. I can think of this as a scale, a double pan balance where one pan, resting on the table, is loaded down with the weight of what we know. The question now becomes how much of what we do not know must be put in the other pan before the weight of a lack of knowledge tips the scale in favor of curiosity. Just the opposite could be true. One pan could be weighted down with what we do not know. The question then becomes how much of what we know must be added to again tip the scale in favor of curiosity.

As an example, we often scan news reports. Based on headlines, we determine whether a particular item is worth our time. Do we read it or not? Consider the headline: "Treatment for uncontrollable epistaxis in a patient with Glanzmann thrombasthenia." I would hazard to guess this is not very interesting; it doesn't spur my curiosity, and unless I suffered from uncontrollable epistaxis, I would probably skip this. Why? Speaking from my personal perspective, I have no idea what uncontrollable epistaxis is or why it would be uncontrollable, why it would afflict a patient with Glanzmann thrombasthenia, and what Glanzmann thrombasthenia is (four don't knows). But there is a treatment (a know). Okay, enough said…for me. For me, the "know" has not tipped the scale in favor of curiosity. Instead, it has done exactly the opposite. It has said there is no need to go further—problem solved. Uncontrollable epistaxis in a patient with Glanzmann thrombasthenia has a treatment. End of discussion!

Has my lack of curiosity invoked the principle of least effort—that is, the most convenient search method with the least exacting mode to find a minimally acceptable result [22], [23]? Am I gravitating to the least demanding course of action? Kahneman [24] says yes, there is an economy of action in cognitive as well as physical exertion, and that effort comes with cost. In this scenario the cost of effort is not offset, or even balanced, by curiosity. So, I go no further. For me, to tip the balance in favor of curiosity, I require something else. I require novelty and strangeness to be present. I would like to know what makes this or any solution unique. Was this a new approach to a familiar problem? Was the familiar made strange to the point that the solution required a different, perhaps nontraditional perspective?

In fairness, the headline did not read as I stated above. It actually read as "Nasal packing with strips of cured pork as treatment for uncontrollable epistaxis in a patient with Glanzmann thrombasthenia" in the Annals of Otology, Rhinology, and Laryngology [25]. And yes, my scale is now tipped in favor of curiosity. Yes, I have added an additional "don't know"; I don't know what cured pork has to do with anything nasal. But I have also added "knows"; I know what nasal packing is, or at least suggests, and I know what cured pork is. But the interaction, the effect of stuffing pork up the nose, is the requisite knowledge that is not retrievable. That is what tipped the scale—the gain exceeding the cost of effort.

Somewhere in my mind, I am inventing scenarios of nitrites, salts, hemorrhaging, astringents, and cured pork tampons, etc., but I am not quite able to retrieve what I need to know to resolve the issue. My curiosity is piqued. I must read the article. I must engage in exploratory behavior.

***

The interesting thing about curiosity is what it does to the mind. The curious mind is not a passive observer. It does not sit idly by watching information pass in front of it, much as parade goers observe marching bands and floats on New Year's Day, being singularly impressed without engagement. The curious mind is an active participant engaged in the multi-dimensional resolution of tasks at hand while simultaneously storing gained knowledge for undiscovered tasks. More importantly, the curious mind has expectations. Expectations of discovery. Expectations of success. Expectations that take it far from sufficiency and into the realm of unrealized recognition. The curious mind will recognize possible solutions as problems arise and possess the potential momentum to move toward innovativeness as a result of the miscellany of information stored as a product of curiosity.

You don't have to have spectacular ideas, you just have to be curious.
—Rangaswamy Srinivasan, coinventor of Excimer laser surgery [26]

I think it is fair to say the curious mind abhors absolutes, as it should. There is no place for a curious mind in a world of absolute "is." However, preface "is" with "what" (what is), and now the curious mind awakens to a world of possibilities. Possibilities bring the excitement of discovery, of learning and unlearning, of digging deeper, of not closing doors. The curious mind thrives on uncertainty and is prepared for opportunities when they arise—that is, making opportunity visible. Chance may favor the prepared mind, but curiosity is the medium, the environment in which chance takes its random walks.

Consider those who engage in survey design and analysis. Do they simply ask a series of object-oriented questions without thought as to why someone would respond in a particular manner? The answer is no because they understand the value of the prepared mind. Those who engage in survey design and analysis (the best designers are also skilled analysts) realize outcomes are a function of directed curiosity and the quality of the questions being asked. If you want to find out if someone likes the car they own, you could simply ask them to respond yes or no to a question of like or dislike. But this limits your understanding. You do not know the model of the car, why they like the car or not, and for what conditions (e.g., great for carpooling but a gas hog on long trips).

Asking a person, or a sample of people, what they like without querying them as to why and under what environmental conditions their response is given is the hallmark of a naive questioner. The lack of curiosity about the environmental dynamics in which the response exists implies the environment does not influence the response, that all responses will be similar or of similar distribution—the response is lock-step and singular in perspective. Thus, more astute survey researchers actively practice the pursuit of environmental questions. This is particularly important if the objective of the survey is to define the sample—and therefore the population—relevant to a problem. The curiosity of the researcher toward the dynamics in which the response exists allows for an appropriate interpretation and inference to the general population and powers the ability to work toward the most creative solutions. Thus, it is with most problems. The environmental dynamics in which the problem exists can define the solution.

Chapter 8: The Daydreamer

Imaginal thought is a cognitive skill that participates in exploration, expectation, and planning.

—Jerome L. Singer,
Professor Emeritus of Psychology
at the Yale School of Medicine [1]

How much of curiosity is enriched by daydreaming? I think it is fair to say that one enhances the other, but I can only speculate on the degree to which this is true. The issue of daydreaming is a fascinating one, and perhaps some insight into this would be a valuable entry into our discussion.

Psychologists estimate that up to half our waking thoughts take one form or another of daydreaming. Additionally—and contrary to my second-grade teacher who poked and prodded me into focusing—daydreaming has been found to be non-pathological and reasonably vital to living an adaptive human life [2], [3]. It is interesting to note that a recent study found about 75 percent of people daydream in the first person (viewing the scenario through one's own eyes). The study conducted by Barlow Soper [4] found that 46 percent are exclusively first-person daydreamers and 29 percent mainly daydream in the first person with some third person mixed in.

Neuroscientists have discovered that neural activity, when one is at rest (a state associated with daydreaming), is more than simple random noise. According to Marcus Raichle, a neurologist at the Washington University School of Medicine, "dispersed brain areas are chattering away to one another." This default mode of the brain consumes about twenty times more energy than when the brain is engaged in a conscious task [5].

Earlier work by Raichle identified the default mode network as always on and always active, no matter if we are zoned out, asleep, or under an anesthetic [6]. Raichle was not the first to notice this. Hans Berger, the inventor of the electroencephalogram in 1924 [7], stated in 1929, "We have to assume that the central nervous system is always, and not only during wakefulness, in a state of considerable activity." As a matter of record, Berger's invention was met with doubt and derision by the medical and scientific establishments at the time.

Many neuroscientists believe the purpose of this default activity may be organization and preparedness—that is, the organization of memories and various systems requiring preparation for upcoming events. If it is organization, the sequencing of content, as psychologists have noted, does not appear to be governed by logical rules. Would this explain the phenomena (incidental benefit) of waking from a night's sleep with the solution to a difficult problem that has been vexing us, or somewhere in the middle of a long drive home having a solution to the problem du jour pop into our head? Perhaps.

The psychologist, Eric Klinger, referenced above, offers benefits to daydreaming. He states daydreaming keeps us organized, keeps our life's agenda in front of us; reminds us of what's coming up, allows us to rehearse new situations (creative problem solving), and plan the future while learning from past experiences [8], [9].

If the curious mind abhors absolutes, as stated earlier, then daydreams should allow it to thrive. The mind, through no course of logic, is subject to a world of possibilities. If prepared for opportunities when they arise, it has the potential for improbable solutions, and in turn, the cognitive evaluation of less than successful ventures leading to the search for successful alternatives.

In the daydream, the individual has the ability to develop a personal narrative free of skepticism or criticism from others. In the daydream, the individual's path can take on many perspectives, all without limitations, all without skepticism, all without hearing the word "no"—that is, risk-free acting out of the daydream scenarios. Simply put, that blank look on a colleague's face during a long and tedious meeting may not represent a vacuous mind. Rather, it may represent the process of creative problem-solving at work—the linking of disparate thoughts generated from curiosity of an unbounded world viewed from other self-generated perspectives, other personalized narratives. I leave it to the reader to give their colleagues the benefit of the doubt.

It has been postulated that as half of human thought consists of daydreaming, it must perform an important function. What comes to mind, from an evolutionary viewpoint according to Klinger, is it is a survival mechanism—the argument being it is too biologically costly not to be.

While we collectively, and from an evolutionary viewpoint, no longer worry about the danger of cave bears and warring clans pilfering from our gene pool, our individual survival depends on processing the stimulus required for complex problem-solving. In the twenty-first century, our corporate survival depends on creative thought leading to innovative processes. It may be fair to say the discouragement of daydreaming has the potential to lead to an overreliance on external sources for problem-solving, outsourcing, and diminishing the potential of the self for creativity.

Section 2: The Changing Landscape

Chapter 9: The Iconoclast and the Changing Customer

It may be fair to say not all businesses would embrace a Steve Jobs personality. In fact, few may. Businesses tend to tie their successes together with strings of like thinking and central themes.

The iconoclast is improvisational, and resultant innovation often appears serendipitous. This conflicts with the canonical regimes expected by companies—that is, adherence to rules and conventions and compliance with dominant corporate values. Thus, in a business environment, becoming an iconoclast or finding those with iconoclastic abilities is difficult.

An iconoclast, such as Steve Jobs, may in fact be a heretic. Consider his idea to incorporate the capacity to store and play music on the iPhone. A great idea to say the least, but it was not well received by his management teams because it would signal a drop in sales of one of Apple's most profitable products—the iPod. Much of Apple's success had to do with the introduction of the iPod in October of 2001. With its introduction, the successful computer company was transformed into an incredibly successful consumer electronics company. So, why would anyone want to mess with such a successful product?

Jobs knew that if Apple did not do this, some start-up tech company would. In other words, to survive, Apple had to put to rest its market leader. A courageous act to say the least, but one that it did in 2007. However, Apple did not kill off its profit maker; instead, it chose to add some of its new technology and call it the iPod touch. With a touch screen and Wi-Fi connection, it could do just about anything an iPhone could do, except make phone calls, and this was what gave the iPhone its advantage [1]. To counter this, Apple lowered the price on the iPod, but the iPod never regained its former success. It went from 40 percent of Apple's revenue in 2006 to 1 percent in 2014 [2].

Apple's act typified creative destruction, and it benefitted from it. In this, we are again reminded of the perennial gale Joseph Schumpeter talked about when warned of the inevitable risk of not recognizing that capitalism is an evolutionary force of continuous innovation and creative destruction [3]. Part of Schumpeter's economic theory is the insistence that large companies should not resist technological changes [4]. Why? Because they are in the best position to be the source of technological change. The threat they perceive comes not from competitors, but from innovators. Therefore, having the financial ability to invest in ideas that seem more of imagination than substance, more extraordinary than ordinary, more nonaligned with the current product portfolio, may pay huge dividends in the long run. The wherewithal to change, innovate, and render profitable products obsolete becomes a survival technique. But, as a rule, too many large companies move forward through the continual repetition of past successful strategies, wagering the averages while often ignoring the tails of the distribution.

***

Repetition of success is the momentum of the company, and it is indeed risky to challenge it. But it is also risky not to. Take, as an example, the case of Kodak, founded by George Eastman and Henry Strong in 1888. Kodak followed a business strategy of selling inexpensive cameras and making large margins on the consumables required for the cameras—film, processing, and paper. To say Kodak was an icon of American business may be an understatement. As late as 1976, Kodak dominated 90 percent of film sales and 85 percent of camera sales in the United States [5], [6]. But then, 36 years later, they sought shelter in Chapter 11 Bankruptcy Laws. Kodak, the giant that popularized photography for the masses, appeared to do everything right. They maintained a highly effective business model, maintained focus on its core strengths, and put out a quality product. But they unfortunately failed to recognize, or at least act on, one very important item. The perspective of the consumer, in regard to imaging, was changing—rapidly.

Most people by now are familiar with the story—that is, Kodak's reliance on film, paper, and chemicals and their reluctance to give this up. But the question that needs to be asked is whether or not Kodak simply underestimated the speed at which digital photography would surpass film photography. The answer, to a degree, is yes, but there is more to that than simple underestimation of a technology evolution, or the prospect of a technology evolution. What they failed to consider was the prospect of a technology revolution. Management, for various reasons, did not recognize the speed at which the digital revolution would disrupt their high margin, but nevertheless declining market.

From their perspective, the reasons not to recognize this were found in the fact they did not have brand supremacy in this market, and also that technical revolutions tend to share the common attributes of falling prices and low margins. From their perspective, i.e., their business model, any strategy to overhaul a business-as-usual model did not require urgency. Why? Because from their 'vantage' point, image sharing still required printing. A person taking a picture with a digital camera would still have to print the image, and Kodak, aside from film, was in the paper and chemical business. What did they miss? Electronic image storing platforms and viewing, and eventually online sharing. Along with the technology change, the perspective of the consumer had changed!

The first online sharing services appeared in the mid-1990s, and this appeared to be an opportunity waiting to happen. The opportunity was the advent of social networks that propelled image sharing into the realm of a commonplace activity. Could this have been predicted? Obviously, it was, but not by industry giants—rather, it was by tech-savvy entrepreneurs.

People still wanted images, but they no longer wanted or needed to print them. Instead, the perspective was changing to electronic sharing, online and instantaneously. But it wasn't just sharing a photograph;

that's too mundane. It was a sharing of lives, of telling snippets of life stories through imagery, at the speed of Wi-Fi—instantly. *Here I am at the beach, right now.* Or: *Here's the guy I'm flirting with; he just bought me a drink.*

The advent of image-sharing camera phones and online sharing fueled social media to an explosive height, and Kodak, the image giant who invented the first digital camera,[G] wasn't part of this [7]–[9]. To indicate how explosive this market was, in 2013, it was estimated that there were approximately ninety-eight cell phones for every hundred people in the world.[H] This may be, in part, the reason that in the spring of 2012, while Kodak was in bankruptcy, Facebook, the social media giant, paid Instagram a billion dollars for the rights to its Android version. Instagram is a photo-sharing service that provides its application, or app, free of charge. Essentially, a billion dollars for intellectual property and customer data! No brick and mortar, no manufacturing facilities or warehouses, etc. The new business platform in town was the app, and it resided on a cellphone. Nevertheless, a billion dollars is a seemingly moderate price to pay to bring the world instantly to their customers. It can be said, and rightly so, that instant online sharing of world imagery is the single largest mediator of social conscience in the world today.

But back to Kodak. What mistake did they make? By most accounts, they became so current portfolio oriented, they failed to focus on customer needs. Kodak's corporate culture maintained a strong belief in a consumer culture that was fading. When this happens in business, focus shifts away from understanding what business you are

---

[G] U.S. Patent 4,131,919 Patent—Electronic Still camera invented by Steve Sasson of Eastman Kodak in 1975 with the patent granted in 1978. The camera weighed eight pounds and had a 0.01-megapixel resolution with the black and white image recorded on a cassette tape. The process took twenty-three seconds. In 2009, President Barack Obama awarded Sasson the nation's highest honor given to scientists, engineers, and inventors, the National Medal of Technology and Innovation, for "*the invention of the digital camera, which has revolutionized the way images are captured, stored, and created, creating new opportunities in commerce, education, and global communication*" [10].

[H] Hong Kong is estimated to have in excess of 256.7 connections per every 100 people while North Korea is estimated to have 12.3 connection per every 100 people [11]

in to the myopic demand to sell more products. These should not be disparate items. Had Kodak paid attention to the perspective of the customer and accordingly reassessed who they were, they would have concluded: images tell stories, and they were actually in the "stories of life" business, not the film business. This is, in part, what Facebook understood when they bought Instagram.

It should be noted there was a film company that knew they were in the stories of life business. That was Polaroid, as acknowledged by their "instant memories" campaign and late 1960s Swinger cameras. Polaroid, founded in 1937 by Edwin H. Land [12] as a way to market his polarizing filter invented a few years earlier, found initial success in their glare-reducing glasses, photographic filters, color animation, and military applications. However, the company leaped to even greater success with the instant camera first developed in 1943 [13]. By 1978, they peaked in employment with over twenty-one thousand employees, and in 1992, they developed a digital camera. However, they did not expand their business into the digital market until 1996.

Why? As mentioned, the digital camera Polaroid developed in 1992 was not released until 1996, a glacially slow product release in an emerging digital age, particularly when they already had a fairly good understanding of their "instant" customer. In the four years between development and release, Polaroid had plenty of time to evolve the business model to accommodate the technology. But in 1992, the evidence suggests they did not place importance on digital technology and certainly did not see it as a disruptor.

In 1992, a meeting was held at Polaroid's Cambridge Massachusetts office complex, known as Technology Square, to discuss the Joshua Project—the code name for Polaroid's newest camera in development for the instant photography market [14]. The meeting was one in a series that had been taking place since 1988. The Joshua camera would compete with 35-mm automatic cameras that were dominating the market.

An advantage 35-mm automatic cameras had was they could take picture after picture without interruption, while the Polaroid camera could only take one at a time with a fifteen-second wait period before the next picture could be taken. Each Polaroid photo needed to be stored somewhere, usually in the customer's pocket.

The Joshua Project camera had several technological hurdles to overcome in order to compete. First, it was believed customers would use the camera more if they did not have to stop after each photo to find a place to store it. Thus, the camera must provide automatic storage. Second, it must compete in camera size, camera price, and film price—and it needed a marketing strategy. To construct a marketing strategy, the Joshua Project looked at all the requisite items. They assessed demographics, current and future economic conditions, and consumer disposable income; they surmised consumers would increasingly look for value in products and services. They looked at the current camera market. In it, they looked at sales and distribution of 35-mm cameras, 110 cartridge and disk cameras, and instant cameras. They looked at film sales in the amateur market, film processing costs, ratings of picture quality, and reasons for taking pictures, to name a few.

From this, the Joshua Project was able to conclude consumers wanted a camera that was easier to operate and easier to manage on vacations and other trips. As for the consumer, they found they would be younger, upscale, career-minded, intelligent, stylish, adventurous, and friendly. Nowhere in the 1992 meeting was there mention of digital photography, even though a digital camera was developed by Polaroid in 1992. Did they think digital photography was not market viable? On any scale? What Polaroid did in 1992 was release its Captiva film camera with the features outlined by the Joshua Project.

Polaroid's technology model can be summed up by a quote from its founder, Edwin Land: "*Do not undertake the program unless the goal is manifestly important and its achievement nearly impossible. Do not do anything that anyone else can do readily* [15]."

Polaroid's business model, however, was not so challenging. It was a simple model based on continuous consumption, much like Kodak—the one-time sale of inexpensive cameras with the continuous sale of film. This was the business model of the Captiva.

The disruptive innovation of the digital market presented a severe challenge to this model. Polaroid could sell the digital camera, but then what? Where was the aftermarket stream of profit? No film, therefore, no profit—or so it was believed. Many, including Polaroid's senior engineers, were reported to be in conflict with management over how to market the technology. Senior management, unable to fully anticipate the impact of digital cameras, did not pursue a new market business model. They apparently believed this technology disruption would be too costly, and the new product would cause more loss than the value it would create.

Organizations do fail when technological changes destroy the value of current competencies. However, they also succeed when responding to disruptive technologies through the development of new and very different skills. Consider the Japanese giant, Fujifilm. As did Kodak, it had a near-monopolistic hold on film in its home country. But when recognizing the revolution in digital photography, it diversified. It sorted through its collection of chemical compounds to move successfully into the cosmetic industry. It dramatically restructured by shedding the more superfluous components of its infrastructure [16]. There was more, but I assume the reader gets the idea.

Joseph Schumpeter (1883–1950), speaking on a much grander scale, referred to disruptive technologies as "*industrial mutations*." In 1942, he wrote, "*The opening up of new markets, foreign or domestic, and the organizational development from the craft shop to such concerns as U.S. Steel illustrate the same process of industrial mutation…that incessantly revolutionizes the economic structure from within, incessantly destroying the old one, incessantly creating a new one. This process of Creative Destruction*[1] *is the essential fact about capitalism* [17]."

Whether you refer to this as a disruptive technology or an industrial mutation, from a purely physical perspective, the reality is it begins as an unstable process influencing a stable process until the unstable process dominates. The stable process is then removed by competition (outcompeted).

Schumpeter was critical of those who assess models and proclaim them predictable because of current stability. In his words (paraphrased), "*Analysis of what happens in any particular part…is inconclusive beyond that.*"

But the development of very new skill sets is difficult. It is far easier to argue innovation is of little worth if it is too costly to implement. This is a common argument used by in-the-box thinkers, but the validity of

[1] For an insightful economic perspective of creative destruction, the reader is directed to *Capitalism, Socialism, and Democracy, Part II,* Chapt VII, by Joseph Schumpeter available online in the Taylor & Francis e-Library, 2003.]

this depends on how far forward the thought process goes. If it is a short-term, next quarter gain thought process, the in-the-box thinker is probably, and momentarily, correct. But the question that must be asked is whether the argument will stand the test of moving forward in time, beyond the quarterly gain, beyond the projections that discount disruptive technologies. For Kodak and Polaroid, there was the assumption of consumer stability. Was this naive? Edwin Land, in the early 1980s, sold off his stock in the company while warning management that the equity of the balance sheet would surely fall off without growth in intellectual capital and arrays of structured accomplishments [18].

At first blush, it appeared Kodak and Polaroid were to become early adopters of the disruptive digital technology. But the unwillingness of management to construct a business strategy around an unproven market demand proved to be their undoing. Both companies lacked the tolerance for moving out of their comfort zones and the curiosity to explore the social complexity of digital technology. They had a shelf space perspective, and as a result, failed to properly assess—perhaps predict is a better phrase—the market potential of a digital imaging platform.

Polaroid, like Kodak, did not understand the social complexity of digital technology and its value to the customer. Polaroid and Kodak had a distorted self-image of how the world viewed them. The identity they perceived was not the identity viewed by the consumer. The distorted view they had of themselves was actually keeping them in bondage to a no longer valid identity. John Hegarty, chairman of Polaroid's advertising agency, put it this way: "*Polaroid's problem was that they kept thinking of themselves as a camera. But the vision process taught us something: Polaroid is not a camera—it's a social lubricant*" [19].

The vision process is an essential component of any successful endeavor, but not necessarily entrepreneurial vision. Entrepreneurial vision in a company is generally patterned on competition within the market and what the company expects to achieve in light of the competition. It focuses on critical tasks pursuant to goals and objectives. It is necessarily lofty and meaningful, challenging with the expectation that management and individual contributors will rise to the challenge. In this, it becomes the glue that binds the company to a common goal.

But the vision process I am talking about is a social vision. In a similar manner to the entrepreneurial vision, to be of benefit to the company, it must be periodically reevaluated.

Social vision is not just how the company perceives itself in a competitive environment—that is, through market share and the ability to develop and exploit competitive advantages—but rather it is the ability to perceive itself or its product offerings in a similar manner as their customers. Hegarty's statement, mentioned above, exemplifies this. Polaroid's customers, as well as Kodak's, no longer saw the camera solely as a mechanism for instantly recording images. They saw images as data to define their lives—perhaps not knowingly, but in their actions, yes.

Images became something not to be tucked away in albums, but instead, day-to-day communication as commonplace as the spoken word. Images were rapidly becoming daily enablers. To be fair to Kodak and Polaroid, much of the social lubricity of digital imaging did not take place until cameras were merged with smartphones. However, digital imaging can be traced back to 1909 and Nikola Tesla. Fast forward to the 1990s and you have PDAs (personal digital assistants) being hybridized with smartphones, Internet connectivity, and e-mail. The handwriting was on the wall. It would only be a matter of time before digital cameras were incorporated into this mix. Did Kodak and Polaroid lack future vision? Social vison? The answer seems to be yes, but when all you can see is the loss of profit through disappearing camera, film, and paper sales, how do you develop a cognizance of social vision and redefine it accordingly? These are difficult questions, and not readily answered.

Social vision is about diversity, one element touching many tangents. It is looking at the products and services in the context of why they are important to society. What purpose is served in their usefulness that goes beyond the face value and practicality of the design? What is the tangential potential? That is, what does it enable? What is its social outcome? These are elements of social vision. Suffice it to say, in today's world, companies and service organizations would be well-advised to develop a social vision to parallel the entrepreneurial vision. As mentioned, in fairness to Polaroid and Kodak, it must be said that tying imaging to cell phones brought a whole new dimension to social vision and communication. Perhaps visual listening is a better term, but this did not happen until Sanyo introduced the first camera phone in 2002—too late for Polaroid or Kodak, but not too late for those with an entrepreneurial spirit and iconoclastic momentum.

Enter Facebook, Snapchat, Pinterest, etc.[J] Their success in social vision, in the image communication business, indicates they did understand this. Tying this into a web-based platform and apps resulted in astronomical success. This typifies the revolution talked about by Schumpeter when he described the process of creative destruction.

***

Let's take a step back in time and consider an example of fundamental social vision. Consider W. C. Coleman, of Coleman lantern fame [23]. As the nineteenth century became the twentieth, electricity illuminated only about 8 percent of American homes. This was partly due to Edison's insistence on using direct current, which was limited in distance, and his claim that George Westinghouse's alternating current was dangerous and commercially unsound. No matter, electrical circuitry needs an infrastructure, and rural America was not equipped, thus large cities may have enjoyed electrical lighting, but a few miles' distance from large urban centers, lighting was restricted to candles and petroleum-fueled lanterns.

Coleman, at the time, was a lantern salesman working for a company called Irby & Gilliland. While Irby & Gilliland made a superior product, selling a superior lantern in a market plagued with flickering, inferior, sooty, carbon-clogging, no-guarantee products was not an easy task. People simply did not trust a manufacturer's claims of the reliability of lanterns. However, Coleman, who was limited in sensory vision (25 percent in one eye and 50 percent in the other) but not social vision, knew he was not selling lanterns. Rather, his product

---

[J] Pinterest has reached 250 million monthly active users as of October 2018. "Pinterest Is a Unicorn. It Just Doesn't Act Like One." *New York Times.* Retrieved 16 October 2018. [20]

Constine Josh, *Snap shares skyrocket on first earnings beat with revived user growth – TechCrunch. techcrunch.com,* Feb 6, 2018 https://techcrunch.com/2018/02/06/snap-inc-earnings-q4-2017/, Retrieved April 11, 2018. [21] 1.588 billion daily active users on Facebook on average for March, 2021 Facebook Reports First Quarter 2021 Results [22]

was illumination, a particularly important product and attractive selling point for store owners wanting a one-up on the competition after the sun went down.

Building on this insight, and much to the chagrin of his employer, he did not sell, but rather rented the Irby & Gilliland lanterns at a dollar a week [24]. While his competitors offered lanterns, he had the social vision to offer a lighting service. While the exchange was still a lantern, he offered something the competition did not—a compelling reason to choose his lantern. At one dollar a week, the financial risk to the customer was greatly reduced. Additionally, this allowed him to convince people he was investing in their community by being part of the community; he was there for the long run, not the quick sale.

The rest is history. He bought out Irby & Gilliland and began to manufacture his own lanterns. Still in business today and having successfully adjusted to the electrification of the world at large, Coleman, bought by Newell Brands in 2005, sells primarily to outdoor recreational enthusiasts.

As a further example, in the early 1930s, an Iowa entrepreneur by the name of George Foerstner [25] designed a line of beer coolers that became a source of income for the Amana Colonies, of which he was a member.

Foerstner, who began his career selling automobile accessories at the age of thirteen, went on to develop this endeavor into Amana Refrigeration, which built home freezers. But this brief narrative is not about his business success. Here is the thing: what makes Foerstner worth mentioning is he was a visionary and a master marketer. He did not sell the freezers directly to the consumer. He knew the consumer would not immediately understand why they needed a home freezer, let alone agree to purchase one. He also clearly understood consumer shopping patterns.

He knew the consumer stocked perishables on a weekly basis—that is, purchased and consumed no more than what could fit into the small freezer component of their refrigerator or icebox. Hence, if consumer patterns provided no real reason to purchase a freezer, how would he convince the consumer to make the purchase? His answer was surprisingly simple. He would provide an incentive for the consumer to adjust purchase patterns. To do this, he first went door-to-door selling the consumer wholesale foods. Once the consumer bought more perishable food than they could safely store (the incentive being a reduction in the cost of consumable goods), he introduced them to his line of freezers [26]. His argument was the reduction in cost over time would pay for the freezer. He sold freezers by first selling the demand.

Much like the Kanizsa triangle discussed earlier—where one imposes the necessary elements to complete the nonexistent image—he imposed the perceived need for a freezer by creating a demand for wholesale perishable foods. Brilliant! Eventually, the Raytheon Company, a tech giant and defense contractor, bought Amana Refrigeration. Not for its successful line of freezers, but rather to gain access to Foerstner's marketing expertise, i.e., his ability to "see" the customer and alter the customer's perception of what was needed.

Raytheon, among other things, built large-scale commercial microwave ovens [27]. Microwave ovens had yet to meet success in the home market due to their large size—in part a construct of high-energy demands and cooling requirements—and the size of the magnetron that generated the microwaves. This was an opportunity awaiting technologies of scale. Coincidently, Raytheon's Japanese subsidiary had recently discovered how to miniaturize the magnetron, opening the way for a marketable home appliance.

Foerstner put his son, Richard, in charge [28]. Richard made major redesign recommendations for the appliance. He insisted it be no larger than the size of a window air conditioner, air-cooled (commercial versions were water-cooled), have a 120-volt operation, a cost to the consumer under five hundred dollars, and no vacuum tubes (to further reduce its size).

George worked on the image of the microwave, moving it from a military and industrial perspective to that of a home necessity. To do this, he hired a team of young women to demonstrate the potential of the oven. He quickly incorporated it into that part of the household—the kitchen—which was almost exclusively a woman's domain (such was the matrimonial and social construct of the time). The microwave oven was woven into the everyday tapestry of a woman's life, and the result was a phenomenal success.

While Richard set about defining the product according to physical dimensions and its primary function, George defined it according to the social fabric of the customer—the customer's perspective. To put this into context, ask this question: what does the product do? Take a picture, as in the case of Polaroid? Yes, and many marketers would stop there and sell the camera and the picture, but for a social vision to take hold, the question must become: what does the picture do? That is the question that needs to be asked and understood. Much like the microwave that could cook dinner, the real question is: what could the microwave-cooked dinner do? Answer: it was a time bank. It could save time, therefore adding time to the day to be spent on other activities.

Much like Cézanne, whose intent was to provide the viewer with an experience of depth different from a single-point perspective, the digital image eroding the film industry became more important than the mere subject matter captured on film. It became a statement of lifestyle. Polaroid came to understand this too late, while Coleman and Foerstner knew from the beginning their products were much more than hardware. They were lifestyle-altering technologies.

Similar arguments to Polaroid and Kodak can be made for the demise of Blockbuster Video, the US-based distributor of video and video game rentals and international phenom. At its peak in 2004, it employed over eighty-four thousand people worldwide [29].

While one may attribute much of Blockbuster's demise to management and unsound acquisitions, it must be said that technology, in the form of video streaming, altered the customer's perspective of how movies should be obtained. Whether Blockbuster recognized this or not, they didn't act on it. Instead, they held steadfast to a revenue-sharing business model that, in the past, was highly successful: studios provided Blockbuster with videos at minimal cost and in return received 40 percent of rental fees, leaving Blockbuster 60 percent. They either failed to understand or simply ignored the fact that the customer expected more than a video.

Due to video streaming, the point of sale was moving to wherever the customer was, not where brick and mortar Blockbuster was. Wherever the customer was, there was also the expectation of access to a library that was always in stock and never charged a late fee. While this may be thought of as Blockbuster's failure to understand the importance of convenience to the customer, it may have been more of a failure to be attuned to the lifestyle changes of the customer.

It appears clear, at least to me, that as customers evolve—i.e., leveraging new technologies, expanding social networking, and altering expectations—traditional product and service consumption has become a thing of the past. As a result, there is a massive reshaping in how products and services are merchandised and distributed. There is no choice in this. Traditional retailing, in the form of brick and mortar and Sunday newspaper flyers, can no longer afford to think of themselves as pillars of the community or anchors of the shopping mall. They must realize competition is coming from outside the geographically local community; the mall is virtual, no longer brick and mortar; and a social presence in the form of social media will, and is, looming larger than shelf presence. Anyone doubting this should look at the Pinterest website that, as of October 2018, reached 250 million active subscribers [30].

Pinterest, for the few not familiar with it, is a social media and website application company. Like other social media websites, Pinterest allows marketers access to data collected on users. This provides marketers with the ability to determine how people respond to a product, making Pinterest integral to corporate-marketing digital strategies. What is interesting is how Pinterest subtly introduces itself to potential customers. A search of the web for the Pinterest site brings up words like "discover," "ideas," "inspiration," and "personalized" in the brief sentences under the web link. These are words that connote the finding of something unexpected, suggesting courses of action, stimulus, and being specific to one's self. Open one of the Pinterest links and you will find something else—free shipping. Once a competitive offering, now a consumer expectation.

Consider Shopko, a Midwest, Western, and Northwestern regional general merchandiser with 360 stores. In January 2019, it filed for bankruptcy, largely due to its inability to compete with online retailers. As Shopko's CEO stated in an affidavit in bankruptcy court, the poor performance was in part due to competition from online sellers, with Shopko having an undeveloped online presence.

"Unfortunately, the Debtors, like many other retail companies, have recently fallen victim to adverse macro-trends, including the general shift away from brick-and-mortar stores to online retail channels. More specifically, retail companies like Shopko, with a substantial physical footprint, bear higher expenses than web-based retailers and are heavily dependent on store traffic, which has decreased significantly as consumers increasingly shop online rather than in malls or shopping centers [31]*."*

In the above statement, we have some insight into why Shopko failed, and that is with the phrase "*adverse macro trends*." Is this what Shopko executives defined online shopping to be—an adverse trend? The move to online retailing and social media has been going for more than two decades. Amazon and eBay were both launched in 1995. The early 2000s saw broadband. By 2003, 20 percent of Americans had broadband in their homes, giving an increasing number of homes access to the Internet and online shopping [32]. This was not an adverse trend. This was a revolution sponsored by disruptive technology, and just as first shots are fired in any revolution, those being shot at need to defend and devise strategies. In this case, the strategy should have been to join the revolution—quickly. But as we have discussed, and no doubt will witness in the foreseeable future, there will be more casualties of this "*adverse macro trend*."

Businesses wanting to compete must realize all is changing. From the sourcing of raw materials to point of sales. The cardinal philosophy of retailing is now that consumer benefits, and the ability to meet changing expectations and patterns of consumerism, are as important or more important than the product being sold.

As a personal example, my wife and I recently visited a local merchandiser with a brick-and-mortar presence of over forty stores in the upper Midwest. I was looking for a particular style of winter clothing I knew the store stocked. However, as luck would have it, this particular store did not have my size. As I was asking the salesclerk if she could find out whether another store had this style, my wife interrupted me and announced she had just ordered this online from Amazon to include next day delivery and free shipping.

Here's the point: a product was purchased from an online retailer while shopping for the product in another retailer's physical store. Here is the question that retailers must answer: do you know where the point of sale is?

***

An industry burying its business model in the sand in the face of a disruptive technology (the crisis) is a business ill-prepared for the challenge. A business denouncing disruptive challenge as little more than short-lived phenomena or trends, without the consideration of alternatives to adjust or replace the business model or current portfolio, is a business at risk. But why would a business do this? Why are some organizations so reluctant to adopt disruptive innovation, so resistant to change?

The easy answer is success in a stable organization is built on the status quo, not the momentum of change. Gain in the face of crisis comes at the expense of entrenched beliefs, dogma, and status quo; it is not just disruptive, it is destructive. Innovation can provoke discontinuity, inducing turmoil in the market. Organizations have standard patterns of behavior that reinforce the organizational identity. They have standard operating procedures in place to direct forward momentum, and what could be called current portfolio inertia. Change would require restructuring mechanisms, directing forward momentum. Organizations, finding they have too much current portfolio inertia, have great difficulty acquiring or adopting new technologies. Thus, they not only risk losing dominance in an existing market, but also often find the market has diminished. They find too late that their perspective of the market is no longer valid. For organizations such as this, it is often only external pressure and survival, recognizing their own mortality, that leads to change, often too late [33], [34].

Consider the words of Milan Kundera, the Franco-Czech novelist: :*We are all prisoners of a rigid conception of what is important and what is not. We anxiously follow what we suppose to be important while what we suppose to be unimportant wages guerrilla warfare behind our backs, transforming the world without our knowledge and eventually mounting a surprise attack on us"* [35].

Chapter 10: The Status Quo

It is fair to say the true iconoclast is not pedestrian and is a contradiction to many business environments where a commonality of thought and philosophy is championed. (Software developers may be the exception.)

According to Jeffrey Dyer of Brigham Young University, and colleagues [1], [2], this is also true generally in society where societies that promote community over individualism are less likely to produce those who will challenge the status quo. Items such as cohesion, directed leadership, strength of purpose, and acceptance or adherence—generally considered from a management perspective as positive attributes—can create a defeating environment for the iconoclast.

This is evident in certain world societies of the last century. One need only look at the collectives and communes of Stalinistic Russia, or China under Mao, to observe the disastrous results of an emphasis on community over the individual. When the emphasis is forced and brutal, the results are tragic. The agricultural collectives and communes of both societies quickly failed in their purpose. Any success Russia had with communes must be considered in the same light as the resources provided to power them. The communes were given land, loans, tax reductions, and the assistance of a cadre of agricultural professionals to meet their goals. In the end, the communes died similarly to many of their countrymen; they were terminated, no longer found suitable. The communes did not improve the quality of life of their members, but this was never an objective. Rather, when they did not provide a visible demonstration of what was possible under communism, they were ordered to cease.

Communes, in reality, may not be where one would look for an iconoclast. Russia did seek superiority in the sciences and technology; however, the lack of cooperation and trust between Russian scientists and foreign researchers took its toll. Some fields of science were considered to be idealist and discouraged, such as relativity theory and quantum mechanics. However, pseudo-sciences, rejected on evidentiary grounds by Western researchers but catering to Russian political venues, were developed, complete with their own trumped-up theoretical basis for being [3].

Foremost in this may have been Lysenkoism [4], named after Trofim Lysenko, who rejected Mendelian inheritance in favor of the Lamarckian view of the heritability of acquired characteristics. Lysenko's proponents offered numerous false proofs, such as weeds spontaneously turning into food grains. But to maintain the theory, many prominent Russian geneticists were repressed, i.e., arrested with internment or executed in an effort to quench the truth about Lysenkoism. Under the cultural revolution of communism, Russian science in the 1920s up to the 1960s was inherently political. The belief that science for the sake of science was discouraged [5].

In the end, Russia played a game of catch-up with the West. Nevertheless, they did accomplish one feat worthy of mention. Yuri Gagarin became the first man in space, and this in itself launched (pun intended) perhaps the greatest technology race in the history of mankind.

Mao's cultural revolution and autonomous Red Guards moved millions into agricultural collectives, threw intellectuals into prison, and closed colleges and universities. The cultural revolution produced what has been referred to as an "ossified produce economy" [6] subject to the commands of Beijing, not the demands of the market. Mao's personal brand of equality for all limited the "rights" of all people, but most notably the capitalistic class. This was the class most likely to demonstrate entrepreneurship, and as a result, the economy began to collapse. When the revolution failed to bring about the desired visible results, blame was attributed to counterrevolutionary forces, absolving Mao from much of the responsibility.

Pol Pot and the Khmer Rouge took the emphasis on community and the dissolution of the individual to horrific lows in their attempt to transform Cambodia into an agrarian utopic society. They classified people according to usefulness, and those classified as depositees—usually the educated or business owners, i.e., those most likely to exhibit individualism—were earmarked for elimination. In Pol Pot's version of the individual, in an agrarian utopia, "to keep you is no benefit, to destroy you is no loss" [7].

These are extreme examples of community over individualism, where the community is expected to permanently flourish as a result of removing individualism. More common examples of diminishing the individual for the benefit of the community are found in the branches of the armed forces of civilized societies' governments. In the armed forces, chain of command over merit of the individual results in the outsourcing of innovation and creativity. To begin this discussion, first we must remember that for the individual, there is only an expectation of permanently residing in such a community when it is the choice of the individual. It must also be noted the authoritarian chain of command over individual needs is essential to the success of military operations; it is, in this environment, a necessarily good thing.

Military communities in the Western world exist through the acceptance of a rigid discipline which, for the majority of servicemen and women, is transient. They come into the military services, perform their duties, and leave after the allotted time—usually three to six years. Only the "lifers" stay, and even for them, there is a mandatory time in which to leave. Thus, someone with iconoclastic tendencies in the military may experience an environment where their particular momentum is not championed or even particularly welcomed, but they will not be a permanent resident of this environment. Thus, military communities successfully exist, in part, because there is a fluidity of membership.

Military communities also exist because they have external sources of funding. They are not expected to fund themselves, to have supportive economies. As a result, there is a mega-billion-dollar industry, sometimes referred to as the military-industrial complex, interactive with the military community that surrounds it. This consists of the taxpayers, politicians, political contributors, lobbyists, a global arms industry, and a host of supportive others all doing their part to maintain and advance the militaries of the world. Militaries are sustained through the efforts of others who see the necessity and demonstrated value in their existence.

Military communities are one thing, but what of communities that do not have sponsored funding or external support? Consider the communes of the 1960s and 1970s in the United States. The communes of this time were intentional communities constructed around an ideology that simpler was better.

To begin this discussion, I must make two things very clear: where the ideology came from and where it went. It came from diversity and vanished into singularity. The large cities and universities of the United States, and elsewhere in the Western world, were hotbeds of diversity, of other perspectives. Not just in the overused phrase of "melting pot" and its mingling of humanity, but in the coming together of philosophies and ideals salted heavily with anger and disillusionment of what was perceived to be the status quo.

The 1960s and early 1970s in the United States were turbulent times, times of rejection of authority and the trappings of capitalism. In the middle of this great ocean of diversity came the thought of not just rejecting authority, but of rejecting diversity. Moving to a simpler life. Rejecting the complexity of life that made the idea of a simpler life not just attractive, but also possible.

There is an irony here. There is also a similarity to military societies in that the communes required an adherence to authority, only here it was the anti-authority of the counterculture. The question in this, as posed by Joseph Manzella of Southern Connecticut State University [8], is how does such a society maintain a sense of identity while being tolerant and permitting individual expression? The answer is, they didn't. Most failed within a few years of their founding, primarily due to the disillusionment with a singularity of perspective—that is, failing to remember the essence of spirit is the experience of diversity.

This is not unlike an authoritarian business environment in which the management culture is a culture of control. To paraphrase GE's former CEO Jack Welch, management functions driven by a focus on control add little in the way of value to their people's capabilities. "*A leader's role is not to control people or stay on top of things, but rather to guide, energize, and excite*" [9].

It is variance that makes the world robust. Diverse systems thrive because of the ability to develop niches for prospering. This results in stability of the system. The same is true for communities. Diverse communities are more likely to confer resilience to the community because of the greater probability of adapting to change. Niches act as buffers against loss; thus, diversity is a stabilizing force. Take this away and you have the recipe for failure.

***

It must be stated that overemphasis on a nondiverse community does not mean creativity and innovation are static. They do happen, but at a much slower rate; hence, they are stagnant. Such economies can be defined by the narrowed focus on community development, where individual effort is directed by current community effort and self-identity takes a backseat to community identity. From a distance, these cultures may look inviting, pastoral, and communal, like a pond of lotus flowers—until one realizes lotus flowers thrive in stagnant waters and can quickly choke life out of their environment, much like how the lack of progressive movement defeats the individual self.

***

On a much grander scale, consider the introduction of mass literacy and its impact on a stagnant medieval Europe. Literacy is a truly disruptive technology. Gutenberg's printing press, movable type,[K] and

[K] Gutenberg, often credited with the invention of the printing press using movable type, printed his now famous Bible in 1456. However, the Chinese artisan Pi Sheng, also referred to as Bi Sheng (AD 990–1051), is more rightfully recognized as inventing the world's first movable type technology between AD 1041 and 1048, during the Song Dynasty. He used thinly cut pieces of clay carved into individual characters and baked them to form a ceramic type. In Korea, the use of movable metal type had been active since 1234. Given the considerable contact Europe had with the East at the time of Gutenberg and in the centuries prior, it is entirely reasonable there was an awareness of Asian movable type printing in Europe. Thus, it may be fair to

ink brought the printed word to the masses in Europe at a time when half the male population and 90 percent of the female population were illiterate [10].

Both governments and the church feared the spread of subversive ideas—subversive being contrary to dogma. The ability to read or write existed primarily in the clergy or those with a professional status, and the written language of choice and decree was Latin. Having a single language for the dissemination of knowledge and restricting knowledge to those wealthy enough to afford an education—or the training of clergy—resulted in like minds and gave a minority control over societies.

Literacy of the masses would have been a distinct disadvantage to those controlling knowledge and keeping economies restricted to the current community status. It must be remembered that the strength of the church was in its resistance to change. Published works and official documentation existing in local dialects or state and regional languages were few. Keeping Latin as the language of choice allowed both civil and ecclesiastic authorities to maintain dominion over knowledge. But this was to change.

Print expanded the distribution of ideas. Soon-to-be Renaissance intellectuals now had a way to move their ideas into the public domain. The pervasion of literacy through the use of vernacular language brought distinct technical advances. In a world on the brink of enlightenment, literacy moved from an indulgence of privilege to a requisite necessity. The world was no longer the single-perspective mechanical process Braque, centuries later, described in his lack of infatuation with art of the day. Rather, the provision of multiple perspectives literacy provided transformed medieval communities into Renaissance societies through the challenge to ritualistic allegiance. Common people now had the tools to be uncommon in thought.

Why was literacy disruptive? Simple: it catered to a new customer, a customer who had previously been a non-consumer, and there were far more former non-consumers of literacy than current consumers. By advocating literacy in the vernacular language and dialects, it remained outside the existing structure. It didn't become mainstream until it was

---

say Gutenberg, and the print revolution associated with him, had its origins or influence from Asia [11], [12].

the mainstream. It was accessible while simultaneously providing access to the world. This made it liberating.

Chapter 11: The Non-Consumer

Catering to the non-consumer is a hallmark of disruptive technology. Consider the telephone. In the nineteenth century, the telephone, while an interesting technology, was not thought to be a viable competitor to the telegraph because it was limited in distance, had no method of keeping a record of communication, and had poor quality transmission. It was thought to have only limited value in communication, perhaps between offices or for "use in factories, mines, and small towns and communities where the amount of the business did not employ the full capacity of the wires" [1]. In other words, it was an auxiliary technology of limited use. But the telephone played to a different consumer.

Where telegraph communication exhibited brevity and played to a sense of urgency and starched communication, the telephone was personal and informal. It didn't require operators to read and translate a message from code or into code. It didn't require a messenger to relay the message to the recipient. The telephone was a personal extension of self—perhaps the first real mechanically assisted extension of self. It allowed the user to disembody the voice to reach out into homes and businesses, thus becoming the first device in history to allow a speaker to be present in two places at one time for the purpose of instantaneous dialogue. It could convey emotion and nuance. It allowed the user to transcend distance in a way the telegraph never could.

Anyone who could put a telephone in a business or home could use it. The only demand on it was the ability to pick it up and speak. The demand on the telegraph required someone to be trained, learn Morse code, and understand the fundamentals of electricity. It was not a household technology. The telephone, much like literacy in medieval Europe, catered to the masses.[L]

It may be fair to say the telegraph companies of the day would not have considered incorporating a disruptive technology like the telephone into their business model due to fear of cannibalization of existing customers. But, as stated, the telephone played to a different audience—the non-consumer of telegraph services—and as such would have made an excellent addition to a portfolio.

An example of disruptive technology closer than medieval Europe or the nineteenth century is the advent of personal computers. In the early 1970s, when I left the military and went to college, computer sciences were a requisite study for anyone in a business, math, or science curriculum—not necessarily for those in liberal arts. The proficient use of a computer required knowledge of assembly or machine language commands.

Demonstration of proficiency in computer programming languages (Cobal, Basic, Fortran, etc.) could be substituted for the graduation requirement of a foreign language.

In other words, the use of computers required a comprehensive learning process and demonstration of expertise, much like the

---

[L] We generally acknowledge Alexander Graham Bell as the inventor of the telephone, but there were others who came before him, and their contributions should be recognized. One notable was the Italian inventor Antonio Meucci [2] who after immigrating to the United States continued to work on a project he started earlier in his life. Meucci, unable to fund a patent application, filed a patent caveat on his invention—an electronic communication device called the teletrofono—in 1871. Because he omitted several key components of the invention, Bell was able to patent his invention in 1876. In 2002, the US House of Representatives acknowledged Meucci's work by issuing a resolution stating, "Whereas if Meucci had been able to pay the ten-dollar fee to maintain the caveat after 1874, no patent could have been issued to Bell: Now, therefore, be it resolved, that it is the sense of the House of Representatives that the life and achievements of Antonio Meucci should be recognized, and his work in the invention of the telephone should be acknowledged."

telegraph. Similar to the telephone, computers for personal use—when first introduced—were not part of the mainstream consumer audience. But personal computers, like the telephone competing with the telegraph, had a distinct advantage.

Anyone could put a personal computer in their home or business. This resulted in not only a major consumer paradigm shift but also a product development shift. This was disruptive innovation at its best—affordable and accessible. The use of personal computers, the demand for what they could do, and the software being developed were as varied as the people sitting at the keyboard. The personal computer also became an extension of self, only now it allowed the user to transcend much more than geographical distance. Where the telephone disembodied the voice, the personal computer disembodied the mind. It allowed the user to move into realms of creativity while search engines sponsored curiosity. It is fair to say this was not immediately recognized.

The first Apple ads were meant for technically proficient hobbyists and talked about fully assembled, tested, and burned-in microprocessor boards and the examination of programs in hexadecimal notation—not necessarily the purview of your average home user today. Marketers across the industry failed to comprehend the creative unleashing potential of the personal computer, particularly prior to the World Wide Web. They often spoke of it as a practicality, a convenient place for a woman to store her recipes (oh yes, they did). But this was going to quickly change. Like the printing press and the telephone, the personal computer was so much more. It was a liberator. Apple's 1984 Super Bowl commercial, "1984" [3], directed by Ridley Scott and still available for viewing on YouTube, demonstrated at least they had come to understand this. The ad shows a woman dressed as a sprinter running into an auditorium and throwing a sledgehammer at a theater screen. On the screen is a face spouting Orwellian drivel. The hammer hits the screen, which then explodes in a flash of light as the audience, depicted in a dull-blue (some say Big Blue) hue, sits with their mouths open, unable to comprehend what is happening. Apple's message—1984 isn't going to be 1984—was loud and clear: personal computers, or at least theirs, would champion the individual as the creative self.

Enter the early 1990s and the advent of the World Wide Web. As a matter of clarity, it should be noted the terms Internet and World Wide Web are commonly used interchangeably; however, the former refers to a global system of interconnected computers while the latter refers to a global collection of documents and resources. With the World Wide Web, the personal computer took on a new dimension, a dimension of global communication, awareness, and literacy. To some, it is the prospect of a global community, a global village, and that the consumer could put this new dimension in their home. A virtual dimension of knowledge and simulation, an immersible multimedia exploration of actual and artificial realities explorable from a desktop.

The last few paragraphs may lead the reader to believe disruptive technologies in part are tangents off existing technologies that exploit the non-consumer of the existing technology, or more precisely, the reasons they are non-consumers of existing technology. This would indeed be correct. To consider what this means, let's explore some of the latest disruptive technologies of the past decade or so.

Put yourself in this scenario. You live in a country where the gross domestic product amounts to one-tenth of 1 percent of the world's total. Your country's 2015 per capita GDP is, in US dollars, under sixteen hundred dollars, and your income is such that you cannot afford to buy a tube of toothpaste; rather, you purchase this when you can from a street vendor by the squeeze. You have no credit, but this is inconsequential as you also have no access to banks. Therefore, you have no ability to securely deposit any acquired funds, let alone withdraw money from an account, transfer money, or pay for goods and services through credit, checking, or debit accounts. Banks and credit unions do not exist for you. You are a non-consumer of conventional banking technology. There are micro-financial institutions in your country, some even locally offer financial assistance to people who want to start small businesses but lack the capital. But you don't have surplus funds for a savings account, and you are not an entrepreneur in need of a loan. Even if you did, you probably couldn't afford to repay the interest. A report by the CGAP in 2013 put interest rates from micro-finance institutions at a nominal 27 percent, citing increased funding costs—that is, the high transaction cost relative to the loan size—as the reason for high rates [4]. Others put rates as high as 37 percent—some cases reaching 70 percent—while other reports have found charges in excess of 100 percent, equating this with legitimized loan-sharking [5].

What you need, like most people around the world living in poverty, is a way to transfer the few and sporadic funds you have to a safe haven, to make purchases or payments without carrying cash in your pocket and without the risks inherent in traveling long, unsafe distances with cash to make a payment or bring money home to your family in a rural village from your job in a faraway city or even another country. You need the safety of financial mobility, no matter how meager it may be.

Enter the M-Pesa. The "*M*" stands for "*mobile*" and "*Pesa*" is Swahili for "*money,*" giving you some idea of where this originated. Using cell phone technology, this innovative idea allows users to deposit and withdraw funds and transfer money for payment of goods and services all through the use of a pin-secured cell phone.[M] Established in 2007 by Vodafone for Safaricom, a Kenyan telecommunications provider [6], with 60 percent of the shareholdings held by the Government of Kenya, M-Pesa is a branchless banking service.

How does it work and where did it come from? The advantage of mobile phone technology is in the cost of communication in the developing world. This does not mean mobile phone technology is inexpensive. Rather, while costs are not minor, they must be considered in conjunction with the reliability of the technology and compared with other technologies such as inadequate landline infrastructures and less than reliable transportation systems generally found in developing countries. This makes cell phone technology an opportunistic technology borne out of inefficiencies inherent in aging, poorly equipped, and badly maintained systems, and a necessary technology to connect developing countries with the twenty-first century. Of note is that of the estimated 2.5 billion people on the planet without access to conventional banking; one billion of these are estimated to have a mobile phone [8].

But how does a cell phone become a money transfer system? The answer is found in a marketing strategy of cell phone providers that has long given the consumer the ability to purchase airtime—that is, prepaid cell phone credit that can be transferred to other users. Cell phone users quickly discovered they could use this to their advantage. They found they could use this to transfer money in the form of airtime. Airtime, as

---

[M] M-Pesa is now in its second generation, dubbed the G2 [7], and has a new service called M-Tiba, which allows the user, via their mobile phone, to set funds aside for health care. Such funds stored in M-TIBA can only be used to pay for health care services and medication.

a proxy for money, becomes a valued commodity, and the sender transfers this commodity to a recipient who, in turn, sells it to a local broker for cash or payment of goods and services—in effect, a transfer of purchasing power [9].

In 2002, researchers funded by the Department for International Development, a United Kingdom government agency responsible for administering overseas aid, found people in sub-Saharan Africa were using airtime as a proxy for money. They discovered airtime was being transferred between friends and relatives and resold as needed. This was the precursor concept of M-Pesa. This led to high-level discussions on how a system of proxy money transfer could be created in Africa—specifically Kenya—and Vodafone was given a grant to pilot a study. Software was developed (through a student project) and the Vodafone subsidiary Safaricom launched the service in 2007. Safaricom is the largest mobile network provider in Kenya at the time of this writing, and the new service allowed a wide range of users to make deposits into accounts stored on their cell phones, redeem deposits for cash, and send balances to others for payment [10].

M-Pesa is not free. Users are charged a minor fee for transactions. But consider this. In 2006, less than 30 percent of Kenya's adults had access to financial services. With the advent of M-Pesa, access was estimated in 2015 at 65 percent with over 20 billion dollars (US equivalent) in transactions. One other interesting aspect of M-Pesa is the not-so-cottage industry that has grown out of it. M-Pesa agents—for whom this is usually a secondary source of income—operate mostly out of their storefronts, kiosks, and roadside stands where they register new subscribers, take deposits, and hand out withdrawals. As of this writing, Safaricom reports more than 160,000 M-Pesa agents operating in Kenya [11].

Since its inception, M-Pesa has expanded throughout Kenya into Tanzania, Egypt, Lesotho, Mozambique, Afghanistan, South Africa, India, and Eastern Europe. In October of 2009, it was reported that M-Pesa is tapping the UK diaspora market controlled by Western Union and Money Gram [12]. In this, Kenyans working in the United Kingdom and sending money home to Kenya will have a more affordable option to do so.

As seen by the success of M-Pesa, disruptive technologies are not only opportunistic, but they also represent a radical departure from convention. In the case of M-Pesa, this was not only a departure from conventional banking, which was not serving the M-Pesa community, but also a departure from cell phone application. It took a component of the cell phone—airtime—and turned it into a commodity—a proxy for money. M-Pesa is not alone in exploiting cell phones.

Consider FinTech—short for financial technology—essentially an unbundling of conventional banking financial services. FinTech is a recent technology, an innovation, an emerging technology competing with traditional financial methods to deliver financial services. Originally a back-office computer technology, it now describes any number of financial activities from cell phone checking, raising money, and managing assets to detouring around banks to apply for credit, to name a few [13].

At least one report, EY's 2018 FinTech Adoption Index, suggests one-third of consumers utilize at least two or more FinTech services, and this will increase as consumers become more aware of the role FinTech plays in their lives. They go on to state, "*This is significant enough for us to suggest that FinTech has reached early mass adoption*" and "*the financial services industry has considerable unexplored potential*" [14].

Studies such as the EY study cited above indicate two attributes of FinTech success. First, a focus on the customer. Services are simpler, more convenient, more transparent, and personalizable. The EY study found FinTech users prefer using digital channels and technologies to manage their lives. Secondly, a willingness to apply technology in what could only be considered by the current financial service institutions as moving away from traditional formalities and embracing novelty. EY found that new services and new players are driving higher adoption, resulting in a ripple effect bringing more and more people to embrace FinTech.

Traditional financial services are seeing a disruption in the traditional way of conducting business. As they struggle with gaining insights into the new perspective of the customer, start-up financial services with little or no infrastructure to unravel and redo are beginning to exploit this environment. They rapidly establish themselves as benchmarks for a new era in financial service with little or no fees attached and the ability to provide new services such as smartphone digital versions of existing financial products.

Consider ClearScore, a London-based financial technology business, and its proposition of "*Your credit report and score, for free, forever*" [15], or PayPal's ability to offer seamless mobile commerce connecting customers and merchants. PayPal may be best described as a distribution channel for global digital commerce.

As successful as FinTech is, it must be said, as a whole, it is still struggling with gaining access to the consumer. But this may be expected in emerging technologies. My personal belief is that the key to all of this is in the multiple perspectives of who the customer is. Traditional financial services had a singularity of perspective—that is, fee and service based upon credit. FinTech must consider their market segments—not just the basic demographics, but rather the changing behavioral patterns of the consumer based upon attitudinal preferences.

***

Since the beginnings of the automobile, there has always been a market for the small- scale entrepreneur willing to provide a ride in their personal vehicle to someone without means of immediate transportation. Inner cities, for decades, have to one extent or the other relied on pirate cabs or, in the vernacular, the hack, or johnny cab. The provision of a pirate cab is simple—a bartered ride to a destination based solely on the degree of the generosity of the driver. Multiple things are at work that make the pirate feasible. The operator takes advantage of the lack of availability of licensed or medallion taxi cabs in the area, the lack of public transportation to a destination, or the unacceptability of mass transportation. The pirate operator is opportunistic. Someone with free time on their hands and the willingness to go out of their way in exchange for the price of gasoline and a margin based on anything from dollars to cigarettes can be in business. Historically, the downside of the pirate is locale. They generally serve a low-income inner-city clientele.

Commercial vehicles for hire such as hackney carriage services can be dated to the early seventeenth century. Motorized vehicles for hire were first seen on the streets of New York City in the waning years of the nineteenth century. Whether it was horse-drawn or motor powered, little changed in the way these commercial vehicles were hailed until the 1940s with the advent of radio-dispatched taxis, considered to be a major innovation in taxi service [16], [17].

While the radio-dispatched taxi lessened the wait time, the structure of hailing a vehicle, for the most part, remained in place. One could stand on the street and wave down a passing vehicle or call for a taxi—once the telephone became a household item—well ahead of the time required for pickup. For the consumer, the structure was fundamentally flawed.

First, it required opportunity—that is, the opportunity to flag down a passing taxi given the possibility a taxi would pass where you were standing. This possibility became increasingly remote the further you were away from a city center. Second, if you placed a call, it required a wait time based on the availability of a taxi. If a reservation had not been made prior, the wait time could be unacceptable but nevertheless necessary. Third, it often required large cash amounts. Any business traveler can confirm in the United States, it is uncommon for a taxi to take a credit card. A taxi from a center city hotel to an airport can be an expensive cash proposition, and as is commonly known, cash is a convenient way for an operator to hide income.

Enter Uber founders Travis Kalanick and Garrett Camp [18] and a modernized premise of the pirate cab. Take a small-scale entrepreneur with some free time and the willingness to provide a ride to a consumer and remove the uncertainty of wait time and the cash-in-hand, pay-at-destination component. This positions these small-scale entrepreneurs between the licensed taxi and limousine services. With this, they have carved a niche. How big of a niche? In 2010, they developed a cell phone app to allow users to hail and track a private car. In 2015, their global presence—estimated at 60 countries and 404 cities at the time of this writing—was worth an estimated 40 billion dollars.

Uber is disruptive, but this may not be immediately apparent. In fact, there are those who would say Uber is not a disruptive technology because disrupters start by appealing to either low-end or underserved markets, that disrupters create new markets where none existed before.

But I disagree. To understand why, one must first recognize taxi companies historically lack innovative DNA. Taxi services have been basically the same thing since the 1940s. It is an industry where prices are controlled by municipal regulations and new taxi permits are expensive making entry into the market often cost prohibitive[N].

Uber disrupts by challenging the static status quo, and this is where it is interesting. Uber crowdsources a task. The task being transportation—the pickup and drop-off of a client. The crowd being anyone in Uber's network with a vehicle and a cell phone willing to complete the task. It provides an opportunity to those not willing to become a licensed taxi driver yet desiring income or additional income through the use of their personal vehicle. Monetary transactions are completed when the client makes a web payment, which prompts the open call and dispatch of an Uber-associated vehicle. This method saves Uber money on employee expenses and eliminates the requirement of employees to support vehicles and facilities. It also reduces or eliminates inventory to include the purchase or lease of big-ticket items, such as buildings and automobiles. In addition, it offers better quality, and this in itself is interesting.

Most established businesses, when challenged by increased quality or service, rise to the occasion by raising the bar, increasing their quality and service to outdo the competition. But what happened when the conventional services were confronted by competition from Uber? Taxi drivers in large cities around the world went on strike to protest Uber's existence. Instead of raising the bar, they have matter-of-factly stated they like the bar where it is and would like regulations to stay in place to keep it that way. To demonstrate this, they were willing to stop the service they now provide, in turn introducing more customers to Uber's service.

But the bar was not simply quality of the ride. The quality of the bar was found in convenience to the client, and the mechanism of convenience was the cell phone app, which changed the way people thought of getting a ride. The call to Uber goes out on the client's cell phone. The charge for the ride is handled on the cell phone (the fare does not change hands with the driver), and the tracking of the ride is provided for on the cell phone. Here is a question, perhaps food for thought: could one short-circuit the typical taxi service through the use of a cell phone app? An app that allowed one to call for a car from one

---

[N] Prior to Uber medallions often cost in the 6 digit range in large cities, and by one report exceeding a million dollars in 2014 in New York City [19].

of the numerous people willing to provide a ride in their personal vehicles. Apparently so! In this, Uber is disruptive.

In deference to those who still disagree that Uber is disruptive [20], it should be pointed out that Uber has, as of this writing, eleven noteworthy competitors in the United States, globally suggesting the market exploitation of the non-consumer or limited consumer of standard taxi services is indeed lucrative [21]. But perhaps we can settle on the term destructive—that is, a creative destruction in the view of Joseph Schumpeter: "the process of industrial mutation that incessantly revolutionizes the economic structure from within, incessantly destroying the old one, incessantly creating a new one" [22].

***

Airbnb

Part of the success of Uber is that the basic business model does not require investments in inventory and facilities. This also is a successful component of Airbnb [23], originally Airbedandbreakfast, a web-based connection service to help people list and find lodging.

Airbnb's growth is not through the increase of physical inventory, but rather the increase in listing potential host facilities and the listing of travelers requiring lodging, where success is the ability to match the requirements of both. The uniqueness of Airbnb is the blurred distinction between customer and vendor. At any time, one can be the other. Airbnb is the portal to which they are connected and which charges a fee for this service. This creates not only a new and nontraditional supply of lodging, but also a market for customers with "other" expectations from that of the traditional hotel booking. Airbnb mitigates risk to both the consumer and vendor by requiring online registration, which includes a personal profile, and providing a format for references, reviews, and ratings. To strengthen its profile, the Airbnb website includes connections to social networking websites such as Facebook.

It should be noted that Airbnb is not without its detractors. Legislators have been accused of discriminating against Airbnb by passing laws requiring residential rentals to be of a certain minimum duration to be legal. Others have cited the potential for breaches in fair housing rules and regulations. Some cities have required those subletting to Airbnb guests to register with the city, carry liability insurance (a prudent thing to do), and pay the cities' hotel tax. Nevertheless, Airbnb continues as a highly successful venture with continued growth through online popularity, mergers, and acquisitions.

Uber and Airbnb are part of what is referred to as a share economy. This may be best described by Benita Matofska, a champion of shared economies, in her blog as a "*socioeconomic system built around the sharing of human and physical resources such as property, knowledge, cars, skills, food, jobs, goods, ideas, responsibility, power, and time*" [24]. However, others have described it as an access economy—that is, consumers paying to access someone else's goods or services.

Renting a room, a house, or a villa directly from the owner can save the renter money while enriching the pockets of the owner. Thus, as a player in an access economy, Airbnb has its competitors. As of this writing, the Internet lists thirteen other global competitors suggesting the nature of travel, whether it be business or tourism, is in reform.

In the four ventures described above, we find a very interesting phenomenon. None of these would have been a likely success if they had tried to compete with the established markets on the playing field set by those established markets. Perhaps it is fairer to say a low potential for success. Why? Because current customers of established markets have an expectation—that is, a sustained and formal level of performance, one they are accustomed to.

However, M-Pesa, FinTech, Uber, and Airbnb could not originally promise this level of performance, therefore they did not cater to this customer. Thus, they were allowed to enter the market with less traditional expectations of performance while offering greater flexibility in customer acceptance. It may seem odd, but sustained formal performance often comes with a price tag of rigidity that excludes those groups with less customer potential. Thus, the more appropriate question may be whether established markets can compete with those just discussed.

Chapter 12: The Dangers of Sufficiency

When faced with the need for a changed perspective in an environment where sufficiency, not creativity, is *di rigor*, managers must develop holistic approaches to problem-solving or innovative thinking. This involves constructing teams of conceptual thinkers and analytic thinkers to put in place the multiplicity of visions mentioned earlier in this book by Alvin Toffler. It may be fair to say the utility of perspective is limited by personal experience; thus, multiple perspectives increase utility.

Managers are cautioned that if the solution team is made up of people more at ease building Gantt charts or reading balance sheets, the team will be systematic and analytically heavy. If the team is composed of designers, stylists, or other free-form-oriented people, then the team will be conceptually heavy. If the team is made up of management types, then the team will likely be portfolio heavy.

Balance of perspective is important, but not always a necessary requirement. However, for a team to achieve an iconoclastic momentum, a dynamic mix is; which may explain why analytically loaded corporate skunk works seldom move past sufficiency. Not that they don't come up with good ideas; rather, that management, aka those who must be convinced, not being part of the "works," are ill-equipped to handle a range of ideas outside of the current product portfolio. There is an unfortunate tendency in management to place an emphasis on push to current market rather than letting the flood of ideas push future needs and opportunities. Critics often cite this as a failing of the idea giant, patent-generating, and Nobel Laureate-producing Bell Labs [1]—that is, an inability to move ideas from invention to practical commercialization.

Not that Bell Labs in its heyday should ever be confused with failing organizations. This was a basic and applied research institution that brought the world semiconductors, transistors, fax transmissions (not invented but first successful demonstration in 1925)[O], long-distance television transmission (1927), photovoltaic cells (1954), and technology for cell phones, to name a few. It had a reputation as being an idea factor. It is just that its ties to its parent company seemingly made it difficult to capitalize on the scope and commercialization of ideas. But there was more. There was an inability, or lack of need, to market itself—to sell Bell Labs as a brand[P]. Bell Labs depended on funding from its parent organization, AT&T. Thus, it may be fair to say this was its Achilles heel. After the breakup of the Bell System in 1984 the

---

[O] The history of the fax machine can be traced to 1843 and Alexander Bain [2], a Scottish mechanic and inventor. However, in 1925, a telephotography machine developed by Bell Labs (AT&T) was used to send a political convention photo long distance for newspaper publication. As fax technology advanced in the latter decades of the twentieth century, US manufacturers had fax machines ready to be put on the market, but research suggested there was no demand. The reason was expense; it was viewed as a telephone accessory costing fifteen hundred dollars or more printing at one dollar a page. However, the Japanese, who came to dominate the fax market, saw this differently. They looked at the growth of the courier market and determined the market for the fax machine was already established.

[P] While Bell Labs was widely hailed as an idea factory it may be fair to surmise that not many of the general population could list their contributions to a world ever increasing their demand on technology. This is not unusual. R&D facilities worldwide place little to no emphasis upon the importance of letting the customer know who they are; to let the customer know it was the Research Labs of ABC Corporation that brought the world Product Z. A lack of visibility in the form of targeted publications and conference presentations that exclude the consumer keep R&D functions and accomplishments hidden from the world of the consumer. If the responsibility of a marketing department is to create customers, then the responsibility of R&D is to give them the resources to do this, and this includes the reputation of the laboratory. Innovation is not just a new product or service. Sometimes it is branding!

purpose of the laboratory was in question. Prior to this, the communication innovations that came from Bell Labs had been channeled into AT&T's business resulting in lack of marketing expertise. As pointed out by Gertner [3], they never had to sell anything, as their ability to compete was a function of the financial success of AT&T, and this may have resulted in diminished forward vision.

***

Successful companies failing in forward vision continue to invest in their existing strengths, thus yielding to the current customer demand and market-driven competition to maintain their current customer base. They wager the averages allocating productive resources to current enterprises, or the crisis "*du jour*," getting little or no more out of this than what they already have.

Peter Drucker, the famed management consultant, educator, and author, perhaps best known for his concept of management by objective, noted, "*The temptation in the existing business is always to feed yesterday and to starve tomorrow*" [4]–[6]. In other words, they invest their resources in building faster horses.

To put this in perspective, one has to revisit Henry Ford and a quote often attributed to him: "*If I had asked the customer what they wanted, they would have told me a faster horse*" [7]. Assuming the evolving needs of the customer are linear, management mandates conformance to accepted norms and the current perspective of the long-range goal, often identified with a vision statement aligned with historically profitable competencies to do little more than what GE's former CEO, Jack Welch, called the dumbest idea ever: "*that the purpose of a firm is to maximize shareholder value*" [8]. Welch had come to believe shareholder value is a result and should not be considered a strategy, something also voiced by Roger L. Martin, director of the Martin Prosperity Institute and a former dean of the Rotman School of Management at the University of Toronto. Martin called the idea that the purpose of every corporation should be to maximize shareholder's wealth tragically flawed. According to Martin, increased shareholder value is a by-product of a focus on customer satisfaction, but not a priority [9].

Corporations should not bet on strategies focused on increased shareholder wealth to open new markets and yield increasing value streams. By this, I mean the production of something that is simultaneously new and genuinely of value. Neither creativity nor innovation exists in the averages, only in the necessity of the future, the forward tail of a moving distribution. It must be understood that creativity and innovation, ideally continual events, are more likely to be passing events. Existing in the future, becoming the average when it is in the mainstream present and then, like a one-trick pony, becoming passé.

The trick is to recognize when they have passed the mainstream. Perhaps few understood this better than Cornelius Vanderbilt, the nineteenth-century industrial icon and one of the world's wealthiest men. For all that has been written crediting him with a passion for conquest, there was, by all accounts, the very real ability to realize the opportunity in the future. As T. J. Stiles said in his Pulitzer Prize-winning book on Vanderbilt [10]—capitalize on the "*unknowability of the future before it becomes the past.*" Perhaps the best example of this is in his development of low-cost, if not lowest cost, transportation routes speeding not only travelers to far destinations but the US economy as well. While Vanderbilt was ruthless and monopolistic, a market manipulator, his railroads opened up new routes, and this opened up new opportunities as well—for investors, entrepreneurs, and consumers.

Companies failing to recognize the future ignore a profound principle of business stated by Drucker: "*Because the purpose of business is to create a customer, the business enterprise has two—and only two—basic functions: marketing and innovation. Marketing and innovation produce results; all the rest are costs. Marketing is the distinguishing, unique function of the business*" [11].

Failing to recognize the future is often the result of the conflict between maintaining tradition and recognizing the need for change. Tradition is an innovation killer, so the questions are: How does upper management uphold time-honored and entrenched values while simultaneously adapting to an environment of change? How does management maintain portfolio control while providing the autonomy required for innovation that may be destructive? Perhaps, more importantly, are the conflicts management faces at the expense of long-term growth—that is, actively investing in growth strategies that have the potential to reduce the ability to meet current or short-term liabilities (decreased liquidity) [12]? These are indeed dilemmas faced every day by the corporate world, and it may be fair to say a company who places emphasis on the quarterly gain is risk averse and trapped in a business model that will ultimately lead to collapse.

***

If, as Drucker states, the purpose of business is to create a customer, then first recognizing the customer is diverse and dynamic is step one in the process of recognizing the future. The customer, collectively, is a collage of culture, ever fluid, and capable of experiencing multiple formats of information simultaneously. In other words, wagering the averages is as antiquated an idea as the idea of a single general marketing strategy; one shoe does not fit all.

In business, teams constructed to avoid the averages must recognize this. They must embrace diversity and the challenges that come with it. Drew Boyd, Director of Marketing Mastery for Ethicon Endo-Surgery, Inc., a Johnson & Johnson company, gives an example of a successful team from Johnson & Johnson where a team, challenged with new product innovation, consists of marketers from different global regions, engineers from different areas (design, mechanical, and manufacturing), clinicians, designers, a sales representative, a customer call service representative, and external partners such as ad agency consultants [13]. In this, singular group expertise does not exist (a good thing); rather, in the variety of expertise there is a cross-functionality in which each member is little more than a novice in the other's domains.

The author, Cynthia Rabe, in *The Innovation Killer* (2006) [14], talks of the value of the perpetual novice. In her experience as the "outsider" on expert teams and, in her words, bringing to the table little more than a litany of annoying "why" prefaced questions pushed the experts to view technology in new perspectives, each with alternate paths. Being the outsider, she was "*not weighed down by the conventions of expertise*" and therefore acted as a "*hyperstimulant for creative ideas.*" Rabe confesses to not bringing any particular skills to the teams other than being able to push the domain experts out of their comfort zone and into different perspectives. Rabe has even coined a phrase to describe herself and others like her in these situations—the zero-gravity thinker.

A zero-gravity thinker is a person or group who aids in the escape of the weight of what is known—again, championing diversity and the resultant different perspective(s). Robert I. Sutton, in *Weird Ideas That Work* (2007) [15], further champions this with what he refers to as ignorant people. He states, "*People who don't know how things are 'supposed to be' aren't blinded by existing beliefs. They can see things that others have failed to notice, and imagine new ideas and perspectives that would never occur to people who develop deep, but narrow, expertise in an area.*" He goes on to say, "*Ignorant people don't know what they are supposed to see, so they can see old things in new ways that so-called experts have rejected, or never thought about.*"

But is this all that is required to make the zero-gravity thinker concept work? It may also be, in a more practical sense, that the zero-gravity thinker, in challenging the expert to explain in terms the nonexpert would understand, forces the explanation in terms of metaphors. Let me explain. A kindergarten teacher, in describing one plus one equals two to her young students, uses a series of values connected by elements of a fundamental arithmetic vocabulary. To get the idea across to a student who does not quite understand what a two is, she may describe it as: *it's like this, if I have one apple and one apple, then altogether I have…* Eventually, apples give way to numerical values and these to even more abstract realizations. However, at the onset, one plus one equals two is an expert explanation of what a two is. In the mind of the young student, this is complex, perhaps little more than gobbledygook jargon, offering little in the way of information or understanding and requiring the metaphor of bringing together apples to make the connection. Whether it is one plus one equals two or the vernacular of particle physics, expert opinion does little to inform or engage a nonexpert audience. Thus the need for metaphor in understanding.

For twelve years, as an adjunct professor of research methods, which is a clever way of disguising a course in statistics for MBA students, I taught all manners of business professionals the art and science of research using statistical methodology. The faculty whom I worked with recognized the business professionals who made up the student body had individual strengths and weaknesses. They had developed as a result of character and, through their personal and professional lives, different learning styles and different thinking styles. To reach all students—that is, first recognizing that analytic abilities are a necessity in a business environment, and not wanting to let students slip by—we actively sought to present information in multiple ways, in multiple formats, and we were successful. Metaphor was a large part of this. Here is a simple truth: to better understand something, we must often change the context in which it is presented.

Metaphors are more than mere language tricks. Metaphors, as a rhetorical device, are a functional basis for understanding, particularly when the subject is complex or involves competing paradigms, as is often the case in the sciences. Terms used within a paradigm are not necessarily of the same meaning in a competing paradigm; therefore, the metaphor is a method of moving to a common ground lest the scientists end up talking past each other.

The unique thing about metaphors is their ability to expand the range of a limiting language. The language of science or the language of engineering are limiting languages in the sense that unless you are schooled in these disciplines, the terms used in the languages are not readily comprehensible. Experts, when confronted with a naive audience, often use terms for one thing to describe another because of the similarity or relationship between things (it's like…). Actually, the use of the word "*like*," or "*as*," defines a simile, but as all similes are metaphors, I will not make the distinction. In this way, the idea expands; it moves tangentially, both in the mind of the expert and in the understanding of the nonexpert with the potential to become an aggressive idea-generating function simply because it forces diversity of thought.

In other words, the engaged zero-gravity thinker develops a personal but alter identification with the elements of the problem freeing him or her from the constraints of accepted definition or wisdom. Thus, the zero-gravity thinker is not so much an annoying challenge mechanism, but rather a necessary medium for thought expansion.

As an example, consider Coleridge's "The Rime of the Ancient Mariner" [16] and the line "*The western wave was all a-flame.*" Taken at face value, the line makes little literal sense as water and fire are incompatible, but as a metaphor, we understand this is a description of the setting of the sun from the perspective of gazing outward across a reflective expanse of water. Metaphorically, it describes a time of day and an environment.

Frank Lloyd Wright once described concrete as cheap and ugly, as living in the architectural gutter. He was referring to the conventional way concrete was being used at the time. But altering the frame of reference in which he was going to use it, he then described it metaphorically as plastic, impressing the imagination, having the ability to weave a building, and the true mass of the architecture. Others have described it as the "*foundation for the massive expansion of urban areas*"—not bad for something more commonly and appropriately defined as a composite material composed of water, aggregate, and cement [17].

Whether one wants to be a zero-gravity thinker or simply ignorant (in the context of Sutton), the concept is simple to understand; the minority dissenting or challenging viewpoint can result in team members reexamining premises by considering more than one perspective and recognizing alternatives may exist (opportunities). The questions effective managers must ask themselves are: Who is on my team? Are they all like-minded, picked because of similar interests and a singularity in perspective? Or have I incorporated those with a minority dissenting and challenging viewpoint?

To further emphasize this point, researchers into group and team behavior, such as Van Dyne and Saavedra [18], have found multiple perspectives generate not only diversity, but also products that are more original. Others have found products generated from multiple perspectives are more complex, more innovative, and of higher quality [19]–[22].

So, the word is out. Diversity of teams, not the similarity of like minds, is a key function of the innovative process. Diversity works because it is multi-perspective. In its collective process, it does not adhere to dogma; it has no single point of origin; therefore, it is not narrowed in focus. It does not accept the status quo and therefore, in a conscious way, is drawn away from the constraints of single-source knowledge. Diversity is an enlightened ignorance, and in this is its strength. Why? Because diversity sources doubt while rejecting absolutism. Managers of diversified teams would be well advised to promote and maintain, on many levels, a chain of multi-perspective culturalism. It is multiplicity, not singularity. It is diversity, not similarity.

***

Diversity was a primary design plan for the Bell Labs Murray Hill research facilities. According to Jon Gertner, author of *The Idea Factory* [23], the buildings, built in the early 1940s, were purposely connected to avoid any geographic delineation, any separation of curriculum; it was not possible for research people to avoid development people. The design, embracing the diversity of employees and entrepreneurial endeavor, intentionally put people in the way of others—theory and application under the same roof. Even the seven-hundred-foot-long corridor that linked the labs to the cafeteria was designed with the intent to allow as many encounters with other scientists as possible. Note: This is also the design of the Isaac Newton Institute in Cambridge, where the layout encourages collaboration and brainstorming. Offices face a central forum. The closing of doors is discouraged, and collaboration encouraged, right down to the installation of blackboards in elevators and lavatories.

The question with such diverse teams is: can confrontation and personality conflicts be avoided? The answer is probably not, or maybe hopefully not. In the words of Jerry Hirshberg [24], founder and president of the award-winning Nissan Design International, now Nissan Design America, "*NDI began life as a cauldron of boiling and colliding cultures, abrading against work styles, rhythms, and priorities…The atmosphere was noisy, intense, irreverent…joyous and abrasive.*" And in all of this was success.

Hirshberg describes his team as being "*unleashed from the traditions and expectations of a single culture.*" He states, "*We could freely envision a fully collaborative environment where the boundaries between engineering, marketing, sales, planning, and design would be blurred, and the natural friction between two different cultures might become sources of energy and ferment* [25]." Hirshberg speaks of a natural friction between different cultures being a good thing. In this, we are reminded of the Edison quote: "*Hell, there are no rules here. We're trying to accomplish something.*"

Here's the thing—conflict in an innovative environment is not a competition; it is not the assertion of a viewpoint at the expense of another where a single winner emerges triumphant. Rather, it is a coming together of ideas, perhaps disparate ideas, but nevertheless ideas that, when merged, result in a synthesis. A whole greater than the sum of its parts. Why? Conflict exposes different perspectives. Different assumptions of what makes the world tick are brought out. These differences are actually necessary components of systems of inquiry into unstructured problems—that is, the difficult problems. The problems lacking algorithmic operators (more on this later).

If team leaders recognize conflict is not a competition, but rather a necessary merging of perspectives for the common good, then the potential for one of the greatest mistakes found in science or in business is avoided—the probability of solving the wrong problem.

Van Dyne and Saavedra worked with groups with designated minority influence and discovered opposing opinions—often considered disruptive and to be eliminated. This did not result in more conflict than control groups, and teams constructed with a designated minority influence engaged in more divergent thinking during problem-solving than control groups.

Interestingly, the Nissan design team did not limit itself to the design of automobiles but consulted on nonautomotive projects under the premise that doing so would place their automotive work in the broadest possible context and allow exposure to a diversity of perspectives.

As the Swedish American entrepreneur Frans Johansson states in *The Medici Effect* [26], the intersection of fields, cultures, and disciplines not only generates combinations of ideas, but also massive numbers of those combinations. In other words, innovation happens at the intersections of diversity. In the case of NDI, they took their cues from Detroit's major weakness—an environment of manufacturing in which unions negotiate and therefore limit individual responsibility (severely restrict may be a better choice of words). Unfortunately for Detroit, this effectively avoids what the innovative process seeks—that is, imagination conflict, a byproduct of overlapping responsibility and competing interest; attributes NDI actively sought and capitalized on.

This position is supported by Paulus and Nijstad [27], who have studied group decision-making and behavior. They point out that research has shown a wider range of perspectives is not only more likely in diverse teams, but also—as noted earlier—provides for more original, more complex, more innovative, and higher quality generation of products.

Similar researchers, such as Kenney and Florida [28], take this position further. Using Japan as an example, they find harnessing worker involvement and intelligence—that is, the integration of a wide spectrum of employees to include R&D scientists, engineers, and shop floor workers—blurs the boundaries between innovation and production, resulting in continual improvement in manufacturing processes. Innovation, as noted, must be a continual process. This establishes an innovation value system in mass-produced commodities. Why does this work? The answer may be as simple as diversity bringing in new concepts and techniques developed and successfully establishing in other fields or disciplines—not necessarily creativity, but rather a new application for an established process.

I am reminded of an ideation team I was asked to participate in a few years ago. The team consisted of like-minded people within a research and development environment, who were asked to limit their thoughts to records of invention within the parameters of the current product portfolio. The team leader, strong and decisive, was a champion of the current constraints of the portfolio. Did the team fail? Yes, indeed! Was this predictable? Most decidedly so.

Why? The team leader acting according to what he believed was the correct manner in which to build and manage the team. He had been schooled in this through continuing education courses and seminars. He did what is common in such cases; he constructed his team in such a way as to sponsor similarity. He picked people of similarity in profession and portfolio knowledge in the belief people with similar professions or jobs will have similar problems and therefore build bonds of trust and respect when attempting to find solutions.

Team leaders often look for similarity in values, beliefs, and attitudes in the belief that such commonality, i.e., homogeneity in the group, is a requisite necessarily leading to quick resolutions, focused ideas, or solutions to problems. It is generally believed homogeneity in the team will lead to relaxed environments—that is, a congenial environment devoid of hostile elements or friction, where it is best to reconcile differences of opinion to sponsor an atmosphere of ready problem-solving. I will say much of this is true. True for the team leader who is tasked with solving for sufficiency. But, in my anecdote above, we were not tasked with solving for sufficiency—that is, finding the quick "it will do solution". We were tasked with ideation, that is, innovation linked to future vision.

An innovative environment will contain a natural friction, an abrasiveness that can become a source of positive energy and ferment. The lack of homogeneity is diversity, and diversity may sponsor conflict. This is to be recognized. But conflict in an innovative environment is not a competition where the assertion of a particular viewpoint, at the expense of other views, emerges as a single winner. Rather, as mentioned, it is a coming together of ideas, perhaps disparate ideas, ideas that, when merged, result in a synthesis. A whole greater than the sum of its parts. Conflict in our team was to be avoided at all costs. This was a mandate by the team leader, but conflict exposes different perspectives, different assumptions of what makes the world tick. These differences are necessary components of systems of inquiry into unstructured problems—the difficult problems. Not those of sufficiency. Our team failed because we were sufficient.

There is a second advantage to diversity and that is the team's ability to mitigate or absorb individual fear, whether that is a fear of failure, fear of rejection, etc. A team composed of thinkers from several perspectives has, by default, several perspectives of fear, each weighted by individual experience, which may not be the collective experience of the group. This allows for individual fears or beliefs to be negotiated by the group. In fairness, though, there is such a thing as evaluation apprehension, which is the fear of a negative reaction by others in the group, of being criticized. This, in turn, can lead to silence or other avoidance mechanisms, which in turn leads to a false consensus of a preferred position as a result of a false cohesiveness or conformity. The result is a limiting of options by limiting perspective, but this may be more common in homogenous teams, not diverse teams.

A great example of the dangers of homogeneity of team members, and its accompanying limiting of perspective, is given by Irving L. Janis [29]. Using the Kennedy-initiated Bay of Pigs decision as an example (a fiasco by any definition), he argues that homogenous, highly cohesive teams (the Bay of Pigs decision team was virtually all Harvard graduates) with strong directed leadership (the President of the United

States) exert their efforts in finding a consensus around a preferred position at the expense of constructive dissent.

David Statt [30], writing on this subject, says, "*The group members had such a high regard for each other's ability that as a group they acted as though they were invulnerable to error. It became unthinkable to them that such bright people could get it wrong.*" Apparently, nobody bothered to suggest fourteen hundred Cuban exiles might be outgunned by twenty thousand battle-hardened revolutionary forces.[Q] Janis refers to this as *groupthink* and warns accordingly of the dangers.

Rabe, however, would call this *expertthink*—groupthink on steroids. The danger in too much cohesiveness or too much conformity is that outsiders, with all of their outside opinions, may be treated with contempt. Information to the contrary of prevailing wisdom may be considered heretical, or at the very least ignored if it doesn't fit the emerging view of the group. But even teams built on diversity need a measure of discipline that will welcome constructive dissent rather than avoid it. Team leaders need to recognize and guard against this if an iconoclastic momentum is to be achieved. If fear, in its many forms, is at the heart of this, then fear-related stress responses are major hurdles that must be overcome if the team is to achieve iconoclastic momentum. Within the mixed-perspective team should be safety in numbers and safety in diversity, resulting in diminishing the far too common team result of sufficiency of action, thus yielding increased imaginative thought processes.

The discussion presented here is readily summed up by the Disney Imagineers [32]—who may very well epitomize the benefits of an iconoclastic team moving with iconoclastic momentum—when they state, "*invite in many perspectives,*" "*nurture your desire to learn,*" "*blend ideas,*" "*be an integrator of thoughts,*" and "*recognize the value of untargeted thinking.*" To this, we may add the words of Robert Bigelow, of Budget Suites and Bigelow Aerospace, who emphasizes the

---

[Q] On April 15, 1961, obsolete World War II B-26 bombers, disguised to look like Cuban air force planes, left Nicaragua to destroy Cuban airfields, but many missed their targets, leaving the April 17 invading forces to come under heavy fire by Cuban aircraft. Within the next twenty-four hours, Castro sent twenty thousand troops to defend the beaches, resulting in twelve hundred members of the invading forces surrendering. The remaining either escaped or were killed [31].

serendipitous nature of discovery: "…*experiment, toy with ideas, try new and different things, and eventually make that miraculous mistake leading to discovery that will change life*…" [33].

Chapter 13: The Nature of Serendipity

Serendipity: the faculty or phenomenon of finding valuable or agreeable things not sought for.

—Merriam-Webster Dictionary [1]

To be clear, serendipity does not mean creative ideas simply pop into the searching or creative mind spontaneously with immediate recognition of what they are and their value. While there are those who would believe such myth—and myth it is—the serendipitous nature of discovery is an ardent effort, coming from being highly motivated in the search for the new and valuable. It favors the prepared mind. The word comes from the English author Horace Walpole (1717–1797). In a letter to Horace Mann, he wrote of a recent discovery of his and termed the nature of the discovery "*serendipity*" after a tale of Italian origin called *Three Princes of Serendip* [2]. In this tale, the three princes search for a lost camel and determine the identity of the camel through discovery and a series of secondhand observations of things they were not in search of.

Serendipity in discovery, or the creative process, stems from an intense gathering of, or exposure to, eclectic ideas and intentional efforts to search out new approaches and pathways to solutions.

Consider the complex path leading to the discovery of radioactivity. In 1857, Abel Niépce de Saint-Victor, the French inventor who worked on photographic processes, observed that uranium salts could darken photographic emulsions and concluded the salts produced an invisible radiation. His discovery was published in 1868 by Edmond Becquerel, the father of Henri Becquerel, credited with being the first person to discover evidence of radioactivity [3].

Did Henri Becquerel know of Niépce de Saint-Victor's discovery through the book published by his father? History does not give us a definite answer to this question, but what is known is Becquerel had long been interested in phosphorescence. Spurred on in his experimentation by the 1895 discovery, by Wilhelm Röntgen, of X-rays, he concluded the radiation came from the uranium itself and not from excitation due to an external energy source. Regarding Röntgen's discovery, for which he received a Nobel Prize in 1901, the materials he had at hand leading to his discovery were borrowed from another physicist, Philipp Lenard.

However, five years earlier, in 1890, Arthur Goodspeed and William Jennings, credited with making the first X-ray photographs, were working in a physics lecture room at the University of Pennsylvania. The two were making brush electrographs of coins. Upon completion of their work, their interest turned to the university's collection of Crookes tubes, a partial vacuum experimental electrical discharge tube. They intended to photograph the glow inside the tubes. What they did not realize was the tubes were emitting radiation, which they discovered only after developing the electrograph plates—shadows of the coins appeared on one of the plates. Unfortunately for them, they did not claim any discovery and missed out on being credited with a noteworthy scientific discovery and accompanying accolades. However, what followed was a period of intense research into radioactivity by the scientific community and the discovery of other radioactive elements such as thorium, polonium, and radium—the latter two by Marie and Pierre Curie with whom Becquerel shared the 1903 Nobel prize [4]–[6].

In this, we find what serendipity truly is, i.e., ardent effort, motivation, and the chance discovery favoring the prepared mind.

Edgar Allan Poe, in speaking of his poem "The Raven," exposed the myth of serendipity when he stated, "*Most writers—poets in especial—prefer to having it understood that they compose by a species of fine frenzy—an ecstatic intuition.*" But he then went on to say he "*would positively shudder at letting the public take a peep behind the scenes.*" Scenes he described as elaborate and vacillating crudities of thought, cautious selections and rejections, painful erasures and interpolations. In other words, a synthesis brought about in the trial and error of a conscious process [7].

Chapter 14: The Desire to Unlearn

One of the biggest and most important tools of theoretical physics is the wastebasket. [1]

—Richard Feynman

Richard Feynman (1918–1988), Nobel Laureate and one of the last century's most influential physicists, was known as the Great Explainer. He once told the story of being a child and having a young friend point to a bird and ask him what kind of bird it was, to which Feynman answered he didn't know. The friend chastised him for not knowing and then proudly recited the identity of the bird (a brown thrush). Later, the young Feynman told his father about the boy who knew all about the bird. His father replied that the boy did not know about the bird at all; he only knew what people called the bird, and that was quite different from knowing about the bird. Feynman's father, perhaps unknowingly, was delivering a fundamentally important message to his son—not to mistake what one knows about a "thing" for the thing itself.

Feynman often credited his father for the way he viewed the world, for the way his mind worked. His father would constantly challenge him to translate what he was reading into some reality of the world to gain a practical understanding. "*Everything we'd read would be translated as best we could into some reality and so I learned to do that—everything that I read I try to figure out what it really means, what it's really saying…*" [1, p3].

In this, Feynman's father was teaching his son an important lesson: knowledge is not a spectator sport, and to truly know, one must often modify that which he or she is attempting to understand.

Feynman came to understand this principle quite well and used it to communicate his knowledge of physics to others less adept in science. He understood words were the teaching tools of science, and this was different from teaching science itself. To this end, he often chose speech, rather than the printed word, to communicate his accomplishments; scientific papers were transcribed from his lectures. He preferred verbal communication, the use of metaphor, and transforming ideas into drawings, allowing the power of storytelling to make his point. Feynman's drawings, in part, are said to be responsible for his Nobel Prize. This has led to something called the Feynman technique: identify the subject; teach it to a child; speak in plain terms; identify knowledge gaps; and organize, simplify, and tell the story [2].

Perhaps this is why Feynman kept a "*notebook of things I don't know about.*" But it must have been a prodigious notebook. Given the rate of growth of scientific inquiry experienced during the latter half of the last century (and occurring today at an even faster speed), such a notebook would have served as a personal reminder of a lack of knowledge or the datedness of knowledge—a humbling experience to say the least, even to a Nobel Laureate. Or as Feynman mused, "*Therefore things must be learned only to be unlearned again,*" recognizing the status of knowledge may be only temporary, based on no more than interpretation and the precision and repetition of the empirical evidence [3].

Feynman, as a scientist, was well versed in the differences between knowledge and proof, or the need to describe a situation and the need to prescribe actions taken as a result of the description. This is the logic of hypothesis testing, to which it is understood the composition of the world is not to be found in a null hypothesis, which is little more than a formal expression of ignorance—that is, a lack of evidence. But a focus on ignorance is to build knowledge given what we know and do not know. This in turn is cyclic; that is, building knowledge exposes more ignorance. When this is put in the context of *learned only to be unlearned*, it is a constant reminder to all that arguments of "*what is*" must be challenged on the amount, validity, and reliability of the evidence. Feynman was adamant about this. "*When I say I know something, that is not equivalent to I have proved it. I don't think proofs are that much better than checking the goddamn formula against a lot of things*" [4].

Feynman was, to say the least, a divergent thinker creating numerous solutions in a range of alternatives, rather than being a convergent thinker in a quest for sufficiency through the emphasis on "no," to find a "best" solution.

For those requiring a more pragmatic approach, perhaps a better way to think about this is to remember when challenged to think outside the box, such challenges are usually premised on the fact that knowledge of what is inside the box is correct. It may not be, or at least it may be insufficient, i.e., limited (generally the case). Nevertheless, detractors exist and will be defensive of the box. Those who would champion the "box" rely on the known composition of the world, or perhaps more appropriately, the world as they know it. This is a platform for arguments in defense of their position and as such, is an inherent position of strength, and one not readily relinquished. It offers the box thinkers strategic advantages and control. Innovation in this context exists primarily in the concept that it is protective of the position and preventive of others challenging the position. The result is that box thinking, in this context, is a short-term exploitive strategy. But in the long run, it does not foster the innovative thinking that is the hallmark of iconoclastic momentum because it does not promote other perspectives.

History is replete with box thinking defenses by people of renown. Those who defend the box appear to be those with the greatest to lose, but loss is not necessarily financial. Consider an extreme example, that of Ignaz Philipp Semmelweis (1818–1865), a Hungarian physician and pioneer in antiseptic procedures [5]. Semmelweis observed that mortality in obstetric clinics could be greatly reduced by the use of hand disinfectants.

Mortality in Semmelweis's world was the result of what was commonly called childbed fever. Of the many observations Semmelweis pondered prior to his discovery of this, the one that may have been the most important was the observation that led to his conviction: "*because these blossoming, vigorously healthy young women had extended periods of dilation, they would die quickly from puerperal fever either during delivery or immediately thereafter.*" Semmelweis kept exacting records and in a short time declared, "*My prognoses were fulfilled.*" Obviously, prolonged dilation meant an increased risk of childbed fever, but why? He then observed: "*women who delivered on the street contracted childbed fever at a significantly lower rate than those who delivered in the hospital. This was in spite of the less favorable conditions in which such births took place.*" He then had cases and controls. What he lacked was evidence of an existing or past exposure to an unknown factor that would be relevant to childbed fever.

Semmelweis's big break in putting all of this together was the result of the unfortunate death of one of his professors, Jakob Kolletschka, a Professor of Forensic Medicine. Kolletschka suffered a small nick in the finger while performing an autopsy. Semmelweis noted the symptoms surrounding the death of Kolletschka were very similar to the symptoms involved with childbed fever. The relationship was made—Kolletschka's death was due to the introduction of "particles" from the cadaver to the wound. Therefore, childbed fever, he reasoned, must also be the introduction of particles into wounds incurred by childbirth—particles adhering to the hands of physicians or medical students who routinely performed autopsies and delivered babies. These particles would not be present with a street birth as there would be no attending physician.

Additionally, the prolonged periods of dilation he observed meant increased contact with an attending physician or medical student. Semmelweis also noted when births were attended by midwives, there was a decrease in mortality; midwives do not perform autopsies. By introducing the use of chlorinated compounds to his medical students for hand washing, he was able to greatly reduce childbed fever and mortality. Despite many publications complete with data, his discovery was in conflict with the established medical community (actually rejected).

Physicians of the day were not just offended at the suggestion they were unclean; they were downright insulted. Such a simple thing, hand washing to save lives, was rejected. An extreme example of defending the box against innovation. It was not until Louis Pasteur's germ theory and Joseph Lister's work in microbiology that hygienic methods became established in the medical community. As for Semmelweis, his was an unfortunate end. At the age of forty-seven, he was committed to an asylum—some biographers say tricked into visiting and then forcibly detained—where he died fourteen days later. The accounts of his death differ. Some say his death followed a beating by guards, and some say it was the result of sepsis incurred as the result of injuries from being restrained by a straitjacket.

The German physicist Max Planck (1858–1947) is credited with perhaps the most skeptical of aphorisms regarding in-the-box thinking. He stated, "*A new scientific truth does not triumph by convincing its opponents and making them see the light, but rather because its opponents eventually die, and a new generation grows up that is familiar with it*" [6]. John Locke, the English philosopher and physician (1632–1704), declared, "*New opinions are always suspected, and usually opposed without any other reason but because they are not already common*" [7]. My own personal dictum—say it loud enough and often enough, and eventually it will become someone else's good idea.

Planck and Locke were referring to the lack of urgency in which scientific or social revolutions take hold. The shift from in-the-box thinking to out-of-the-box was, as they knew it, a slow and difficult process—a paradigm shift of near glacial velocity. Fortunately, the world of Locke, and later Planck, no longer exists in its capacity for paradigm shift. Ours is a world of resource mobility. Online chat rooms for every walk of science and technology exist in which scientists, engineers, and inventors in general can bounce ideas off each other and explore technologies. We have online venture capital colliding entrepreneurs with investors. Patent histories can be easily researched with access to country-wide data registries. Global markets can be identified. Ideas can be investigated and expanded through simple key words thrown into search engines such as Google or Yahoo.

Nevertheless, it is difficult to invent the future when vision is turned to the present based on past accomplishments. The box represents current experiences, skills, and knowledge. Therefore, thinking inside the box does not require redirecting competencies or changing focus. As a result, a team with greater diversity working within these constraints should at least be able to build a bigger box.

David Baltimore, Nobel Laureate and co-discoverer of reverse transcriptase, essential for the reproduction of retroviruses, wrote, "*You can take a piece of information, and you can do lots of things with it. You can try to publish it; you can try to develop a practical aspect of it, like a therapy, or a machine...I guess I've always considered those a kind of continuum of ways that information becomes valuable, and ways that I take information and then try and go further with it* [8]." Baltimore was advocating building a bigger box with the expectation of understanding that gaps in knowledge were the links to discovery.

Before we move on, we should elaborate a bit on Baltimore's discovery, also credited to Howard Temin, for it is worth considering in the context of this book. Temin, for years, had been advocating what he called his provirus theory and what others called heretical and pornographic. The provirus theory stated RNA viruses actually made DNA. This was heretical thinking because the dogma of the day, known as central dogma (named by Francis Crick), provided a flowchart for the transfer of information in one direction only: DNA to RNA. The reverse was not considered possible—that is, RNA to DNA. Baltimore and Temin, working independently but simultaneously, overturned this, and Temin shared the Nobel Prize with Baltimore in 1975.

In this, we are reminded of Feynman when he stated, "*You <u>can</u> doubt the experts once in a while...you have as much right as anyone else...to judge whether a reusable conclusion has been arrived at*" [9], or George Bernard Shaw; "*The reasonable man adapts himself to the world, the unreasonable one persists in trying to adapt the world to himself. Therefore, all progress depends on the unreasonable man.*" [10].

Chapter 15: The Value of Disparity: Integrating Disparate Thoughts

Robert Sutton's writing in *Weird Ideas That Work* effectively argues that companies requiring people to do things in a proven way should avoid variance—variance in people, knowledge, activities, thought, etc. [1]. Manufacturers concerned with product quality understand this. They understand occasionally there are unanticipated or sporadic glitches in the manufacturing process that affect quality, but more importantly, they understand there is also noise.

Noise, or more appropriately, random variation, results from a variety of factors to include people, material, methods, measurement, machines, and the environment. This is, to a great extent, controllable variation, and controlling this variation is key to quality control and the six-sigma process. But Sutton also argues that companies championing creativity and innovation need to recognize variation is the key to success. This is not a paradox or a conflict in his arguments, nor does it mean Sutton opposes performing routine activities with proven methods—which would affect quality control. Rather, in the context of a changing world, there is a deep need to challenge assumptions, explore options, and even reconsider practices considered destructive or misguided.

By doing so, he contends organizations and people have the opportunity to "*challenge existing dogma and generate counterintuitive ideas*." But this requires leaders to live with uncertainty for long periods of time; more importantly, they must be able to stand up to criticism and take the heat from both inside and outside of their organizations. Not something that many are willing to do, and certainly something that even less are prepared to do.

There is short-term safety in retreating into the in-the-box corporate success model. Short-term corporate success relies on predictability. It structures itself around the ability to manage, set priorities, and meet deadlines. It teaches its managers the core curriculum of creating, implementing, monitoring, and controlling projects defined in terms of deliverables, all under the guise of increasing personal productivity. But this is really community productivity, and as mentioned earlier, community over individualism is less likely to produce those who will challenge the status quo. Maintaining the status quo is betting on the averages. It ignores the dynamic potential of the tails of the distribution.

Consider Borders, the book retailer giant with, by all accounts, an inventory system that could predict what consumers would buy [2], [3]. At the same time, as much of the industry was going digital, Borders was expanding its on-the-shelf programs. It was also expanding and beefing up its physical operations while its chief competitor, Barnes & Noble, increased its online sales. Borders, ignoring online sales, outsourced this to Amazon. Did it believe the Internet was little more than a short-term phenomenon (also responsible for the demise of Blockbuster Video)? The Internet—not just a great example, but perhaps the epitome of disruptive innovation—has, since the 1990s, spurred creativity and innovation, improved processes and services, by design, for global consumers ready and willing—or not—to move away from convention.

Borders understood well their method of doing business and adhered to their own dogma, but as Marvin Minsky, the American cognitive scientist, once stated, "*You really don't understand something if you only understand it one way*" [4]. Borders relied on their conventional manner of doing business while the consumer changed its purchase perspective. Upon filing for bankruptcy, the Borders Group gave as a reason for the company's lack of liquidity an environment of curtailed customer spending.

But the customer had not curtailed its spending! What it did was shift its spending—to the Internet. As mentioned, Borders outsourced to Amazon while investing in CD and DVD programs at a time when Netflix, iTunes, and assorted file-sharing networks were gaining in popularity. It continued its emphasis on shelf space, ignoring the rise in popularity of the virtual space of eBooks. It wanted to be a premier big-box bookseller, when in fact the Internet was becoming a superpower in large-volume sales. It underestimated the transformational power of the internet. To which Mike Edwards, the CEO of Borders was quoted as saying in a lessons learned manner "...you can be the best ice salesman in America until the refrigerator comes out"[5].

Could they have taken advantage of the Internet's potential? That is difficult to say. But what can be speculated on is they failed to recognize that the advent of disruptive technology—in this case the Internet—not only could predict demise, but also predict a revolution, or in many cases an evolution. An evolution in the way traditional businesses operate and the traditional way products are consumed.

***

The recombinant process

Disruptive technologies are not always immediately recognized as being predictive of the demise of traditional ways of doing business. Some disruptive technologies are more accurately described as evolving technologies. The change sponsored by such evolving technologies can be slow, barely perceptible, moving at the proverbial snail's pace, often viewed as a random series of unrelated events. But progress is not random; rather it is a "dynamic" waiting, the sorting and ordering by time.[R] New ideas are not generated from nothingness, but rather pieced

[R] One of the oldest known inventions that waited for its time was the seed planter. Jethro Tull (1664–1741), an English-born lawyer-turned-farmer, is credited with the invention of the seed drill in 1701 [7]. The seed drill consisted of a horse- or oxen-drawn hopper containing seeds that were moved via a rotating cylinder to grooves cut into the hopper, which passed the seeds into a funnel. The seed then fell into a narrow furrow dug by a plow at the front and covered by a harrow at the rear. Up until this time, seed planting, referred to as drilling, hence the name seed drill, was done by hand. However, found in Chapter 11, v22, of the Book of Jubilees, an ancient

together from what is known, challenging why they are known and exploring what is not known. Thus, disruptive technology becomes a recombinant process requiring a broad or other perspective to move away from sufficiency. It is only during periods of challenge that scientific or other communities of discovery get to view their progress holistically.

To explore the recombinant process, let's take some time out from our 'in the present' discussion to retreat far back into history. To look at examples of what happens when existing dogma is not challenged. Then, moving forward through the centuries, view the strength of shared ideas to see that innovation, and invention as Lemley wrote in *The Myth of the Sole Inventor*, is incremental and largely a social, not an individual, phenomenon [6].

***

Over eighteen hundred years ago, in Western civilization, the Roman physician Galen's writings on anatomy and physiology appeared to address all that ever need be said on the subject [9], [10]. Galen, born around 130 CE in Greece and living for approximately seventy years, some say even into his eighties, was a great supporter of observation and empirical reasoning—which he used to develop his understanding of medicine and the human body. He advocated prognostic medicine, which was contrary to divination and mysticism—the standard of care at the time—although he was a believer in the humoral theory of medicine that stated healthy people resulted from a balance of four vital body fluids, aka the humors. The humoral theory of medicine persisted for much of the last millennium and gave rise to the proto-psychological theory of the four temperaments. If you have ever undergone a DiSC assessment, you have, in some manner, been exposed to analogs of this theory [11].

Jewish religious work, sometimes referred to as "Lesser Genesis," and written around 100 BC, is the following passage: "*Abram taught those who made implements for oxen, the artificers of wood, and they made a vessel above the ground, facing the frame of the plough, in order to put the seed thereon, and the seed fell down therefrom upon the share of the plow, and was hidden in the earth…*"[8]

Much of Galen's observations and views of anatomy came from the dissection of animals. Aside from some early training in Alexandria, a culture with a more liberal view toward autopsy than Rome, and his role as surgeon to the gladiators of the High Priest of Asia, his knowledge of anatomy came from dogs, pigs, and primates (Barbary apes). As Galen became a highly respected physician, he often incorporated personal philosophies into his teachings. His crowning achievement, entitled *On the Natural Faculties,* remained the authoritative and undisputed source of medical knowledge for fifteen hundred years. This was in part due to its similarity to the ecclesiastic view of a system ordained by nature, but then came the sixteenth century, the Reformation, and challenges to ecclesiastic views.

Andreas Vesalius, an anatomist in the sixteenth century, may have been the first to challenge Galen's authority. While Vesalius's contribution to knowledge and understanding of the human body is widely hailed, his greater contribution may exist in the challenge to knowledge itself because it broadened the perspective in which the human body was viewed.

> "*Indeed, those who are now dedicated to the ancient study of medicine...are beginning to learn to their satisfaction how little and how feebly men have laboured in the field of Anatomy to this day from the times of Galen, who, although easily chief of the master, nevertheless did not dissect the human body; and the fact is now evident that he described (not to say imposed upon us) the fabric of the ape's body, although the latter differs from the former in many respects.*" [12]

This, in turn, leads to other challenges such as William Harvey's (1578–1647) [13] challenge to Galenic views of blood circulation.[S] Harvey studied under Hieronymus Fabricius (1537–1619) at the

[S] It is noteworthy to mention there were important medieval Islamic contributions to the study of anatomy, such as the contribution prior to Harvey of Ibn al-Nafis's discovery of pulmonary circulation. Did Harvey have access to these? What is known is that in the early 1500s, there was considerable movement of Arab documents between Damascus and Padua. Harvey may well have been influenced by early Islamic knowledge [14], [15].

University of Padua. Fabricius was a professor of Surgery and Anatomy at Padua and is credited with the construction of the university's first anatomical theater that still bears his name. This is where Vesalius received his doctorate in 1537 and subsequently was offered the chair in surgery and anatomy.

In 1543, Vesalius published De humani corporis fabrica (*On the fabric of the human body*). As this work was seven volumes in length, he also published an abridged edition for students. Vesalius took advantage of the technical development of printing and refined woodcut methods to distribute his works by enlisting the services of one of the foremost printers of the time, Johannes Oporinus of Basel. Much like letting the cat out of the bag, with this new perspective, medicine and health care began to climb from the static bins of antiquity. This is to an extent Lamarckian inheritance[T]—learned and passed on to generations, albeit here through education and publication, capable of transmission across cultures, across lineages, and promoting rapid change.

***

[T] Lamarck's views, sometimes identified or confused with soft inheritance, puts the emphasis on the organism, or for our purposes on the individual, to pass on characteristics acquired during a lifetime to drive adaptation. Lamarck believed modifications acquired during the life of a parent organism were then transmitted to their offspring. Darwin's work based on natural selection diminished this theory, and perhaps rightly so in a genetic context, as a reaction to a physical world. But if we put this in the context of learned and passed on—that is, influencing with ideas and capable of transmission across cultures—what we have is prototypic networking where the influencing idea is the node and the link is the method in which the idea is bridged to other nodes—that is, transmitted from node to node. Early on, in human evolution, bridging consisted of grunts and gestures. Oral language, as a bridge followed, and then written language, allowing our ancestors greater capability to expand to other nodes. The printed word accelerated this, as did wireless communication, all leading to a virtual integration of thought. Individually, we do not know everyone on this planet, but thanks to the Internet, we now have immediate access to their ideas.

The University of Padua

When discussing iconoclastic momentum and its associated innovation and creativity, one would be remiss to not mention the University of Padua. One of the oldest universities in the world, the University of Padua was founded in 1222 under the premise of academic freedom.[U] At the time, the establishment of a new university required a decree by the emperor or pope. This was not the case with the University of Padua, which was established somewhat spontaneously by scholars dissatisfied with the University of Bologna. The city of Padua may have been chosen for the site of the new university due to Padua's (northern Italy) reputation for the cultural richness and liberal atmosphere.

During the fifteenth century, the university, under Venetian rule, actively attracted an international community of scholars. This continued over the centuries as evidenced by eminent physicians and scientists—well known for their contributions to the advancement of science and medicine, attending and teaching at the university, and establishing its reputation as one of the most influential schools in Europe [17]. Names such as Galileo, Copernicus, Vesalius, and Harvey are some of the more notable, as well as Elena Lucrezia Cornaro Piscopia [18], one of the first women in the world to receive an academic degree and the first to receive a doctorate in philosophy.

The University of Padua was not only an active participant in the Renaissance and the Enlightenment, but also a major champion of the translation of Arab documents and the transmission of knowledge they contained. While much can be said about Muslim scientists and engineers and their creativity and innovativeness, perhaps their most

---

[U] When speaking of academic freedom, the Flying University of Poland [16] should also be mentioned. Operating between 1885 and 1905 in Warsaw, its purpose was to provide Polish youth with an education free of the censorship and ideology of the governing authorities. The Flying University was aptly named due to its secrecy. Held in private houses throughout Warsaw and beginning with a series of "conspiratorial" educational opportunities for women, it eventually became a university open for both sexes, albeit an illegal university. Among the most famous of its students were the Nobel Prize winner Maria Skłodowska-Curie and Zofia Nałkowska, a prose writer, dramatist, and essayist who served as the executive member of the prestigious Polish Academy of Literature from 1933 to 1939.

important contributions come from the fact Islam was a repository of lost knowledge—that is, lost to Europe. This is not to say Islam was only a passive participant in the sciences and medicine, but rather to acknowledge their vital role as archivists during the centuries in which Europe endured an intellectual coma.

Islamic scholars preserved not just Greek math, science, and astronomy, but also that of China, India, and Babylonia, and improved upon much of it. This knowledge was brought to Europe by Islamic scholars by way of the University at Padua and consequently was spread throughout the Renaissance. It can be said Western science owes much of its evolution to Islam and the academic freedom of the University at Padua.

As an example, William Harvey, credited with describing the circulation of blood, published his book, *Exercitatio Anatomica de Motu Cordis et Sanguinis in Animalibus*, in 1628. However, the circulation in the lungs is first described by the Damascene physician Ibn al-Nafis in the thirteenth century [19]. Ibn al-Nafis's work can then be traced forward to Michael Servetus, who published *Christianismi Restitutio* in 1553. This, in turn, can be traced to other scholars, such as Valverde and Colombo in the sixteenth century. In deference to Harvey, his is considered the first complete account of the circulation of blood. Was Harvey aware of these earlier works? Almost certainly.

Then there is Copernicus, who is thought to have borrowed much from Islamic scholars, although to what extent is still debated [20]. What is evident is that his book, *De revolutionibus,* cites Islamic authors, and there is growing recognition that a number of mathematical models used by Copernicus have Islamic origins.

Among the more noteworthy of the Islamic scholars is Al-Razi (AD 854–925/935), who was critical of classical Greek theories of medicine and challenged Galen's work, which in turn influenced the later works of Vesalius [21].

What was my point in discussing this period of history? To emphasize that innovation and discovery are not spontaneous, but rather products founded in communication and sponsored by challenges to dogma.

***

Consider Newton's rejection of Descartes's model of the circular motion of planets around the sun [22]–[23]. Descartes's claim that planetary motion was explained by the phenomena of swirling vortices was widely hailed as true. However, Newton rejected the vortices explanation, suggesting instead that gravitational forces act upon the planets and even more distant bodies such as comets.

He stated, "*The motions of the Comets are exceedingly regular, are governed by the same laws with the motions of the Planets, and can by no means be accounted for by the hypotheses of Vortices. For Comets are carried with very eccentric motions through all parts of the heavens indifferently, with a freedom that is incompatible with the notion of a Vortex.*"

What is important is the phrase, "*governed by the same laws.*" Newton's rejection of Descartes was based on, among other things, a simple observation of eccentric motions being incompatible with the notion of a vortex. Nevertheless, he was widely criticized for bringing in occult agencies (vacuum and gravitational forces) into science.

Newton, in Book III of *The Principia,*[V] wrote, "*Gravity acts on all bodies universally and is proportional to the quantity of matter in each.*" He was stating all bodies are acted on by the same laws. However, the concept of force was a particularly confusing one to Newton's contemporaries, who did not understand how to fit it into their perspective that bodies consisted only of the properties of size, shape, degrees of solidness, and motion. Descartes's model did not need "occult" agencies; hence, it was a sufficient model. It offered a plausible explanation. Descartes built a model to fit the observation and then devised rules to govern the model. Newton's challenge was brought about by inductive reasoning—that rules, whether they apply to orbiting bodies or apples, are universal and models must first fit the rules, and this will explain the observation.

To further understand this, one must understand Descartes's vortices were circling bands of particles in which the planets reside. For Descartes, our solar system consisted of stratified bands, each

---

[V] *The Principia* or *Philosophiæ Naturalis Principia Mathematica,* Latin for *Mathematical Principles of* Natural Philosophy, is comprised of three books by Newton containing his Laws of Motion. Newton's laws are considered the foundation for classical mechanics—that is, the motion of macroscopic objects.

containing a planet circling the sun at various speeds. Planets come to rest in the vortex band when their centrifugal force is balanced by the smallest particles making up the ring. Planets out of balance in a ring ascend or descend to the next vortex in which equilibrium is reached.

For Descartes, circular motion was necessary because empty spaces do not exist: no empty space, no vacuum. Just space filled with particles. Descartes argued that a vacuum was impossible, but his argument was more metaphysical than physical. According to Descartes, the essence of body was extension (matter), and this is an attribute. It follows then that if a vacuum is nothing, then nothing cannot possess attributes; therefore, "*nothingness cannot possess any extension*" because extension must consist of the presence of something, and vacuum is a contradiction of extension [24-26].

This argument was contrary to Newton's ideas and another reason Newton's concepts were originally rejected. In Newton's concept of space, vacuum occurs, and gravitational forces act on planetary bodies regardless of the distance of emptiness. For Newton, planets are drawn toward their respective centers by a centripetal force.

Now, if this were all there was to the story of Newton's challenge to Descartes's model, it would be an interesting story, but an incomplete one, for there is something much larger here. Newton's ideas were generated from observation and from what was known. He then challenged the known and, in turn, explored the unknown. The challenge to the known here is the challenge to the Cartesian view of natural philosophy.

Cartesian philosophy was grounded in logical analysis and a mechanistic understanding of nature, and at its core was the distinction between thought and extension (mind and matter). Cartesian philosophy, firmly entrenched when Newton was a student at Cambridge, had replaced Aristotelian views held in place for centuries, but Newton's observational methods and universality of laws challenged this. In turn, his influence on the eighteenth century was not that of a single idea or of a brilliance in mathematics (co-discoverer of calculus), but rather the controversy surrounding his ideas that drove not just discussion, but rigorous philosophical debate for decades.

We generally do not think of Newton when discussing the philosophers of the day, such as Leibniz, Spinoza, Locke, Hume, or Berkeley, but his influence on them was profound. Not that they immediately rejected Cartesian philosophy and accepted Newton's experimentalist views. Quite the contrary, and this is what is important, Newton's views were not just challenged, but fell under an intense scrutiny that would continue in one form or another for the remainder of the century. Thus, his challenge became a recombinant process requiring scientific and philosophical communities to view their perspectives holistically—hence, progress.

In the examples above, the process of challenge and change often required decades if not centuries (after Galen), but what of the more recent integration of thoughts?

We leave this chapter with a parting thought—a quote from Nikola Tesla. "*Deficient observation is merely a form of ignorance and responsible for many morbid notions and foolish ideas prevailing*" [27].

Chapter 16: Inefficiency Breeds Opportunity

Inefficiency ➡ opportunity ➡ exploitation ➡ creativity ➡ innovation ➡ market ➡ repeat

Inefficiency breeds opportunity. Given our previous discussions, this is an interesting but nevertheless very true statement. But let's take this discussion further with continuing our retreat into history and centering our thoughts on the opportunities brought about through the inefficiencies of communication.

The inefficiencies of communication provide ample and obvious examples of opportunity. Communication is language, be it verbal, signs and signals, illustrations, etc., and if the sender communicates in a language the receiver fails to understand or fails to receive in a timely manner, the communication fails.

Communication begins with the need to inform others. The earliest methods of communication among humans were no doubt survival cues—the pitch of grunts or the posturing of the body to indicate a social acceptance, danger, or food source. But whether it be from a primitive ancestor in the savannahs of Africa, shrieking and gesturing to inform others in their band of a welcome visitor or encroaching danger, or modern man highlighting the events of the day through the medium of the live video streaming, communication is information. It is the value of the information which has made possible the evolution of human society.

The inefficiency of shrieking and gesturing, in time, gave way to verbal communication in the form of primitive languages. This, in turn, gave way to more formal structured language and in turn the evolution of symbols to represent the verbal language. Structuring language in the form of symbols, with rules to govern the symbols, meant information provided by one person could be carried over long distances to others without misinterpretation. This meant devices for constructing the symbols and carrying the symbols, such as carving tools and clay tablets, would give way to papyrus, paper, and quill pens. Along the way, mankind added in more abstract forms of communication, such as song, dance, and art. This in turn would eventually give way, through opportunity brought about by inefficiency, to communication as we know it today.

Much of the time, we tend to think of communication in its more untailored form, that of general discourse used to casually interact with the world around us, but as we know, communication is far more. It is a current in which a flow of information can create overnight kingdoms. It can be a sanitizing flame or a destructive inferno. It is a web that binds the power of business, communities, and empires.

In the sixteenth century, as Europe raced to colonize the New World, communication was weak by any standard, even those of the day. Dictates and decrees took frustrating months to be delivered trans-continentally, and even more to be answered. For a world bent on discovery and empire building, the long-distance mode of communication was a sail upon a sea; an inefficient medium for global communication, but it was the only form of truly long-distance communication available at the time.

Voyages from England to North America could average two months, although ninety to hundred days or more were not uncommon, provided the ship was not lost at sea. Two ships leaving England on the same day could arrive off the coast of the New World weeks apart. Storms, prevailing winds, the experience of the crew, and the gulf stream all were hazards to the journey, although typically the return trip was quicker.

Fast forward to the nineteenth century. Enter the steamboat, or the sail steam hybrid. The SS *Savannah*, a sailing ship/sidewheel steamer, leaving Savannah, Georgia, in 1819, crossed the Atlantic, under a combination of steam and sail power, to Liverpool, England, in approximately twenty-nine days. However, the *Savannah* was not a commercial success due to the space required for her large engine and fuel capacity at the expense of cargo. She was converted back to sail after her return from Europe. Nevertheless, the genie was uncorked.

The *Savannah* demonstrated the time spent in the transit across the Atlantic could be greatly shortened, meaning such ships could make more trips annually. Economically, this meant the return on investment was greater while the time to payoff was reduced.[W] This also greatly decreased the time for transoceanic communication, although it was still not enough for a turbulent world.

Within plus or minus a handful of years from the SS *Savannah*'s departure for Liverpool, Mexico gained its independence from Spain, creating the first Mexican Empire; Greece won independence from the Ottoman Empire; Antarctica was discovered; British India absorbed much of the remainder of the subcontinent (the Maratha Empire); the British Empire annexed Burma; Peru won independence; and of course, James Monroe introduced the Monroe Doctrine to control European influence in the Americas—later invoked by John Kennedy during the Cuban missile crisis 140 years later.

While sail with steam was somewhat better than sail alone, this was still an inefficient medium for communication. As previously stated, opportunity rides the crest of inefficiency, and opportunity came in the form of submarine telegraph cables. But, before entering into this discussion, we must back up a few years to discover what was in place, and how it came to be for this opportunity to be fortuitous.

Samuel F.B. Morse (1791–1872) was a graduate of Yale University and an aspiring artist in the first third of the nineteenth century [1]. He studied art at the Royal Academy of England and was establishing

---

[W] It would take thirty years before other steamships were constructed to make transatlantic voyages. Of the first were the *Great Western* and the *Sirius*. The *Great Western* averaged sixteen days for her westward crossings and fourteen days for the eastward passage. The *Sirius* took eighteen days for her maiden voyage across the Atlantic.

himself early on as a painter and sculptor—having reached a fair amount of acclaim by winning, in 1813, the Adelphi Society for the Arts' highest award for his model of the *Dying Hercules*. His *Gallery of the Louvre*, 1831–1833, is now part of the collection of the Terra Foundation for American Art in Chicago, while his portrait of John Adams, 1816, can be found in the Brooklyn Museum's collection. But then, in 1837, he conducted the first successful land wire transfer and recorded messages.

How did this come about? According to John Mullaly, 1858, in his report on *Laying of the Cable* or *The Ocean Telegraph*,[X] the idea came to Morse during a transatlantic passage aboard the ship *Sully* in 1832.[Y]

In one of the many social gatherings taking place on the ship, the conversation turned to Benjamin Franklin and the circumstance in which he was able to cause electricity to pass through a great length of wire for the purpose of measuring its velocity. According to Mullaly:

> *In one of the many social gatherings which took place among the company, a conversation arose in regard to a subject which was at that time extensively discussed among scientific circles—the obtaining of a spark from the electromagnet, which showed the identity of electricity*[Z] *and magnetism, a fact which had often been supposed to exist, but the existence of which had not been conclusively proved by actual experiments. In the course of conversation the well-known circumstance of Franklin's having caused electricity to pass through three or four miles of wire, for the purpose of measuring its velocity, was related, and it was this particular circumstance which led the Professor* (speaking of Morse) *to an investigation of the subject, with the view of employing the subtle agent as the messenger of man. He made the observation,*

[X] Mullaly and Morse were on the US Frigate *Niagara* during the first of the cable laying voyages.

[Y] James Fenimore Cooper, the author and friend of Morse, contradicts this. He states, "*Our worthy friend first communicated to us his ideas on the subject of using the electric spark by way of the telegraph. It was in Paris during the winter of 1831–1832*" [2].

[Z] A term first used by the English physician William Gilbert, in the year 1600, from the Latin *electricus* to describe the forces exerted when certain substances are rubbed together [3], [4].

> *that "if electricity can be made visible in any desired part of the circuit, there is no reason why a system of signs could not be devised by which intelligence might be transmitted between distant points." The remark excited little or no attention at the time but the idea took such firm possession of his mind that he devoted the greatest part of his leisure time to the invention of an instrument by which, what was before but an idea, was to be converted into a fixed fact* [5].

Apparently, the idea did more than spark (pun intended) his imagination as he did devise just such a device. In 1835, at a time in which he was becoming disillusioned with the art and the art world, he exhibited a model of his invention to his students in New York.

In 1837, Morse applied for a patent, and in 1838, he asked Congress for an appropriation for the construction of a telegraph line between Washington DC and Baltimore. Congress acted slowly as the line did not go into operation until May of 1844. Note: A Dr. Charles T. Jackson later claimed he had given Morse these ideas and should be considered a joint inventor of the telegraph [6].

But history credits Samuel Soemmerring [7], of Bavaria, with inventing the crude telegraph in 1809.[AA] Soemmerring, a physician, anatomist, anthropologist, and paleontologist, whose anatomical investigations into the human eye, nervous system, and lungs made him one of the more important anatomists of the time, was also an inventor. His telegraph, based on electrochemical current, was able to transmit a distance of 3.5 kilometers.

However, it is reported Soemmerring was influenced by the Spanish physician and experimenter Francisco Salva, who among other things improved the lightning rod conductor invented by Benjamin Franklin [8], [9]. In 1795, Salva presented a report to the Barcelona Academy of Sciences entitled "Electricity Applied to Telegraphy," and in 1804, five years before Soemmerring, he demonstrated a working model to the Barcelona Academy.

[AA] Soemmerring's device was electrochemical—that is, a current was passed through a series of wires, one for each letter of the alphabet and one for each of ten numerals. The wires were connected to electrodes immersed in an acid bath at the receiving end. Completing the circuit resulted in hydrogen bubbles to be released at the electrode that corresponded with the appropriate letter or numeral.

Whether Morse knew of Soemmerring or Salva is unclear, but Morse could well have been influenced by Harrison Dyar, who, in 1828, used electrical sparks to burn dots and dashes in chemically treated paper.[BB] He was no doubt aware of William Sturgeon [10], the British inventor who in 1825 demonstrated the power of the electromagnet.

The electromagnet's use in the telegraph is a simple one. A transmitter sends an electric pulse. At a receiving end, some point distant from the transmitter, an electromagnet is powered by the electric pulse; the pulse opens and closes the electric circuit, creating a magnetic field when the circuit is closed. This, in turn, attracts a small lever, causing a mechanical action to place marks on a piece of paper. Sturgeon, in turn, probably got his information from the French physicist André-Marie Ampère [11], who found parallel wires with currents flowing in the same direction attract each other while currents flowing in opposite directions repel. Ampère was furthering the work of Hans Christian Oersted [12], of Copenhagen, who in 1819 laid the foundations of electromagnetism when he placed a compass needle parallel to a wire conducting an electric current and observed the deflection of the needle in the direction of the wire.

While Oersted may have laid the foundations of electromagnetism with this observation, he was not the first to observe this. Benjamin Franklin, experimenting with electricity, described a similar experience brought about by electrifying iron shot and repelling a cork ball, then reversing the polarity and attracting the ball to the shot: "*...if you present to the shot the point of a long slender sharp bodkin, at six or eight inches distance, the repellency is instantly destroyed and the cork flies to the shot.*" Franklin, along with William Watson (1715–1787), an English physician and scientist, is credited with naming the type of charges: positive and negative [14].

However, Charles François de Cisternay du Fay, a French chemist, earlier reported the positive and negative charges but termed them vitreous and resinous [15] Interestingly, Franklin acknowledged, in September 1747, in a letter to Mr. Peter Collinson of London—a Fellow

---

[BB] By at least one account, it is said Dyar abandoned his experiments due to "*conspiracy to carry on secret communication,*" which smacked of witchcraft to the people of the time [13].

of the Royal Society and supporter of Franklin—that he might not have been the first to observe this phenomenon.

He stated, "*In my last I informed you that in pursuing our electrical enquiries, we had observed some particular phenomena, which we looked upon to be new, and of which I promised to give you an account, tho' I apprehended they might possibly not be new to you, as so many hands are daily employed in electrical experiments on your side of the water, some or other of which would probably hit on the same observations*" [16].

Indeed, Franklin was correct in this acknowledgment. Otto von Guericke (1602–1686), a German scientist, inventor, and politician, is credited with the discovery of an experimental method for demonstrating electrostatic repulsion. Using a device consisting of a sulfur globe attached to an iron rod and activated by rubbing with one's hand, he produced a charge that would attract and repel [17], [18].

Then there was Stephen Gray (1666–1736), a somewhat self-educated English scientist and astronomer, who was apprenticed to his father in the cloth dying trade. Gray's observation that a piece of cork generated an attractive force on paper scraps and dust when rubbed piqued his curiosity. Through observation and experimentation, he found he could transfer the "charge," i.e., carry it over a distance, around bends, and transmit it to metal objects. While Gray went on to perform numerous other electrical experiments, the importance of his work and his contributions to the subject did not receive the recognition it should have. He died destitute and was buried in a pauper's grave [19], [20].

There were, of course, other contributors to the telegraph at this time. Francis Ronalds, an English inventor, in 1816, put down eight miles of glass-insulated wire in his garden. He then sent electrical pulses along the wire to transmit messages (actually the discharge of air pistols). This experiment gave way to further discovery in which he concluded: "*any required words could be spelt and figures transmitted*" [21]. While this may have been the first "practical" working telegraph, the modest Sir Ronalds asked his publishers to state, "*He disclaims the appellation of original inventor of the electric telegraph, many schemes of the kind having preceded his*" [22].

Then there was Joseph Henry, who in 1830 took Sturgeon's electromagnet one step further—or perhaps that extra mile would be more appropriate phrasing—when he demonstrated its usefulness in long-distance communication by sending an electric current the distance of a mile to activate an electromagnet, causing a bell to ring [23].

In 1832, Baron Schilling von Canstatt—also known as Paul Schilling—invented a telegraph consisting of sixteen keys for the purpose of switching an electric current and demonstrated a short-distance transmission of signals between two rooms in his apartment in St. Petersburg. While this may have been a minor contribution, it caught the attention of both the English government and Nicholas the First of Russia (Schilling was born in Russia) [24]. Schilling was indeed influenced by Soemmerring, having seen his telegraph, perhaps in 1823, while visiting Soemmerring and subsequently developing a relationship he maintained over a period of years.

In 1835, William Fothergill Cooke saw Schilling's invention while a student at Heidelberg University. He took the idea to England, improved upon it, and co-patented it with Charles Wheatstone, the English scientist and inventor famous for his Wheatstone bridge used to measure electrical resistance [25].

Now, here is where the information gets a little dicey. Samuel Morse was acquainted with both Cooke and Wheatstone [26], [27] and through these relationships may have learned Schilling devised a method of replacing letters with points and lines (dots and dashes). A method Cooke and Wheatstone did not employ. Supposedly, this is what Morse patented in 1840 but substantiating Schilling's method with this had proven futile. What can be substantiated is that as early as 1832, perhaps during or shortly after the *Sully* voyage, Morse was working with the idea of dots, spaces, and dashes. But if Schilling had actually conceived of this prior, the question is why did Schilling not patent his work? The answer may be simple.

Schilling was a Russian and Nicholas the First did not permit patents in fear other nations would usurp their ideas. Apparently, they did. Note: there are others who would claim the famous code belonged to Alfred Vail, but Vail never claimed he had anything to do with devising it, and in letters to Morse referred to it as "*your system of marking*" [28].

Vail's contribution remains in dispute, but according to his son, in a pamphlet published in 1914 [29], "*It is not claimed that Vail invented the telegraph, but his work shows Morse invented 'a system of telegraphs,' not the telegraph*." Interestingly, in this same pamphlet, which traces a history of the telegraph, there is mention of a Jesuit from Rome by the name of Famianus Strada, who in a 1617 publication, *Prolusiones Academicae*, alludes to communication with a distant friend with the help of a lodestone: *"Take a plain, round, flat disc, and upon its outer rim mark down the letters of the alphabet, and traversing upon the middle of your disk, have a needle, which has touched a loadstone, so arranged that it may be made to touch any particular letter, ad libitum."* Strada then says to make an identical disk and give it to a friend; then on a prearranged date and time, "*turn your finger to the disk and touch the easy moving needle...your distant friend...learns [sic] your meaning from the interpreting needle.*" Signaling without wires? If not in reality, then certainly in the mind, and no doubt grounded in some form of observation. Strada exclaims, "*Oh! This style of writing were brought into use*!" [30]

Assigning an invention or discovery to one person at one point in time is misleading because of the seemingly arbitrary complexity of invention or discovery. Discovery requires not only recognition of the thing, but also recognition of what the thing is. These are often disparate issues.

For instance, the Vikings discovered North America, as evidenced by the discovery of a thousand-year-old settlement in L'Anse aux Meadows, Newfoundland. But as the Vikings did not recognize the New World for its potential for the interchange of cultures and resources, or perhaps were simply indifferent to their discovery, they are generally given only a casual acknowledgment for this.

As we have seen with the telegraph, and will continue to see in this text, invention and discovery are long-drawn-out processes of communication and conceptualization. Consider the discovery of DNA often attributed to James Watson and Francis Crick in the 1950s. Tracing back the origins of DNA, we find a Swiss chemist by the name of Johann Friedrich Miescher [31] who, in the 1860s, chanced upon a substance he called nuclein (now known as DNA) when he added acid to white blood cells. He called this substance nuclein because he believed it to come from the nucleus of the white blood cells. Furthering his investigation into nucleins, he found it was composed of hydrogen, oxygen, nitrogen, and phosphorus with a unique ratio of phosphorus to nitrogen. His discovery played a vital role in the identification of nucleic acids as carriers of genetic information; however, Miescher was never able to identify this.

This would be left to others such as Albrecht Kossel [32], a German biochemist who received a Nobel Prize in 1910 for determining the chemical composition of nucleic acids. Fast forward to 1944, we find Oswald Avery and colleagues published a paper that outlined the nature of DNA as a transforming principle. This paper, in turn, was read by Erwin Chargaff, who, inspired by Avery's work, published two papers in 1950 regarding the chemistry of nucleic acid. More precisely, he determined the number of guanine units is equal to the number of cytosine units, and the number of adenine units is equal to the number of thymine units, and DNA composition varies between species.

In 1952, Rosalind Franklin, an English chemist, working with X-ray crystallography produced high-resolution photographs of DNA fibers, which paved the way for Watson and Crick [33]. A colleague of Franklin's, Maurice Wilkins, received a high-quality image of DNA from her. Wilkins, in turn, showed this to James Watson, who along with Crick and research reports from Wilkins and Franklin, deduced the double helix structure of DNA. Watson and Crick, along with Wilkins, were awarded the Nobel Prize in 1962. Some, including Watson, say Franklin should have also received the Nobel Prize for her work, but as the prize was given in 1962 and Franklin had passed away in 1958, she was not so honored: the Nobel Committee was not disposed to posthumous nominations.

Back to our previous discussion, given all those who had a hand in the invention of the telegraph, and the numerous methods in which it could function, why is Morse given popular credit for inventing it? The answer lies in the fact Morse's invention was simple, a single circuit, and it didn't just send a current—it sent a message; he was able to transfer and record. It was this exploitation of the work of others that led to the practicality of the telegraph. Throw in the famous code and now you have a commercially viable product.[CC] Decades later practicality

---

[CC] Of note is that Salmon P. Chase, Chief Justice of the US Supreme Court, at a dinner in 1868 honoring Morse, also spoke of the achievements of many of the notables mentioned above for their contributions to which brought about the telegraph. Chase, who was the leading counsel against Morse in a previous lawsuit, introduced Morse by stating, "*Many shining names will occur…in the history of the*

and commercial viability would be the hallmark difference between two of the nineteenth century's greatest minds: Thomas Edison and Nikola Tesla.

Edison's inventive success was governed by use to the consumer and cost of production, while his contemporary, Tesla, was more driven by ideology and the grandeur of the idea. While both of these men were caught up in the novelty and usefulness of the invention, Edison moved quickly from the novel idea, and hence novelty, to the usefulness stage of invention. In Edison's words, "*a rapid and cheap development of an invention*" [34]. Tesla deferred, preferring to remain in the world of novelty while keeping usefulness at a future distance. While Tesla provided the world with solutions to basic scientific problems, it is often forgotten solutions to problems in themselves provide no direct economic contribution to society; rather, it is the application of the solution that has value.

***

Let us redirect our discussion back to the original topic of communication. It was communication that was changing the world, and in the nineteenth century, the major influencer was the submarine telegraph cable. To quote Daniel Headrick, author and historian, "*It was an instrument of power...intertwined with the power struggles of the time: private enterprise and governments; the dominance of the Western nations over the non-Western world*" [35].

The first cable was laid across the Atlantic in 1858 and failed miserably due to thin wire, poor reception, slow transmission, and a very short life span. Siemens, the multidisciplinary twenty-first-century technology giant, laid its first transatlantic cable between Ireland and Newfoundland in 1874 with a ship, the *Faraday*, specifically designed for such a task.

As technology improved, cable designed specifically for underwater use increased the efficiency of transmission from not more than thirteen words a minute in the late 1800s to fifty words a minute by 1900. By the 1920s, this was between four hundred and five hundred

---

telegraph. Among them, Volta...Oersted...Ampere and Araga... Sturgeon...Henry, and...Steinheil" [6, p238].

words a minute. As efficiency increased, so did the demand for use, resulting in an inefficiency and, of course, opportunity. It might be fair to state opportunity was, in part, ushered in by paranoia.

Governments wanted exclusive control over the cables, free from message interception, censoring, and vandalism (a polite term for overt cable cutting). Enter opportunity in the form of an expensive but wireless method of communication. A bit of background: wireless communication was first postulated as waves of electromagnetism traveling in space by James Clerk Maxwell. This was verified by Heinrich Hertz as early as 1880, and in 1897 Marconi patented a complete wireless system. It should be noted that wireless and radio, for many years, described the same thing. The choice of terms depended on which side of the Atlantic you were on. The British preferred the term wireless as there were no wires connecting the transmitter to the receiver. Americans preferred radio because the transmitter radiated electromagnetic waves.

In the very early 1900s, the conventional wisdom was that longer distances required longer wavelengths[DD] for transmission, requiring enormous transmitters and fields of high masted antennas.[EE] But as telecommunication technology advanced, demand increased, despite the cost, and inefficiency once more appeared.

In 1897, Britain awarded Marconi a patent for *Improvements in Transmitting Electrical Impulses and Signals and in Apparatus Therefor*—his initial patent for the radio. But Marconi did not develop his ideas in isolation. He built on the decade-earlier work of Heinrich Hertz,

---

[DD] Radio waves were first predicted by Maxwell in 1867, when he described light waves and radio waves as waves of electromagnetism traveling in space.

[EE] In 1900, Tesla proposed a world system of wireless transmission, which would bring together existing telegraph, telephone, and other signal stations for the purpose of transmitting signals, characters, and messages (to include music and photos), to any part of the world instantaneously. A plant was constructed on Long Island consisting, in part, of a tower 187 feet high and 68 feet in diameter. In April 1917, President Woodrow Wilson, due to America's entry into the war in Europe, issued a proclamation taking control of all radio stations. Those not within the Navy's wireless system were to be rendered inoperable. Fearing the tower could be used by German spies, it was destroyed in 1917. Tesla contradicted this in later years, maintaining it was in the interest of the US government to preserve the tower as it could be used as a submarine location device.

who in turn built on James Maxwell's 1860's *A Dynamic Theory of the Electromagnetic Field.* Interestingly, Hertz did not see the value of his ideas: "*I do not think that the wireless waves I have discovered will have any practical application.*" [37] Note: Hertz is given credit for conclusive evidence of wireless transmission, but David Edward Hughes, the British-American inventor and professor of music, may have been the first to successfully demonstrate radio transmission. In 1879, while working on induction balance (think metal detectors), he noticed his experiments caused a bad contact in a nearby Bell telephone to spark. Further exploring this, he discovered he could reproduce this phenomenon, which he called aerial waves, up to a distance of five hundred yards. Unfortunately, prominent scientists of the day convinced him that his discovery was nothing more than electromagnetic induction, not aerial transmission, so little more was made of this [38], [39].

Marconi was also well aware of the work done by Nikola Tesla. Tesla proposed that messages could be transmitted without wires, and in 1893, he demonstrated this at the Franklin Institute in Philadelphia. So, here was Marconi, a self-styled inventor who had been schooled in the laboratory of Augusto Righi, who in turn is credited with being the first person to generate microwaves (think radar and ovens).

Marconi took his knowledge base and added to it by reading the accomplishments of Tesla, who was a mechanical engineer, electrical engineer, and by many accounts, a futurist, if not a self-styled prophet, who in later years was unceremoniously given the role of a mad scientist.

Add in Hertz's contributions, but let us not forget with Hertz, one must also credit Maxwell. And in speaking of Maxwell, we should not forget Michael Faraday. Faraday is credited with being a scientist, physicist, and chemist, and indeed, he made great contributions to these fields in spite of his limited education. More importantly, Faraday was an experimentalist, perhaps best known for his demonstration that changing magnetic fields produced an electric field. This became known as Faraday's Law, but as his mathematical abilities went little beyond simple algebra, it required Maxwell, years later, to mathematically model it.[FF]

Marconi is credited with the invention of the radio, but as described above, this is not entirely accurate and also a credit Tesla openly disagreed with. Others who came before Marconi, including Tesla, must be credited with principles used by Marconi.

Tesla believed Marconi was not using the Hertzian apparatus to generate waves as described in his 1897 patent application: "*Signals are sent by means of a Hertz radiator, and are received by a tuned receiver*." Rather, he was using his (Tesla's) apparatus for transmission. Tesla questioned the validity of the patent in a letter to his attorney in which he stated, "*I have noted that the signals have been described as being due to Hertzian waves, which is not the case*." He goes on to state the patent describes something different from what actually takes place and then asks the extent to which this affects the validity of the patent [40]. Even Marconi's 1909 Nobel Prize in Physics, shared with Karl Braun, a German physicist and inventor from whom Marconi borrowed much from Braun's patents, stated, "*in recognition of their contributions to the development of wireless telegraphy*"—no acknowledgment of invention, but rather contribution.

Marconi was, among other things, a businessman and entrepreneur. Although it can be said he built upon the work of others, it should not be forgotten this is how science works. Marconi was truly innovative, but his real contribution, and perhaps the reason for his credit, was the commercial success of the radio. He founded the Wireless Telegraph and Signal Company shortly after receiving his 1897 British patent.[GG]

[FF] Maxwell translated some of Faraday's discoveries in electromagnetism into sets of differential equations. Maxwell used this to fit a hypothesis of his own, which by manipulating the equations gave a wave equation indicating the velocity was that of light. He concluded light is an electromagnetic disturbance. Hertz, drawing from Maxwell's equations and what must have been considered Maxwell's "prediction" of wireless electromagnetic waves, set out to produce the waves experimentally and to also calculate their velocity. One must credit Maxwell's math skills as the inspiration for Hertz's discoveries. As a side note, both Faraday and Maxwell never considered bodies existing without anything between them but distance. This in turn gave rise to the space filling concept of ether, eventually abandoned in favor of curved space time.

GG In 1943, Marconi's 1904 US patent for Apparatus For Wireless Telegraphy, filed in 1900, was ruled invalid by the US Supreme Court; Marconi Wireless Tel. Co.

The success of this company is well documented, and it remained in existence until 2006.

On the other hand, Tesla, who many now recognize as the real "father" of radio, appeared to be content with lecture hall demonstrations of his techniques. On several occasions, he turned down invitations to demonstrate the real-world practicality of his devices. Tesla preferred to stay in his laboratory while Marconi, perhaps fully realizing financial success was tied to the practicality to the consumer, brought his ideas to the street.

But all was not well with wireless communication. It was, from a practical point of view, inefficient at long distances. Early wireless communication took advantage of what is known as surface wave propagation and low frequencies. With radio, the surface wave, more precisely ground wave, had its efficiency in the ability to be diffracted around obstacles due to their long wavelengths, allowing them to follow the curvature of the earth. Unfortunately, they also dissipated with distance. Enter opportunity in the form of the short wave. The short wave utilized skipwave propagation, in which the wave is reflected off the ionosphere and back to Earth, allowing communication around the earth.

The problem with shortwave communication up to this time was it had a habit of disappearing and then reappearing continents and oceans away from its origin. Its reappearance was not predictable. It was considered a useless bandwidth until the early twentieth century when Ambrose Fleming, an English electrical engineer and physicist, and former student of Maxwell, used a diode tube to detect radio signals.

Diode tubes are a form of thermionic valves. Decades earlier, in 1873, the British physicist Frederick Guthrie had described what was

---

v. United States, 320 US 1. The Court stated, "*The broad claims of the Marconi Patent No. 763,772, for improvements in apparatus for wireless telegraphy—briefly, for a structure and arrangement of four high-frequency circuits with means of independently adjusting each so that all four may be brought into electrical resonance with one another*—held *invalid because anticipated. P. 320 U. S. 38. Marconi showed no invention over Stone (Patent No. 714,756) by making the tuning of his antenna circuit adjustable or by using Lodge's (Patent No. 609,154) variable inductance for that purpose. Whether Stone's patent involved invention is not here determined*" [41]. The Stone patent of 1900 references a radiotelegraphy communication system, while the Lodge patent references new and useful Improvements in Electric Telegraphy.

referred to as thermionic transmission—that is, an electric current could be controlled through a vacuum (the vacuum tube). The reference to a valve comes from the fact that the flow of current is directional, and by applying a change in voltage, one can increase or decrease the current. Fleming, who earlier had collaborated with Marconi on wireless transatlantic transmission, wrote to Marconi, in November of 1904, "*I have been receiving signals on an aerial with nothing but a mirror galvanometer and my device*"—that is, the diode [42]. He patented this in 1905, and protection was granted for the use of the valve as a rectifier of oscillations and as a detector and receiver in wireless telegraphy.

The detection of radio signals, coupled with the directional antenna, gave shortwave communication the reliability the world needed, and as a result, submarine cable networks lost their dominance. Today, there are an estimated 1.5 billion shortwave receivers, in various forms, in use [43]. But even this amount of usage does not offer security for the future of shortwave transmission. The future of shortwave communication may be relegated to enthusiasts. The development of direct satellite broadcasting, bandwidth crowding, and electrical interference from common household items such as cell phones and computers have decreased its popularity (sounds suspiciously like opportunity). While shortwave continues to be an accessible medium for international communication, some like Andy Sennitt, former editor of the *World Radio TV Handbook*, consider it a legacy technology whose glory days have come and gone [44].

While I have greatly understated and omitted much of the technology of wireless transmission, today wireless transmission, in its multitude of forms such as microwaves, is a part of all lives. We commonly recognize it in the form of Wi-Fi, cell phones, and Bluetooth, but a quick search of the US Patent Office finds it in a broad spectrum of devices such as parking meters, pipeline detectors, ultrasonic mammography, remote pregnancy monitoring, and navigation systems.

We carry it in our pockets, can buy it in disposable throwaway form, and use it to find restaurants in unfamiliar cities, all arising from the inefficiency of an earlier system—from sail to steam engines, to cable transmission, to wireless transmission. Along the way, and riding on the opportunity spawned by the inefficiency of communication, were the great advances of the latter part of the twentieth century and continuing into this century.

I remember quite well, in my youth—I was born in 1948—of those predicting what the new century would bring. There was talk of domed cities, weather control, flying cars, Martian colonies, and unlimited food supply. There was never talk, let alone prediction, of a future dependent on communication, more exactly wireless transmission—person to person, person to machine, machine to machine.

Note: I use the term machine loosely to define any technology capable of transmission or reception of a signal, whether that signal be purely electronic or in another form—such as an infrared pulse passing a binary code to a receiver that passes the code to a microprocessor (TV remote control). One can only speculate as we move further into this century what the new crests of communication inefficiency will sponsor in the way of opportunity. Hertz may have thought his discovery little more than a curiosity with no practical value, but the lesson in this is do not discount the curiosities.

Chapter 17: Crisis and Novelty

If inefficiency sponsors opportunity, then crisis sponsors novelty, or rather, it should. Novelty is the creative, perhaps innovative, response to a crisis. The crisis may arise from a lack of preparedness, a shift in a business model, a response to a failed experiment such as in the sciences, or an awareness that a disruptive technology will render the current business model and/or portfolio obsolete.

To understand where novelty comes from in the face of crisis, we must first understand where it is not found. It is not found in structure. Why? If crisis sponsors novelty (the premise of the argument), then the crisis comes from the fact the problem or dilemma is not structured—that is, the problem space (the presentation of the problem) lacks operators. It will have an origin, the reason for the crisis, and it will have an objective, i.e., complete the goal, but it lacks the conditions in which the problem must be solved—that is, operators.

Consider an exercise that has operators such as a student solving algebraic problems. The rules of algebra are well defined, and if the student works within the rules, a solution is inevitable. The same is with paint by numbers. The exercise is to fill a canvas with colors of paint so it identically resembles the picture on the box. If one follows the rules—

that is, applies paint color "x" to all spaces defined as x on the canvas, and so on—the picture as shown on the box will be reproduced on the canvas.

On a more complex level, if a manufacturing engineer wants to optimize the production rate of an extruder line while minimizing the amount of rejects, he or she would (or should) follow a path outlined by the operators of designed experiments (DoE). This is what operators do—allow an exercise to be solved efficiently and sufficiently. Operators allow for the exploitation of current knowledge.

I have a small greenhouse in my backyard. A few years ago, I ordered a kit. Using the architectural renderings accompanying the instructions, I was able to solve my dilemma (how to build a greenhouse) in an efficient amount of time. But none of this is novelty because the exercise space was structured. It contained operators that allow for a solution. Operators are limiters. They define the parameters for solution-finding. In this, operators are limiters to novelty. The fact is their presence precludes the need for novelty and in turn redefines what one may consider a crisis.

To understand the creative process sponsoring novelty that evolves from a crisis, we must understand structure in the form of operators does not exist at the origin of the problem; as a result, neither do familiar solutions at the outcome. Novel solutions will generally not have familiar outcomes. This should go without saying, but I mention it because it has been my experience there are solution seekers who will not recognize a solution if it is not in the familiar—that is, have a familiar outcome. Some of you, no doubt, by now, recognize operators tell us how to look and where to look, and only how and where to look; hence, novelty and crisis solutions are highly unlikely in the presence of operators.

At this point in the dialogue, I must introduce a second premise. The premise is fairly simple: Most of what we refer to as problems are not true problems, but rather exercises in which the singular sufficient solution is found by drawing upon past experience. Thus, there is only one right answer with the expectation it will be found through the manipulation of proper algorithms.

Recall our discussion much earlier in this text, that answers of value are derived from a procedural activity involving the retrieval, from memory, of some algorithmic process, a computational model, and then a decision as to the value of the effort. It is this that gives senior management confidence in their teams when directing them to "not come out until everyone is in agreement to the solution."

Most—but not all—business dilemmas are not original. They have occurred prior, in part or parcel, and deriving a solution is found in recalling the similarity of prior experience, allowing everyone to be in agreement. As an example, supply chain problems, staffing, regaining market share, capital expenditures, layoffs, and downtime, etc., are all recurring dilemmas facing businesses. Experienced managers and MBA students studying case histories will have experience (real or academic) in the singular sufficient solution.

So, what then is a true problem? According to Ian Mitroff [1], an organizational theorist and professor emeritus at the University of Southern California, a problem is not singular in its solution. Rather, problems will have as many unique solutions as there are perspectives of the stakeholders. Stakeholders are not only affected by the problem but also affect the problem. In other words, there is no such thing as one right answer to a true problem. Why? As Braque, Picasso, Wright, Hemingway, and so many others discovered long ago, the singular perspective does not capture the complexity of variance required to define the problem and understand the solution is multifaceted.

Consider problems such as poverty, addiction, terrorism, or global environmental changes. There is no one particular perspective on this and no singular solution. As an example, in 2010, CircleofBlue.org, an information resource with a focus on water and its relationship to food, energy, and health, listed nineteen solutions to the global freshwater crisis [2]. Stakeholders in this are supply chains of major global corporations, energy producers, agricultural consumers of freshwater, economists, governments, and lawmakers within governments, etc. In fairness, not all nineteen items listed are solutions; some were simply recognitions of potential, but the point is made. The problem is complex, and any solutions brought forth are as varied as the stakeholders whose perspectives range from population growth, urban development, farming, climate change, competition for freshwater, etc., all of which will vary the perception of the value of fresh water.

Consider the 1995 heat wave in Chicago with temperatures reaching 106 degrees Fahrenheit, resulting in an estimated 739 deaths [3]. Mapping the crisis indicated this was a problem entrenched in poverty and victimizing the elderly. Substandard housing and little if no neighborhood cohesiveness made the fear of crime a reality and kept many from performing such simple heat relief-giving tactics as opening windows. The city itself, the urban center, was responsible for as much as four additional degrees of the heat being produced (known as an urban heat island[HH]). Additionally, power failures were generated, and a temperature inversion that kept stagnated polluted air at ground level was also partially responsible for the deaths and heat-related health problems. Epidemiologically speaking, the crisis was referred to as a mortality displacement, meaning a certain proportion of the excess death was to be expected (about 26 percent), although disproportionally riskier for Blacks.

Can this happen again? Almost certainly. Why? Because the multiplicity of perspectives as to why death occurred in the face of extreme heat have been recognized but not resolved.

Understanding the numerous reasons why the problem exists is not a solution to the problem. It is only the recognition of the need for a multifaceted solution. But multifaceted solutions are complex, highly variable, and almost always come with multiple stakeholders.

Mitroff, mentioned earlier, provides the example of the loss of jobs within a society to outsourcing as an illustration of a complex problem without a singular solution, stating, "*Anything that is well structured and relatively independent of context and culture...can be done by someone who is not a member of the society in which the problem arose* [5]"—that is, it can be outsourced.

Outsourcing is a shift of jobs and income-producing responsibilities from one society or community to another. Its immediate effect on the sector being outsourced is unemployment. While generally used for nonfundamental roles, i.e., rote-driven support roles within corporate

---

[HH] Urban heat islands are cities or areas within a city that are warmer than surrounding areas. According to the U.S. Environmental Protection Agency, daytime temperatures in urban areas can be 1–7°F higher than temperatures in outlying areas and nighttime temperatures between 2-5°F higher [4]. Recognized problems associated with urban heat islands are increased energy demands, air pollution, greenhouse gas emissions, heat-related illness, and mortality. Proposed solutions to urban heat islands range from planting trees, green roofing (planting vegetation on roofs), reflective paints, asphalt coatings, and evaporative cooling systems such as rooftop sprinklers.

functions, Mitroff argues effectively that knowledge-based professions and academic disciplines are also at risk. Why? Because the promise of a singular focused career in which only one knowledge or experience set is needed no longer exists; thus, as the nature of work changes, the nature of knowledge changes; this is a societal and cultural revolution. Solutions to this, according to Mitroff, will only come with the realization and acceptance that this is a problem lying outside the current academic, professional, and corporate disciplines. Does this sound ambiguous? Here is the thing: true problems are ambiguous.

Now that you have a bit of background in where I want this to go, let us ground ourselves in problems of a more practical nature. The problems found in the following paragraphs will not be structured (no defined operators) and will have multiple stakeholders and solutions. They are all, in their own way, a crisis borne of necessity, albeit not necessarily immediate. These are not checklist exercises. They are not structured by "if this and this and this, then this." Let's see how they are handled.

Assume you urgently need some money, fast. Not a large amount of money, maybe just a few hundred dollars. The money is to help out a friend or neighbor in need, but you have nobody to lend you the money because you do not plan on paying the money back. You believe charity is its own reward, and maybe it is, but life events based on good intentions are generally not negotiable in financial arenas. So, where do you get the money? Your rich uncle won't give it to you, and neither will a bank. Charitable organizations won't help because their money is earmarked for other endeavors. It would seem obtaining money legally requires you to fill out forms and follow certain social and economically regulating rules, but your particular crisis doesn't entertain rules; hence, you have no operators. You have a crisis. You need to raise money for what can be best described as an urgent life event. What do you do? You need a novel solution.

A decade ago, you could have held a fundraiser such as a community dinner and asked for donations. Or stood on a street corner, holding a pickle jar with a hole punched in the lid and "Please help" scrawled in crayon across the outside, but such efforts often underfund. Enter crowdfunding, the online global method of getting the urgency of your project in front of hundreds of thousands, if not millions of viewers for the purpose of instant funding. Websites such as GoFundMe are an innovative endeavor to help those in which other avenues of funding are closed. They allow users to raise money for whatever purpose by sharing their particular project though integrated social websites. Those on the websites then view the project and can decide if it is something they would like to donate money to. They do this through debit or credit cards and can track their funding and leave reviews, making the websites self-policing.

For this service, websites such as GoFundMe (www.gofundme.com) take a modest percentage of each donation to offset costs. I say modest because it truly is when compared to what large national charities remove for administrative costs from each dollar pledged to help. Who uses crowdfunding? According to Wikipedia, the millennials' source of all knowledge and the e-version heir-apparent to the baby boomer's fictional *Junior Woodchuck Guidebook*[II], crowdfunding is used by those who want to save people from financial crisis[7]. Those who would help someone avoid eviction or otherwise lose their home, those building a trust fund for a child of a good Samaritan, those purchasing a wheelchair for the neighbor down the street, those looking for tuition money, etc.

Websites such as GoFundMe have a business model that is surprisingly simple—keep the project singular, that is, no projects that fund other projects, but allow donations for personal causes and life events.

To be clear, crowdfunding is not new. It has been around in one form or another for well over a hundred years; as an example, Joseph Pulitzer's 1885 newspaper campaign to fund the Statue of Liberty's base raised over one hundred thousand dollars in six months [8]. The term, however, was coined in 1997 by a British rock band trying to raise money online for its American tour [9]. Shortly after this, entrepreneurs, seeing advantages in crowdfunding over traditional financing, moved the platform into the investment market as a result of the JOBS Act, which allowed nonpublic investment companies to market to the public

---

[II] The Junior Woodchucks are a fictional scouting organization the Disney triplet characters Huey, Dewey, and Louie (Donald Duck's nephews) belong to. The guidebook, depicted as a small paperback, is remarkable for the wealth and depth of knowledge it contained, detailing information and self-help about whatever scenario or dilemma the Junior Woodchucks would find themselves in [6].

for the first time since the Great Depression. This, in turn, opened other doors such as in real estate, where investors are paired with opportunities.

But not all crisis spurs novelty that is so obviously an immediate need as financial help. As an example, what do you do if you are the National Basketball Association in the 1970s, and your fan base is eroding? You have lots of very tall players standing under nets, dropping in two-pointers, and not a lot of defense to make the game enjoyable. Television ratings, and as a result revenue, are dropping. Your current business model based on the rules of the game is showing signs of coming apart. You are not at a crisis point, but you recognize a need to do something.

Enter the three-point shot, first introduced in 1945 in an NCAA game between Fordham and Columbia. History has it that it was proposed earlier that year as a bonus shot to limit the effectiveness of taller players. Suffice it to say, it did not fare well and had an on-again-off-again existence for several years, finally surfacing in the professional leagues in 1961 in the short-lived American Basketball League. In 1967, it was reintroduced by the American Basketball Association (ABA, now also defunct) and immediately chided as a gimmick to help a struggling league, and this may have a ring of truth to it. Nevertheless, it is now considered a premium skill and a method to equalize the height advantage that some teams have from their seven-foot-plus players who easily stand under the basket or layup two-pointers.

When the ABA adopted the three-point shot, the NBA, the premier league, chose to maintain the game as is, as they perceived the status quo to have fan value. But the NBA's two-point shot game was a slow game, and the fans were decreasing in numbers. To overcome this, the NBA increasingly brought in new and taller talent. It became a game of very large men in large man's world standing near the basket and easily scoring. More of the same with the rules of the game resulted in a not too terribly exciting game and a stagnant market. Disillusioned fans could be quoted as saying, "*Give each team ninety points and ten minutes to play. Then call it a day.*" It is not clear whether the NBA believed the three-point shot would drive away purist fans, but it is apparent they underestimated the growth of a fan base that would evolve from a faster, longer range, and higher-scoring game.

The ABA saw its demise nine years after its inception, but the merger of the two leagues at its death resulted in four of the strongest ABA teams, and the three-point shot, merge with the NBA. The result is a matter of historical record. Once the current scoring rules were set aside, the three-point shot became an offensive weapon. Coaches increased the percentage of shots from beyond the arc, and teams began drafting, as a matter of cost-efficiency, increased numbers of smaller players (smaller is a relative term in basketball) proficient in the skill of distance shooting; the three-pointer is worth 50 percent more.

To combat the three-pointer, defenses opened up. Statistics indicate the three-pointer has evolved in the game from a strategy to come from behind in the last minutes of play to an integral part of the overall game plan, moving from approximately three attempts per game to an average of twenty-four. It is fair to say the three-point shot forever changed how the game of basketball is played. The three-point shot was, by nature of the game, a novelty resulting from a lack of growth that became a mainstay [10].

Had the three-point shot not been adapted by the NBA, the game may never have had the professional success it now enjoys. Some scenarios would suggest it may have been relegated to a game found only on the courts of high school and college campuses, but these are scenarios of failure and built on speculation.

To further our discussion, let's move from basketball into the physical sciences and consider the failed experiment. What happens when scientific experiments fail? The researcher has the option to move on to other venues or seek other paths for success. Why? Because failed experiments tend to close off pathways. Science is replete with such examples. Seldom is failure also the right stuff for success, or as Monty Python might say, "*Now for something completely different*" [11]. But this is naive. Failures can lead to unexpected and otherwise unavailable discoveries or breakthroughs because failures are always informative and can sponsor curiosity. Failure is an important factor in scientific success. Perhaps the most important factor.

In 1938, Roy Plunkett, PhD [12], was working in DuPont's Jackson Laboratory in New Jersey. His task was to develop a safe alternative to the ammonia and sulfur dioxide refrigerants of the day. More specifically, he was tasked with increasing the usage of Freon® in automobile production for General Motors. Freon is a fluoropolymer, and Plunkett was working with pressurized cylinders of the gas. Upon inspecting one such small cylinder of tetrafluoroethylene, he found it contained no pressure. Curious, he cut the cylinder open and discovered a slippery white powder coating the inside.

At this point, Plunkett could have considered his experiment a failure and moved on, that tetrafluoroethylene under pressure did not give him the results he needed. Instead, he became curious as to the nature of the powder. Further investigation determined it had a high melting point and when it did melt, it would not flow. Neither did it dissolve in anything or react with acids or bases. It didn't obey the rules, did not appear to be useful, at least for the time being.

Nevertheless, Plunkett was granted a patent for his discovery on February 4, 1941. Enter World War II and the need for corrosion-resistant materials for uranium enrichment. Plunkett's white powder became part of the Manhattan Project. This gave DuPont the impetus for further research, and by the end of the war, Teflon® had wide industrial applications. By the 1960s, the failed experiment in automotive refrigeration had moved into the world's kitchens and became part of everyday household usage.

Of the last three scenarios, the first two are interesting from the view that conventional algorithmic solutions were not available; thus, there were no dots to connect to lead to a path of success. Success had to be found from another perspective. The last scenario found success in waiting for an application to arrive—the dynamic waiting we discussed earlier that is so common in technology advancement. However, there is one more example that needs our attention, and this involves not only failure, but also incorporating the failure into the algorithms of success.

In May 2016, Paul Raccuglia and colleagues published in the prestigious journal *Nature* the results of using what they called dark reactions—that is, failed or unsuccessful experiments collected from archived laboratory notebooks, along with validated information to train a machine—learning model to predict reaction success [13]. They were able to successfully predict conditions for inorganic product formation. Of interest is that their machine-learning model, when tested, far outperformed traditional human strategies.

Why?

To answer this, we must return to our discussion of multiple perspectives. Many scientists trying to devise such a solution would turn to the rational perspective of looking at what has led to success in the past. Instead, Raccuglia and his team from Haverford and Purdue, in devising a solution to their problem also took the perspective of viewing failure as a necessary path of inquiry. This is not only another perspective it is also a path of conflict spoken to by Hirshberg when he talked of *blurred boundaries*. The initial problem was to develop an algorithm to predict conditions for inorganic product formation. In this they succeeded, but even more so, they developed a conceptual model of the problem relying on the perception of success and failure.

Much of science would be well advised to take note of this and stop relegating failure to archived laboratory notebooks. Rather, let failure be taken advantage of by artificial intelligence, such as IBM's Watson, a supercomputer combining artificial intelligence and analytical software, with the ability to read, understand, and categorize the unstructured data found in scientific and health care journals. Perhaps there should be a call to store all publicly funded research, failed and successful, in repositories available to researchers and artificial intelligence.

Chapter 18: Visionaries and Futurists

There is one contradiction to the predictions stated at the end of Chapter 16, occurring decades before my youth, that is of note. Nikola Tesla talking about wireless communication predicted:

It will be possible for a business man in New York to dictate instructions, and have them instantly appear in type at his office in London or elsewhere. He will be able to call up, from his desk, and talk to any telephone subscriber on the globe, without any change whatever in the existing equipment...to hear anywhere, on sea or land, music or song, the speech of a political leader, however distant. In the same manner any picture, character, drawing, or print can be transferred from one to another place. Millions of such instruments can be operated from but one plant of this kind. More important than all of this, however, will be the transmission of power, without wires...the wireless art offers greater possibilities than any invention or discovery heretofore made. [1]

Tesla made this statement in 1908, and the future he was predicting was, by his own design, taking place and ready to demonstrate in a matter of months. This did not happen.

In 1926, he further postulated, "*When wireless is perfectly applied the whole earth will be converted into a huge brain, which in fact it is, all things being particles of a real and rhythmic whole. We shall be able to communicate with one another instantly, irrespective of distance. Not only this, but through television and telephony we shall see and hear one another as perfectly as though we were face to face, despite intervening distances of thousands of miles; and the instruments through which we shall be able to do this will be amazingly simple compared with our present telephone. A man will be able to carry one in his vest pocket*" [2].

Really! Was Steve Jobs actually Nikola Tesla reincarnated?

Tesla also believed in Martians, as did many notables of the day. William Pickering (1858–1938)—the American astronomer and observatory builder for whom an asteroid and craters on the moon and Mars are named—claimed to see canals with vegetation, lakes, and clouds in the Martian atmosphere. Percival Lowell (1855–1916), businessman, mathematician, and astronomer, advanced the speculation of a higher civilization on the Red Planet. The tycoon, John Jacob Astor IV (1864–1912), who perished in the sinking of the *Titanic*, wrote a fictionalized account of space travel and predicted magnetic railways and wind turbines for generating electricity. In his 1894 novel, *A Journey in Other Worlds: A Romance of the Future*, he wrote prophetically, "*This period A.D. 2000, is by far the most wonderful the world has as yet seen. The advance in scientific knowledge and attainment within the memory of the present generation has been so stupendous that it completely overshadows all that has preceded*" [3].

However, Tesla, for a brief period of time, also believed he was in communication with Martians. In 1899, while observing the electrical activity of the Earth, he began to pick up rhythmic signals he could not identify, except to call them "*disturbances being intelligently controlled signals*," and in this he was correct. But in calling them "*greetings from one planet to another*," he was not. He was right on the first count, wrong on the second. The truth, after much speculation about correspondence with other planets, particularly Mars, was he picked up the signals being transmitted by a competitor, Marconi, experimenting with the transmission of the letter S in Morse code [4].

Of all that Tesla was, iconoclast, inventor, electrician, theorist, genius, mad scientist, and futurist, there is one description all should agree on. He was a visionary. He believed in the omnipotence of electricity and saw the future of mankind in it. He saw it relieving future generations of needless toil through the remote control of automatons. He demonstrated a wireless-controlled model boat in 1898.

He saw electricity controlling the weather, enhancing agriculture through the propagation of plants, and facilitating nitrogen into the soil. He envisioned a not-so-peaceful end to warfare through the creation of sweeping arcs of electricity capable of incinerating whole cities and all of their inhabitants to include even the sterilization of the soil in which they stood.

He envisioned instantaneous wireless transmission of photographs and verbal communication. He designed electrical propulsion systems that he believed could power aircraft and propel men beyond the confines of the earth. He believed in the ability to obtain electrical energy directly from the sun. He believed in the wireless transmission of energy: "*I can conceive of no technical advance which would tend to unite the various elements of humanity more effectively than this one...*" [5]. In this, Nikola Tesla predated, in practice, at least two of A. F. Osborn's rules for brainstorming—that is, think freely and generate ideas [6].

Osborn (1888–1966), an advertising executive and originator of the creativity technique called brainstorming, was a proponent of the novelty of ideas while Tesla was a practitioner. But there is little to suggest Osborn thought brainstorming should move in the direction of usefulness (more on Osborn later).

Tesla, the practitioner, reveled in idea generation and visions of future technologies, but was not particularly driven to bring any of this to a practical and consumer-oriented fruition. It is unclear whether Tesla ignored the practicality of usefulness or actively disliked it. Perhaps a better phrasing would be "did not hold it in favor," even though he did pay lip service to it.

Robert C. Litchfield [7], an associate professor of business at Washington & Jefferson College, argues that actively choosing to either ignore or disfavor usefulness can affect the "*range and skew of ideas generated.*" He makes the point that extreme ideas can affect problem framing, which is exactly the difficulty Tesla had. This was exploited by much of the popular media of the day, and maybe why many of his wealthy benefactors—businessmen such as John Jacob Astor and J. Pierpont Morgan—lost their faith in him and turned their backs. His benefactors wanted utility. While his benefactors were entertained by the novelty of his ideas, they were also firmly grounded in a return on investment. Had they been able to wait fifty to one hundred years, they would have seen the marvel of his ideas come to pass.

It is often debated everyone has the potential for creativity, and this may be so, but not all potential is realized, and not all realized creativity has value. Thus, we could ask: *do those who realize creativity have the ability to frame their creations within usefulness (innovation) or the return on investment?*

There is one other reason Tesla's investors may have turned their backs. His investors were powerful men, ruling the US industry and influencing world economies. They were industrialists. The manner in which Tesla promoted his wireless system was clearly a threat to established industries on a number of fronts, in particular to the reduction in the value of copper and obtaining energy without the consumption of natural resources (heavy industries prospered on the consumption of resources). But it wasn't just his wireless system that was flaunted in their faces. It was energy in general. Consider this 1896 quote from an editorial in *The World Magazine*, entitled "A Way to Harness Free Electric Currents Discovered by Nikola Tesla."

> *The scientist-electricians who have for years been trying to master the mystery of electrical earth currents with which the ground beneath your feet is filled, are on the threshold of success. The success of the experiments they have under way means much to them, but vastly more to the people. It means that if Nikola Tesla succeeds in harnessing the electrical earth currents and putting them to work for man there will be an end to oppressive, extortionate monopolies in steam, telephone, telegraphs and the other commercial uses of electricity, and that the grasping millionaires who have for two decades milked the people's purse with electrical fingers will have to relinquish their monopoly.* [8]

Tesla, perhaps, should have used some of his income to purchase the services of an image consultant or publicist. He seemed to have forgotten, or perhaps simply ignored the fact the principal encouragement of the day for men of science came from profit-based societies and growth industries, i.e., sponsorship of technological development. Industry of the day, looking into the future—for this was a future-driven era—was not averse to giving financial support to the sciences in hope that new ideas and inventions could be turned into a revenue stream, but destructive technologies—that was a threat.

Editorials aside, what Tesla was proposing, here and throughout his lifetime, was a new worldview. Not just revision or a shift in technology—that was already happening through the usual processes of questions put to accepted theories leading to extensions or rejections of such theories. From this, any formulation of new theories resulted in changes to scientific and social generalizations, attracting the next generation of practitioners. The old school disappeared and there was the emergence of a new school—a paradigm shift. But what Tesla the futurist wanted was more than technology shifts; it was a revision in the way the world defined itself and thought of its future. The world, as we might expect and was borne out, was not ready.

Most innovation, if not all, will threaten the status quo, make people nervous, and even topple established industries: consider typewriters, VCRs, and Kodachrome, or other metaphoric buggy whip industries. To a lesser extent, innovation means we no longer carry enough change in our pockets to make a phone call. The lesson in this is twofold: 1) innovation is good, but innovation with current utility is better if you are looking for investors; and 2) innovation is good, but innovation based on current utility is of questionable value if you are looking far into the future.

So, now we have the invention and innovation process spanning only a few decades between the late nineteenth century and the early twentieth. The ideas of people in different countries were brought together by the printed word, by publications, even though at least one person (Hertz) could not see the practical need for his work. It was the printed work of these men, the publications and patents, exchange of letters, that became the network that bound them together. This network allowed for two very important things to happen; first, it allowed for the bridging of distant worlds, and second for the taking apart and reassembling of the ideas.

Andrew Hargadon [9] of the University of California, Davis, calls this recombinant innovation: "*Wherever...networks of people, ideas, and objects come together...they become the raw materials for others to exploit in their pursuit of innovation.*"

Thomas Edison, for example, did not invent the light bulb. But he networked with those who were influential in the invention. Note: networking does not imply an actual one-on-one collaboration, but rather the knowledge of others and the exploitation of that knowledge.

Of other knowledge and influence, consider Humphry Davy and Warren De la Rue. Davy, a Cornish chemist and inventor, demonstrated an electric arc in the first decade of the 1800s [10] by connecting two wires to a battery and using charcoal strips as electrodes. This created sufficient light for illumination, which upon further advances in this technology led to the streets of London being illuminated by carbon arc lamps. Warren De la Rue, the British astronomer, chemist, and inventor, enclosed a coiled platinum filament in a vacuum tube and by passing an electrical current through it produced light in 1840 [11].

In Edison's case, the incandescent bulb came about twenty years earlier from a modest yet prolific inventor by the name of Moses Farmer of Boston [12]. Farmer, an electrical engineer educated at Dartmouth, invented an electromagnetic locomotive, a process for electroplating aluminum, and several forms of incandescent lighting. Farmer is said to have illuminated his home with electricity, generated from a dynamo of his own design, as early as 1859. But from what history tells us, Farmer's religious beliefs kept him from profiting from his inventions. Farmer patented an early light bulb, which was later bought by Edison.

Joseph Wilson Swan, of England, is also credited with inventing the incandescent light bulb. He enclosed carbonized paper filaments in an evacuated glass bulb to create a light bulb in 1850 (Edison was born in 1847) and by 1860 was able to demonstrate a working device and obtain a UK patent [13]. The device was inefficient at best; however, in 1878 he demonstrated an improved incandescent carbon lamp, and a patent was granted in 1880 [14].

Edison was well aware of Swan's work but did not collaborate with Swan as is sometimes noted [15], [16]. Rather, apprehension over patent infringements and the potential for lawsuits resulted in Swan's company, the Swan United Electric Light Company, and Edison's company to merge and form the Edison and Swan United Electric Light Co. Eventually, Edison acquired all of Swan's interest in the company.

Edison, however, is credited with the first commercially viable incandescent lamp and filed his patent application in 1879, which was granted in 1880. Of interest is that Edison's first patent application was rejected because it infringed on a patent caveat filed by J. W. Starr, of Cincinnati, Ohio, for a *divisible light*, in 1845.[JJ] Starr, who sought US, British, and French patents, did not continue with his work, having died of tuberculosis in 1846.

So, is invention (innovation?) and discovery the work of pure genius, or is it an assembly function derived from networking? The arguments so far presented would strongly indicate networking. From our previous discussion, we know invention and discovery are timeworn processes of conceptualization. While genius may or may not be involved, it does appear to be a function of those prepared to take advantage of networks, and the argument can be made that the iconoclastic view of the world, in their sense of practicality, is that of connectivity.

They are simply better connected (an active effort); even if the connectivity does not include a one-on-one collaboration, there is an overt awareness. This describes what can be thought of as iconoclastic capital, that is, in part the beneficial value that social and professional connectivity has on invention, innovation, and discovery. I say in part because iconoclastic capital must be a value function of individual attributes working in conjunction with social and professional networking. The question then is: *Can anyone become an iconoclast, or can any team develop iconoclastic momentum?*

We have seen how networking can take decades, if not centuries, and in this time is a boundary; time limits knowledge, or more exactly, the ability to distribute and access knowledge. But for more current and

---

[JJ] Starr and his business associate, Edward Augustin King, were granted a British patent for their invention. Two styles of lamp were described: in one, a platinum strip (or filament) was enclosed in glass (no vacuum), and in the other, a carbon strip was enclosed in a vacuum above a column of mercury (required for vacuum). By replacing the carbon strip when it failed, the lamp was made renewable [17]. Starr died in 1846 of tuberculosis.

practical methods, how is this done? How does one bring together or create a network of people to provide the raw materials for others to exploit in an immediate sense? One example may come from a resolute woman by the name of Cheryl Gartley, whom I met a number of years ago. Cheryl is the founder and president of the Simon Foundation for Continence, a nonprofit organization whose purpose is to find solutions for those with urinary or fecal incontinence. But perhaps Cheryl's real claim to fame, at least among those who know her, is her tenacity and the fact she has a way of getting things done, sometimes in the face of limited resources.

A few years ago, Cheryl—I suspect somewhat dismayed at the lack of innovation by clinicians and medical device manufacturers[KK] who serve the burgeoning population of people suffering from incontinence—had an idea. What if you could bring together people from around the world, people from different walks of life, people with different perspectives, and put them in a room for a few days and see what happens? Not just people with incontinence and not just manufacturers of health care products, but truly different people.

The purpose of this was, of course, to spur the innovative process to the benefit of incontinent sufferers. So, Cheryl, along with Alan Cottenden—currently Emeritus Professor of Incontinence Technology at University College London—gathered some industry sponsors and began to invite people—such as students and recent graduates of engineering schools. Those with widely varied engineering interests, venture capitalists, inventors, health care professionals, and yes, those suffering from incontinence. More importantly, those invited to attend did not have to even know what urinary or fecal incontinence was. Cheryl told of many such people hanging up on her, thinking her initial phone call offering an invitation to attend was little more than a crank call.

From the original meeting in 2007, the biennial meeting has attracted experts from all walks of life: people designing zero-gravity toilets for use in space, scientists developing nanotechnology, biofilm

---

[KK] In a recent conversation I had with Cheryl, she relayed a discussion she had early on in her career with the vice president of a major manufacturer of incontinence products, who confessed he had never met, let alone talked with, a person suffering from incontinence.

technologists, developers of ballistic protection fabrics, health economists, experts in medical implantables, surface technologies, smart chips, olfactory detection, quality of life, microbiology, hand washing, and even an expert on presentation skills.

The meetings have one objective: put these people together under a central theme and see what happens. The inventive process is a slow process from the record of invention to patent filing to production, so it is still too early to know the outcomes of the conferences, but time will tell. The important point here is the success of the meetings will not come from a solitary focus, but rather from the connectivity of networks. Each of the participants, whether they be active or passive participants, come from varied and diverse backgrounds, and in such each has their own specialty networks. Thus, connectivity goes well beyond the immediate conference participation. Cheryl Gartley is indeed exploiting the network process as a strategy for solutions to the problem of urinary and fecal incontinence.

Perhaps the most striking example of bringing together disparate ideas is what is referred to as open-sourcing—or the open-source principle found in the software industry—which promotes the sharing of concurrent yet dissimilar agendas and dissimilar methods; often at the expense of intellectual property rights to promote product development. Open-sourcing takes advantage of the Internet and a socio-technical system, which provides countless thousands of developers/innovators a format for near-instantaneous collaboration (or usurping). But one does not have to be a software developer to take advantage of open-sourcing.

The online and instantaneous access to large data libraries, patents, publications ranging from books, peer-reviewed journals, and blogs allows anyone with the ability to enter some key phrases into a search engine access to a multitude of perspectives—to bridge distant worlds and to take apart and reassemble ideas. However, this is not without difficulty. The Internet is truly a technical superorganism, where the greatest challenge may be intelligent information retrieval from a very nonlinear flood of information, forcing the retrieval process to operate at the "edge of chaos" [18]. But chaos is inefficiency, and as stated prior, opportunity rides the crest of inefficiency.

For some years now, companies have taken the concept of online access further to sponsor what is known as e-brainstorming. In this method, participants tasked with generating solution ideas do so remotely on a computer screen, which contains a second screen (split screen). Simultaneously, other remote participants also generate ideas on screens. The result is that all ideas are instantaneously shared on the second screen, allowing the participants to build on the work of others without the problems associated with face-to-face brainstorming sessions.

E-brainstorming takes advantage of the individual insights for idea generation by putting people in a virtual community. Research indicates the groups using e-brainstorming produce more ideas per person and do not suffer from individual productivity loss when compared to nominal groups [19], [20]. Online sharing and rapid participation seem to have the ability to amplify collective problem-solving.

Consider Tim Gowers, a Royal Society Research Professor at the Department of Pure Mathematics and Mathematical Statistics at the University of Cambridge, and a Fellow of Trinity College, Cambridge [21]. He is also a blogger. In 2009, he used his blog to determine if massively collaborative mathematics was possible; an experiment in social networking no less. Picking an important but unsolved mathematical problem—in this case finding a new combinatorial proof to the density version of the Hales-Jewett theorem—Gowers and a few colleagues posted this in his blog and invited people to comment.[LL] Gowers stated, "*Suppose one had a forum for the online discussion of a particular problem…that anybody who had anything whatsoever to say about the problem could chip in…you would contribute ideas even if they were undeveloped and/or likely to be wrong.*"

The premise was more minds working collaboratively from multiple perspectives are more powerful than the single perspective of a mind in isolation. What is interesting is the invitation was open to any and all; thus, people from different fields of expertise could comment and contribute. Comments, suggestions, and ideas could be solicited from multiple perspectives.

It took over seven hours for the first comment to come in; however, over the next thirty-seven days, eight hundred mathematical comments

---

[LL] Hales-Jewett theorem: a fundamental combinatorial result concerning the degree to which high-dimensional objects must exhibit some combinatorial arrangement, where it is impossible for such objects to be completely random [22].

were received totaling over one hundred seventy thousand words. It wasn't just that comments were received. The timeline showed ideas introduced and accepted or rejected. Sometimes revised. Mistakes made and corrected. Tangents pursued and determined to be false. And in all of this came a scattering of understanding, of comprehension. Thirty-seven days after the post, the problem was considered solved.

The idea generation collective demonstrated by Gowers gives further substance to the concept of a technical superorganism. Fortunately, Gowers and colleagues had the intellectual wherewithal to sift through the wealth of specialized information that came in through the comments. As stated above, the greatest challenge may be the sifting through of information, and not just the intelligent information retrieval from a very nonlinear flood of information, but also the synthesis of this information.

Suffice it to say that when speaking of innovation, nothing exists in isolation, nor as a singular entity, but rather the pieces that comprise the complexity of the innovative process or invention are in one manner or another inexplicably bound to each other prior to their assembly—waiting their time in the shadows to be brought forth by those with the ability to bring them together. This is not a task for like minds constrained by the perspective of the box.

As an example, consider Edwin Land, who in the 1920s invented sheet polarizers [23], [24]. This had little practical value at the time, but in the 1990s, it became instrumental in the liquid crystal displays of the pocket calculators and digital watches. This waiting in time, revisiting old ideas and experiences, Land termed "atavistic"—that is, a revisiting of old problems to gain new insights.

Land's term, "atavistic," could be applied to much of the creativity of the nineteenth and twentieth century. Electric-powered cars were introduced in the nineteenth century. Robert Anderson, a Scottish inventor, devised a crude electric carriage in the 1830s. His prototype electric-powered carriage used a non-rechargeable battery [25], [26].

Throughout the nineteenth century, other inventors devised their own versions of electric-powered vehicles. Ferdinand Porsche introduced the P1 in 1898 [27], which was powered by a three-horsepower electric motor with a cruising range (time) of three to six hours. A year later, the first hybrid car, the Lohner-Porsche Mixte Hybrid, was introduced [28]. It had in-wheel electric motors and onboard gas engine to recharge the batteries. But all of this would fall out of popularity in favor of petroleum-powered vehicles.[MM] It would take an energy crisis and rising fuel prices of the twentieth century to make this form of transportation again popular in the first decades of the twenty-first century.

History, of course, is filled with such examples. Prior to the twentieth century, the timeline between invention and widespread use was measured in decades. During the early years of the twentieth century, this improved somewhat, but things like refrigeration, electrical heating, and the aspirin still averaged thirty-three years before commercial use [29].

We must, of course, recognize the difference between Gowers's online problem-solving mentioned earlier and the timelines mentioned in the preceding paragraphs. Gowers's problem was intellectual and those mentioned above involved materials, manufacturing, marketing, and the waiting for technology to catch up with the idea. Nevertheless, the point is made. As stated earlier, innovation does not exist in isolation, nor as a singular entity. The pieces that comprise the complexity of the innovative process, invention, or problem-solving are in one manner or another inexplicably bound to each other prior to their assembly, waiting their time in the shadows to be brought forth by those with the ability to bring them together. This gives cause to wonder what other futuristic ideas lie buried in the patent applications of long past.

It is the responsibility of the iconoclastic team to provide the links; not necessarily bridge the gaps, but more importantly, fill them in. This is a near Herculean task when teams charged with innovation are of a similar ilk—that is, lacking diversity.

A point of interest: to think about networking, one must remind himself or herself about graph theory introduced by Euler almost three hundred years ago to describe the Königsberg bridge problem; Euler viewed the bridge problem as nodes connected by links, aka a network.

[MM] Electric vehicles have been around, in one manner or the other, since the 1830s, and had their greatest popularity in the 1890s and the first decade of the 1900s. Their popularity came from the fact they were quieter, did not have exhaust fumes, were not noisy, and did not require gear changes as did the internal combustion engines of the time. However, this popularity declined due to improvements in roads, affordable gasoline, and faster speeds of internal combustion engines, all offering greater range than that provided by electric vehicles.

Fortunately, this gave us the graph theory. Unfortunately, the problem has forever been viewed within the dimensions of a page.

In deference to Euler, his node and link "proof" of the bridge problem stated graphs with two or more nodes and an odd number of links do not have a continual path solution. Something the people of Königsberg discovered for themselves one hundred forty years later when they built an additional bridge—that is, a continual path. Changing the perspective, as described in Chapter 5, adds a link, but not a bridge, per se accomplishing the same thing. The moral of the story: do not confine your networks to a single perspective.

But it is not just innovation that exploits networking; return on investment, both time-sensitive and cost-sensitive, can also take advantage of this. The trick may be not in making this more efficient, but rather to recognize inefficiency sponsors opportunity. As advanced technology feeds increased consumer use, utilization efficiency decreases as a result of an overload on the system; increased demand (consider bandwidth) resulting in a need for further advances. Once further advances are put in place efficiency increases. However, the resultant rise in users of technology may increase at a rate greater than the advances in technology, leaving the users of technology always at the brink of inefficiency providing ample opportunity for iconoclastic momentum.

Previously, work was built upon the ideas, processes, and technology of others over an accumulated span of decades or even centuries of opportunity waiting to happen. Research opportunities can now be explored through open-sourcing, and carried out by a network of sponsored industries, graduate students, post-docs and faculty, and experimentalists no matter what the affiliation. All linked instantaneously for the sharing of ideas, and therefore not limited to thesis or antithesis, but rather focused on the syntheses of next-generation products, leading-edge technologies, and strategies for leveraging investment. It is safe to say societies will no longer be satisfied with waiting great spans of time for singular events. If there is any doubt about this, one only has to watch the change in stock prices at AAPL at the mere mention of a new product. Thus, the demand for the variance-oriented, multicultural, multi-perspective network in the moment team has arrived—that is, the iconoclastic team.

Consider a quote from the essay "As We May Think," published in 1945, by Vannevar Bush, head of the World War II US Office of Scientific Research and Development (OSRD).

> *Consider a future device for individual use, which is a sort of mechanized private file and library. It needs a name, and to coin one at random, "memex" will do. A memex is a device in which an individual stores all his books, records, and communications, and which is mechanized so that it may be consulted with exceeding speed and flexibility. It is an enlarged intimate supplement to his memory.* [30]

This excerpt is visionary, as is the entire article. Published shortly after Germany's unconditional surrender on May 8, 1945, it expresses Bush's concern of scientific effort being directed toward destruction instead of understanding and the need for mankind to have a machine that would make knowledge more accessible to the masses—a machine that would convert the information found within the world to knowledge.

Bush coined the term "memex" to describe ultra-high-resolution microfilm, that when linked with a collective of screen viewers would provide more than information. The links would allow the reader multiple perspectives, hence the potential for the synthesis of knowledge. In a manner, Bush was predicting hypertext and hyperlinks. Hypertext and hyperlinks, as we know, are the key components of the World Wide Web. Today, web pages written in HTML (Hypertext Markup Language) allow the user to connect to a variety of methods of viewing published information through the click of a mouse. It is the nonlinearity of the links that allow a multiplicity of information to provide the reader with the ability to transform data into knowledge. Bush's memex machine stopped just short of what may be the web's most important feature, the instantaneous sharing of ideas.

Chapter 19: Creative Abrasion and Dissension

This is a story that has been told many times, but it is worth repeating here. In 1979, Motorola, the American multinational telecommunications company founded in 1928, was taking a long hard look at itself. It had lost market share in key segments. Bob Galvin, president and CEO, wanted to know why. The question was asked, "*What's wrong with our company*?" The answers were to be expected, i.e., the economy, Japanese competition, poor R&D, etc., were to blame. The usual litany of politically correct, shift-the-blame responses.

One lone voice, that of Art Sundry, a sales manager, dissented. "*Our quality stinks*," he is quoted as saying. In most politically charged corporate boardrooms, this would be enough to have one fired, but Galvin listened to him and entertained his candor. Then, to validate Sundry's opinion, he went to the factory floors and talked to the employees, not the managers and directors, but the shop workers and machine operators. Then he went to the consumers. Their opinion was Sundry's opinion. Quality did indeed stink [1].

Galvin was well known for his belief that business performance was closely aligned with quality, so it came as no surprise when he implemented a stringent quality improvement program. And it came to pass that Six Sigma, a focused implementation of data-driven quality principles and techniques for eliminating defects in any process, was born, or perhaps reborn. I say reborn because the statistical methodology for Six Sigma was known prior to its popularization in the mid-1980s by Motorola. Walter Shewhart (of Shewhart Chart fame) demonstrated, in 1924, that a manufacturing process should require correction when it deviates more than three sigma (standard deviations) from the mean[NN] [2]. But the origins of standard deviations can be found in the concept of a normal distribution introduced by Carl Gauss, a German mathematician and physicist, in 1809 [3].

However, a Motorola engineer by the name of Bill Smith is credited for coining the term Six Sigma, and the term is now a federally registered trademark of Motorola. Motorola went on to realize a reported sixteen-billion-dollar savings as a result of improving quality and reducing costs through strict attention to business and operational metrics.

***

Near the end of World War II, William Shockley [4], [5], a young physicist on leave from Bell Labs, was asked by the War Department to prepare a report on the probable casualties to be incurred from an invasion of the Japanese mainland. His report, in part, influenced the bombing of Hiroshima and Nagasaki. When the war ended, Shockley was tapped, along with chemist Stanley Morgan, to form a solid-state physics group at Bell Labs. This led, through a series of failed experiments, changes in focus, patent infringements, and squabbles with colleagues, to the invention of the transistor and a shared Nobel Prize for Shockley in 1956.

It may be fair to say Shockley was a complex man with a myopic view of his environment. From most accounts, it is reasonable to express the opinion that congeniality was not one of Shockley's long

---

[NN] The term Six Sigma comes from the field of statistical quality control, which evaluates process capability. Processes that operate at a six sigma level (standard deviations from the mean) are assumed to produce long-term defect levels below 3.4 defects per million opportunities. By contrast, Shewhart's proposal of correcting the manufacturing process at three standard deviations would allow for 66,807 defects per million opportunities.

suites. Increasing workplace friction resulted in his leaving Bell Labs and moving to Palo Alto, California, in 1955. As a visiting professor at Stanford University, he decided to begin his own manufacturing concern and opened Shockley Semiconductor under the sponsorship of Beckman Instruments.

By September 1956, the concern had thirty-two employees handpicked by Shockley to either build and tune equipment or conduct pure science and applied research. Five of his employees were assigned to work on field-effect transistors, which were of interest to his sponsor; however, Shockley was not interested in this and spent much of his resources on his own devices (diodes), which were commercial failures.

It is generally agreed on by historians that Shockley was not an astute businessman, nor a successful manager. He trusted no one and at one point, demanded his entire lab take lie detector tests; they refused. In 1957, eight of his people (known as the traitorous eight) left [6]. They soon found a collaborator and willing investor in Sherman Fairchild, founder of Fairchild Aircraft and Fairchild Camera, and started a new company, Fairchild Semiconductor.

By the early 1960s, as Shockley Semiconductor was failing, Fairchild became the undisputed leader in the semiconductor market, in part due to an 1872 legal provision in California's laws stating "*every contract by which anyone is restrained from engaging in a lawful profession, trade, or business of any kind is to that extent void.*[7]"[OO]. This meant the eight could move from business to business, bringing with them prior skill sets and techniques without worry of legal repercussion due to conflict of interest.

Fairchild later lost their leadership position to Texas Instruments. Two of the traitorous eight, Gordon Moore and Robert Noyce, left Fairchild Semiconductor in 1968 and went on to found N-M Electronics, which a year later became Intel, where Noyce was instrumental in overseeing the development of the microprocessor. Of note is that Marcian "Ted" Hoff, the twelfth Intel employee, is credited with the idea of a universal processor rather than custom-designed circuits leading to the microprocessor revolution of the 1970s.

[OO] Much credit is given to the success of Silicon Valley as a result of California's long-standing disdain for noncompete clauses, allowing for the mobility of employees and the transfer of ideas.

But let's step back to 1957 for a moment and ask the question of where Shockley went wrong. After all, he was an extremely intelligent man, had the right background, had financial backing, and had hired some of the most brilliant minds he could find. By all rights, he should have created an innovative empire, the likes of which had not been seen before and perhaps would have equaled or outstripped that of Microsoft and Apple. But he did not! Instead, he created a risk-averse culture. Not that the people he hired were risk averse. They were young, energetic, highly educated, and initially excited at the prospect of working with a Nobel Laureate.

Shockley came from a successful career at Bell Labs, where the research environment had freedom generally seen only in academics, where communication between basic researchers and the product developers was encouraged. But in his lab, Shockley discouraged the sharing of ideas, even between colleagues; he kept people in project silos of his own making. He not only ignored the ideas of those he had hired, but he also often offered little but discouragement to those with their own investigative initiatives; there is reason to believe that Robert Noyce missed out on a Nobel Prize because of such discouragement.[PP] Shockley held steadfast to his idea of a product portfolio essentially consisting of a single product and allowed little or no room for deviation in his singular perspective. From what we have discussed up to this point, this would appear to have all the hallmarks of eventual failure,

---

[PP] In 1956, Noyce framed the concept that quantum tunneling is a quantum mechanical phenomenon, where a subatomic particle passes through a potential barrier[8]. Quantum tunneling has important applications in the tunnel diode, a type of semiconductor diode that has negative resistance. Quantum tunneling is projected to create physical limits to the size of the transistors used in microprocessors, due to electrons being able to *tunnel* past them if the transistors are too small. Noyce postulated that tunneling could be demonstrated in a simple P-N junction, i.e., the interface between two types of semiconductor materials, a positive type and a negative, inside a single crystal of semiconductor. The positive side contains an excess of holes, while the negative side contains an excess of electrons in the outer shells of electrically neutral atoms, allowing electrical current to pass through the junction in only one direction. Noyce, while working for Shockley, brought this to his attention, but Shockley was not interested and dismissed the idea. Seventeen months later, Leo Esaki (Japan) published an article describing the same negative resistance diode. In 1973, Leo Esaki shared the Nobel Prize for physics for his work on the negative-resistance, or tunnel, diode.

and it did. By 1963, it was over. He took a creative environment with creative people and fostered a constrained culture. When this was shown to not work, there is little evidence that he acknowledged the need to change. Indeed, much of this carried over into his personal life, where in later years he was often criticized as a racist. He became an outcast in scientific and academic circles and, at one point in his life, advocated the sterilization of those with IQs less than 100 (the average for the general population) [9].

And what of the traitorous eight? Their legacy is well documented. They reinvested their capital, became venture capitalists, and in twelve years had spun off more than thirty companies and funded many more. By 1970, more than twelve thousand people were employed in the "chip" business in Silicon Valley as a result of their efforts. Much of this was due to Robert Noyce, who perhaps taking a cue from his disenchantment during his employ with Shockley developed a corporate philosophy of denying the hierarchical culture of traditional American business.

The point here is the iconoclast or iconoclastic team is not a singular entity with a singular focus. In the case of Motorola, prior to implementing quality change, they labored under the singular portfolio perspective of managers and directors to put a product on the market at the expense of quality. Art Sundry ended this with his abrasive outburst of "*Our quality stinks*." Shockley held steadfast to his own portfolio-driven ideas while actively discouraging the sharing of ideas of those around him. The dissension in ranks that ultimately came from this, led by the traitorous eight, is now collectively known as Silicon Valley.

Chapter 20: The Customer

A few years ago, a colleague and I set out to explore the use—by a postsurgical patient sample—of a medical device designed to facilitate bodily waste removal in those who had lost the ability to vacate bowel and bladder normally. Our idea was a simple one, ask the patients to perform various everyday tasks that involved the device. We would then observe and record the tasks being performed. As the devices attached to the abdomen of the patient, we were particularly interested in application, removal, and disposal of the devices.

We contracted with a university that had facilities that would allow us to duplicate a "real world" setting inside a laboratory. This allowed us some control over the test environment and reduced variability in our observations. We received Institutional Review Board Approval to conduct the study, gathered the appropriate informed consents, and enrolled people with the medical condition that required the use of the devices.

All patients were familiar with the devices having been not just a user of the device for more than one year, but also at the time of surgery instructed in the proper use of the device by a clinician specializing in this. The study design was observational; a panel of clinicians, engineers, product developers, and marketing professionals would observe the study subjects performing routine tasks involving the devices. The sessions would be videotaped, and personal interviews would be conducted. The tasks in this study were as mentioned, common tasks involving the application, removal, and disposal of the devices.

Medical devices such as the one we were interested in are developed with the Voice of the Customer [1] (VoC) in mind, and this particular observational study was part of that process. VoC is a process for summarizing customer requirements by producing a prioritized set of customer wants and needs relative to their importance and satisfaction with current alternatives. With the type of device we were interested in, there are several customers to consider, each with their own perspective and desire for the product to have certain attributes.

Two are of interest here. First, there is the clinician who will recommend the device to the patient. The clinician will, of course, approach this from a clinical perspective. The clinician has several requirements for such devices and based upon the manufacturer's ability to meet those requirements, will select and recommend a device for the patient. Second, there is the patient who must use this device twenty-four hours a day, often for the remainder of their lives. The patient's perspective, aside from the efficacy, is to a great extent a quality-of-life perspective.

The study began early in the morning, and what happened during the course of the day was a great surprise to some, but to others was to be expected. Each patient arrived at a predetermined time to avoid meeting another patient or a patient's family members. Anonymity was a part of the informed consent to participate. The patient was brought into the "set," which simulated a home environment, and asked to perform the tasks. The panel of observers was positioned behind a two-way mirror—reflective on one side and transparent on the other—so the patient could be observed without being influenced or intimidated by the panel.

Before going on, there are a few points to remember. The clinician specialists on the panel are the ones who helped select the patients. They are the clinician's patients and as such were previously instructed in the proper use of the devices by the clinicians. As the clinicians are also customers of manufacturer, the engineers and product developers on the panel are influenced by the clinicians. But to what extent? The marketing professionals were on the panel to observe not only the patients, but also the response of the clinicians, engineers, and product developers.

As the patients were brought in one by one and began to go through the tasks, the response from the clinician specialists was perhaps predictable. Almost to a patient, the clinicians exclaimed, "*That's not what they were taught to do*!" What happened over the time between being instructed on the use of the devices and the time of observation (one year or longer) was the patients had altered the instructions—and thereby the process—to accommodate their physicality and fit their lifestyles.

The response from the engineers and developers was also, I believe, predictable: "*Isn't that interesting. We should have known that. Why didn't we think of that*?"

The engineers and developers of the devices developed their products from a solution-engineered perspective, i.e., the product must do this and this and this, with only minor deference to the benefit of the patient. What do I mean by benefit? Simply, what does it mean to the patient in terms of attributes? Consider this question being asked of a patient: *If the product has this, what will it mean to your life, your relationships, your family, your work environment, etc.?* Note: this is different from simply asking a consumer: *do you need this*, or *does it work*? Developing a product solely on the basis of "do you need this" or "does it work" runs the risk of commoditization—that is, developing a product indistinguishable in terms of attributes from other products in the eyes of the consumer. The product becomes undifferentiated, resulting in a weakening or negating any pricing leverage other than the cheapest.

In regard to attributes, it is worth noting the question of which attributes are important is not always easy to understand prior to the development of a product, particularly when multiple customers (stakeholders) are involved. Thus, it is difficult to determine importance unless you have some idea of the purpose of the attribute. In the scenario given above, two different types of customers were given: the clinician and the patient, each with distinct requirements and some overlap of needs. But there are also the manufacturing and cost requirements of the engineers to be considered and the ability to sell the requirements of the marketers. If we take the time to list the attributes, we find we can question the attributes or find there are alternate attributes, such as what if the attribute did not exist or offered a different function. Cost of manufacturing, as an attribute, is almost always an overriding factor in product development, but what if it did not exist? Would this change the marketer's perspective of the customer? Clearly it would, but in most cases, it does exist; therefore, obtaining an understanding of the customer and an emphasis on the voice of the customer cannot be understated.

As an example, ask a consumer if they need a car and they may answer yes, but this does not tell you how to design a car. However, asking the consumer what the car means to their life or how it will impact their life may elicit one or more of the following response phrases and terms: financial responsibility, personal freedom, enhanced relationships, liberty, opportunity, convenience, fun, etc. Framing the question this way adds dimension to the consumer, and framing the response in terms of attributes and then drilling down on these adds understanding and a multiplicity of perspective.

Take for instance the phrase "personal freedom." Drilling down on this leads to insights into consumer needs such as not having to depend on others, not having to depend on public transportation, the convenience of going when and where I want, the opportunity to be whimsical, etc. This, in turn, provides styling and marketing insights. Additionally, clustering the attributes based on their significance can result in a geometry of importance resulting in an entirely new perspective. The question we must ask ourselves is do we always see the obvious. The answer is no, we do not, at least not until we have an appreciation for the perspective of others.

To the marketing professionals observing our study, their reaction was also predictable. The successful marketing of a product can be based on a product's packaging and features. But this is only part of it. It is also based on how you believe the consumer perceives their world, or more precisely, how the consumer believes the product, from a holistic perspective, will benefit them within their world. In this scenario, the reaction of the clinicians and engineers/developers meant the customer's perception of the world, relative to the device, was not necessarily what they were led to believe. The reaction by the clinicians and engineers/developers meant the dimension(s) of customer needs and how customers form preferences and order importance according to those needs had changed and, accordingly, also the minds of the marketers.

Successful product development requires identifying customer needs, which in itself is a multi-perspective task, particularly in the events just described where there is more than one type of customer perspective to consider. Identifying customer needs is almost always a qualitative research task with the goal being to integrate the experience of the customer(s) into the customer's use of the product. Of course, all of this comes with caveats. In this case, the engineers and product developers must balance the cost of satisfying the customer need with the customer's wish to have the need fulfilled. But even this has a caveat. The customer may not know of a need to be fulfilled, something certainly not lost on Steve Jobs when he stated, "*A lot of times, people don't know what they want until you show it to them.*" Something he would say quite often, as in this conversation Jobs had with Edwin Land [2]:

> *Land: "I could see what the Polaroid camera should be. It was just as real to me as if it was sitting in front of me before I had ever built one."*
> *Jobs: "Yeah, that's exactly the way I saw the Macintosh. If I asked someone who had only used a personal calculator what a Macintosh should be like, they couldn't have told me. There was no way to do consumer research on it."*

Consider our earlier discussion of the light bulb. Edison's light bulb was not just a safe and inexpensive alternative to natural gas, candles, or oil lighting of the day, which certainly filled a customer need, but what else did it do to fill the customers' needs? What were its attributes? Edison's light bulb didn't just bring light; it also extended the length of the day at the flip of a switch. No longer were people synchronized to the rotation of the earth to determine work from rest. Light could be controlled. It could be directed. It could be turned up, turned down, and altered to provide ambiance and mood. Controlling light means new dimensions of convenience, opportunity, productivity, and personal freedom. What would the line of questioning need be to tease this out of the customer?

***

Food for thought: What Jobs was talking about when he stated, "*A lot of times, people don't know what they want until you show it to them*," is the creation of want where want does not exist. This idea was first mouthed more than seventy years ago as a moral dilemma and critical of consumerism through advertising by Herman Wouk (*Aurora Dawn*). "*But what does an advertising man do? He induces human beings to want things they don't want...the creation of want where want does not exist...Doesn't it seem the worst sort of mischief*" [3].

As we are discussing creativity and innovation, this is not a critique, but a question asking: Is there anything more creative than this, i.e., the creation of want where want does not exist? Is this the ultimate creation? Perhaps anyone believing their work is innovative should ask of themselves this simple question: Am I truly innovative if I cannot first create demand?

Chapter 21: The Value of Untargeted Thinking

Earlier we discussed fixation and the positive and negative attributes associated with it. At this time, we should again turn our attention to this topic.

Anyone who has ever opened a math book and tried unsuccessfully to solve a problem, even when the correct answer is listed in the back of the book, knows full well of the problems associated with fixation. The book provides an example and tells us this is how the problem must be solved. But, putting pencil to paper we fail to solve the problem, so we repeat the process. If we are unsuccessful frustration sets in. Finally, the book is closed, and we justify our failure to be successful by claiming an error in the book or our own lack of competence.

The real failure just may be the instruction given in the book, the instruction given by the teacher, or a combination of both. To understand why, we need to explore the concept of fixation. As mentioned in earlier chapters, fixation can be thought of as convergent thinking—a part of ordinary problem-solving, that is, making use of prior history, stored knowledge, and algorithms. While this may have benefit and offer solutions, is this the best way to approach a problem?

In 2003, Steven M. Smith, of Texas A&M, wrote, "*The first ideas to be considered during creative idea generation can have profoundly constraining effects on the scope of the ideas that are subsequently generated. Even if initial ideas are intended to serve as helpful examples...the constraints of initial ideas may be inescapable*" [1]. This followed a decade earlier research-based article by Smith and colleagues about the constraining effects of instruction on idea generation [2].

In their study, two groups of people were given identical idea-generating tasks. In one task, the groups (test and control) were asked to invent new toys that had never been seen before. In the other task, they were asked to draw and describe new forms of life, such as that which may be seen on another planet. The difference between the two groups was that prior to being asked to perform the tasks, one group, the test group, was given examples of toys (electronic involving physical activity and a ball) and life forms (four legs, two antennae, and a tail). The test group now had prior history and stored knowledge. The control group saw no such examples.

While both groups generated a similar number of ideas, the test group, aka, the fixation group, was more likely to incorporate the examples they were shown into their ideas than the control group. Smith, Ward, and Schumacher refer to this as a conformity effect—that is, the inability to disassociate the examples from the idea-generating process, thereby biasing the process, artificially introducing a creative block into problem-solving. A similar result occurred with a study performed by Jansson and Smith [3] in which engineering design students and professionals were given different design problems and tasked with generating as many solutions as possible.

While the total number of designs produced were similar, study participants receiving examples of solutions prior to the task showed a propensity toward greater conformity to the elements of the examples. Evangelia Chrysikou and Robert Weisberg [4] of Temple University took this one step further, wanting to know if expertise—say that of engineers—played a role in fixation. They hypothesized nonexperts, when confronted with a similar problem as the experts, would have demonstrated negligible fixation—that is, the ability to disassociate the examples from the idea-generating process. What they found was "*fixation due to pictorial examples is a general phenomenon that occurs across individuals and is not a result of expertise.*"

Those leading creative problem-solving teams need to be aware of this, need to be aware of fixation occurring during problem-solving—that fixation may be the unnecessary result of the method in which the problem is presented, that it can result from an unhelpful reliance on past events when what is needed is a new perspective.

So, instruction in itself can act as a hindrance, or perhaps a creative idea block is a more appropriate term. But aren't all groups given instructions when tasked with problem-solving? According to the works described above, task managers, not skilled in the psychology of presenting problems, may in fact be part of the reason innovative solutions are difficult to reach; that is, they may unwittingly drive their teams to convergent thinking, resulting not in creative solutions but rather in solutions of sufficiency.

This is not to say convergent thinking is a bad thing. It is not. Rather, it is a conscious problem-solving tool. Convergent thinking is thinking that focuses on a single, well-established answer to a problem. Convergent thinking emphasizes the linearity of logic based on accumulated stored information to lead to a single "best" answer, as compared to divergent thinking that explores multiple possibilities and the generation of creative ideas [5].

Convergent thinking also, in a much subtler form, has value for much of our day-to-day existence. In this context, we may only be slightly aware of it. It is this that helps us move through the day with some degree of accomplishment. Convergent thinking allows us to avoid distractions. It allows us to focus, act, and accomplish. It keeps our lives on track and orderly. Convergent thinking definitely has its advantages. Consider the business perspective of convergent thinking—which in this context, I believe is more appropriately addressed as targeted thinking. In this, the problem at hand is how to put the right product in front of the right consumer at the right time to initiate a purchase. The solution comes in the form of targeted advertising.

Since the advent of online shopping, retailers have discovered the benefits of targeted advertising, where the common belief is online advertisement must be immediately relevant to the viewer. To take advantage of this, unimaginably large databases are constructed to compile consumer profiles, in real time, to personalize ads to the individual viewer. Anyone using a search engine to find some miscellaneous item understands how well and sometimes how annoying real-time targeted advertising can be. Search for something once, and any subsequent searches will find pop-up advertising for the item and for related items.

The jury is still out on the benefits of targeted advertising. Those who are proponents champion this method because the ad is designed solely to create specific purchases from a specific source. However, those who are not proponents of this method of advertising argue the lack of information presented in this marketing technique provides an imbalance of information—that is, the seller knows more about the consumer than the consumer knows about the seller. Nevertheless, for the marketer taking advantage of the data being accumulated on the consumer, the benefit is the ability to put in front of the consumer things they want or think they need, based on their recent targeted online search or purchase histories.

In convergent thinking—or targeted thinking—the information at hand, used to cue the teams, is central to the idea formulation and belief in the appropriateness of the solution. Convergent thinking, to maintain focus, relies heavily on the use of the word "no" to define parameters, to control the focus. The word "no," in this context, is a negative affirmation. Successful managers must ask themselves: is the use of "no" a valuable contribution to the task at hand? If the task is one of sufficiency, then I suspect the answer is yes, and convergent thinking is appropriate to the task. But if sufficiency is not your target solution, if you find you are denying alternate pathways that offer a multiplicity of solutions, whether solving or presenting the problem, then perhaps not. If sufficiency is not your target solution, then avoid being predisposed as to how the problem should be solved.

The lesson here is when faced with a difficult challenge, first understand the perspective of the problem giver, then construct your solutions from multiple perspectives to seek the perspective(s) that makes "no" a refutable position, i.e., challengeable. Always remember when given a difficult or seemingly impossible task, or unsolvable problem, one option may be to eliminate "no" as a solution limiter. What is needed is a process to generate creative ideas by exploring a multiplicity of perspectives and possible solutions—that is, divergent thinking.

***

In 1957, the advertising executive A. F. Osborn [6] (Applied Imagination) brought the idea of brainstorming into mainstream problem-solving and creative idea generation. He did this by effectively arguing brainstorming could double the number of ideas generated from that of more conventional techniques. Osborn argued that teams tasked with idea generation spent too much time in evaluation and criticism and not enough time on idea generation.

To encourage creativity, he proposed each member of a group generate as many ideas as possible, regardless of how impractical they might be—quantity over quality. He employed the rule that no one was allowed to offer an opinion on the quality of an idea, not even the person who generated the idea (avoid criticism). He did allow group members to take the ideas of others and expand on them (build). Finally, he stated the group was not to reach a conclusion on the adoption of ideas (unimpeded creativity).

Osborn's rules generated quantity without criticism and allowed others to build on ideas, resulting in unimpeded creativity. Apparently, that was enough for the corporate world; brainstorming not only caught on, it went uptown, not just with those who believed in its effectiveness, but also with researchers who wanted to understand if indeed it was effective. After considerable research into this method by numerous researchers, they concluded there was minimal to no support for brainstorming claims [7]!

Researchers found that brainstorming groups did not generate the expected number of ideas and that the ideas were usually of lesser quality than those of individuals working alone.

Why? Were artificial blocks or biases unknowingly incorporated into the problem-solving processes of groups? Were Osborn's rules discounted?

Seldom are instructions given to a group that are as simple as that outlined by Osborn, although most brainstorming texts acknowledge Osborn's rules for successful efforts. Perhaps no one is reading these. It has been my experience that instructions are usually given in the context of a product portfolio or mission statement by a strong leader; that a practicality be achieved, and a consensus reached, and the group remains harmonious in its interaction. In this may be the real reason for failure.

Brainstorming requires interaction—that is, the utilization of human resources—the very thing that proponents tout as a strength. But Michael Diehl, of the University of Mannheim, and Wolfgang Stroebe, of the University of Groningen, found that because brainstorming usually involves an interactive effort requiring attention to others, it does not promote idea generation. Rather it results in low productivity and an accompanying lesser quality in idea generation [8].

So, the question becomes: is brainstorming, as customarily practiced, simply structured incorrectly, even if the rules, as written by Osborn, are followed? Almost all of this book opines the benefit of interaction and multiple perspectives, so let's revisit Hirshberg and NDI to see if we can find some insight.

Hirshberg said Nissan Design International intentionally restricted its early brainstorming sessions to the search for "*creative questions*." He said, "*We find it useful to halt the meetings just at the point the questions become provocative*." Why? He purposely wanted no clear route to a solution. No closure. Not at that point in time. Instead, the group was put on *pause*—intentionally left with uncertainty, a lack of balance, and a simple command: "*...not think about the subject for a while*" [9].

In this, NDI allowed for mental time and space for the preconscious to join in, and this may be an important difference. NDI, under Hirshberg, promoted the individual creativity by first exposing members to the multiple perspectives of the group. Then, at what would seem the most inopportune time, the time of closure, removed them from the risk of groupthink. Instead, NDI gave individual creativity time to marinate in a broth of multiple perspectives while allowing irrelevant information to clear from short-term memory along, with its potential to subvert the benefits of group interaction. NDI, wittingly or not, moved through the creative process as described by Julian Jaynes (1920–1997), an American psychologist best known for his controversial theories of consciousness. Jaynes's creative process includes a preparation phase that is a conscious problem identifying and solving endeavor, an incubation phase in which conscious concentration is removed and then illumination justified by logic. Jaynes argues very effectively that "*the dark leap into huge discovery*," as he puts it, has no representation in consciousness [10]. But no representation in consciousness does not mean unconscious. What Jaynes is saying is while the preparation, materials, and end results are consciously perceived, the actual process of thinking is not.

Discovery, or creativity, is not simply a spontaneous bursting upon the scene. Nor does it mean we possess some singular hidden source or wellspring of creativity waiting for that one chance "aha" moment to be unleashed, and then quietly receding into some dark recess of the mind. If there is serendipity in creativity, it is the preparedness of the individual, or group, to respond to the chance appearance of the appropriate information.

Some explanation is required, and we find it in the writings of Albert Rothenberg, an American psychiatrist and researcher into the creative process, who has spent a great deal of his career investigating and writing on the subject of the creative process. In *Creativity and Madness*, he writes that creative thinking is nonconscious in that the creator is generally not aware of the "*specific structural features of the unusual modes of thought when they are producing a creation*" [11]. In other words, a non-realization. Nevertheless, as he states, the creative person is fully conscious and in possession of their senses.

Rothenberg states for creativity to occur, there must be an interest in discovery, there must be motivation, there must be a willingness to explore alternate paths, and more importantly, there must be the ability to fantasize. Fantasy requires abstract thinking, and while the thought process may move freely about in fantasy, the creative person in Rothenberg's words "*is constantly alert and prepared to select and relate his thoughts to the creative task*" [12].

While we have no real conclusive evidence, that is, hypothesis directed, that NDI's methods worked, their success does speak for itself. Much like the individual tastes of tomatoes, peppers, oregano, and red wine, when mixed together and allowed to simmer all day, the cook is rewarded with a sauce of extraordinary flavor.

Food for thought: could the above be the reason so many managers tasked with an innovative process fail? That is, the unwitting removal of the incubation process through naive coercion such as unreasonable time demands or performance expectations.

The evidence supports it is a false belief that simply working with others promotes greater idea generation than working alone. Secondly, there is the false premise (expectation) that personal productivity within the group will be enhanced by the group, hence the belief that upon completion of the group task, individual productivity has increased. But this doesn't mean interaction with a group should be discounted; rather it needs to be put in the proper sequence of events required for idea generation.

Paulus [13] et al, writing on the effects of information exchange and verbalization in human performance perception in group brainstorming, also found there may be a false sense of contribution; individuals may take credit for a disproportionate amount of brainstorming activity in groups. They go on to conclude the illusion of productivity in brainstorming groups may carry over to other similar group activities.

Indeed, Silver and Thompson [14] found, in a study of identifiable needs, that one-on-one interviews were more cost-effective than focus groups and yielded similar results. They determined two one-on-one interviews were about as effective as one focus group in identifying needs (51 percent versus 50 percent) and four interviews were about as effective as two focus groups in identifying needs (72 percent versus 67 percent). Furthermore, they were able to demonstrate at nine interviews, over 80 percent of needs were identified, comparable to what was found with eight focus groups.

Griffin [15], as part of her PhD work at MIT, showed similar findings, but is quick to point out the "*data suggests interviews with twenty to thirty customers should identify 90 percent or more of the customer needs in a relatively homogeneous customer segment.*" The key phrasing here is "*relatively homogenous customer segment.*" In this, she is recognizing the importance of understanding diversity in the customer and targeting the appropriate customer segment. Those conducting such interviews in hopes of identifying customer needs should be diligent in selecting participants to interview, lest selection bias skew their results.

Advertisers have known this for years. Advertisers do not target all people equally, nor do they listen to all people equally. There is no intention of satisfying the wants and needs of an entire population, but rather to focus on the desires, known or unknown, of the target segment, and so it is with the selection of participants for one-on-one interviews. Common sense? One would hope so.

So, why is it one-on-one interviews appear to be more efficient than focus groups? Some of the answers may be found in Nijstad, et al [16], who, in writing on innovation through collaboration contend the time spent on irrelevant information- such as having others in the focus group listen to it-blocks idea generation in two distinct ways. One, it blocks activation of mental imagery and two, it decays trains of thought. They state the activation of images requires attention and cognitive capacity and delays such as the distraction of irrelevancy negatively affect this, and that trains of thought are prematurely aborted when there is not the immediacy of expression.

Much of the criticism of focus groups is directed toward irrelevancy—that is, group members engaging in socialization, influencing one another, talking over others, and avoiding controversial topics. As an example, a number of years ago I was an observer during a focus group involving six nurses. The nurses were all members of a particular health professional society and were, with the exception of one, certified in their specialty. The nurses varied in age from their late twenties to retirement age. The focus group, at first, was cordial, allowing all members to have an equal say. At this point, the moderator was in control of the group, but early on, the group members began to socialize around a common topic—that of their certification.

When the group discovered who the nurse was who was not certified, they immediately began to discount her ideas. They were openly critical at times, talked over her, and in general dismissed her as not having anything to say that was of importance. However, later in the discussions, one young nurse, having just received her certification, asked the nurse without certification why she never bothered to obtain her specialty credentials.

The nurse, who was the oldest in the group by many years, simply replied that it wouldn't be fair. When asked why, she replied, "Because I'm a member of the committee that writes your exams."

Her experience in this specialty predated certification. From that moment on, no one said anything until the oldest nurse spoke first and then only to reinforce her opinions. Is this reminiscent of brainstorming sessions—that is, engaging in socialization, influencing one another, talking over others, giving way to authority? In other words, spending time on things other than idea generation. Was idea block at play here? Certainly, time spent on first discounting the oldest nurse was a matter of introducing irrelevancy as was time spent on confirming her opinions. Additionally, while the oldest nurse was not giving instructions for the group to follow, she certainly represented, in the mind of the other participants, structure and rules that defied the reduction in inhibitions and welcoming of "wild" ideas that Osborn championed.

The question becomes: what would happen if the "bad" aspects of discussion were eliminated, and time was spent only on idea generation? There are those who advocate time spent only on idea generation, to eliminate bad habits. Their techniques prohibit all verbal interaction and/or require participants to generate ideas in isolation with group interaction only allowed at the selection process.

There is a variant of brainstorming that needs mentioning here. Recall Tim Gowers and his massively collaborative mathematics problem in which a solution was found using the Internet. It can be said the success of his experiment can be found in some of the reasons brainstorming fails. As mentioned earlier, it is a false belief that working with others promotes greater idea generation than working alone, as is the expectation that personal productivity within the group will be enhanced by the group. Thus, if the individual working alone can outperform the brainstorming group, we need to question the value of brainstorming, particularly as this activity remains a popular idea-generating activity within organizations. In Gowers' experiment, the success was due to a community of Internet users, each working alone, generating ideas from multiple perspectives, with anonymity and without criticism. Note: Gowers' method, which earlier was referred to as e-brainstorming, cannot rightfully be called brainstorming due to its lack of structure. E-brainstorming, as used here, may be a poor choice in terminology.

If brainstorming groups are usually outperformed by individuals working alone, should we quit forming brainstorming groups? Or is there a way to brainstorm together while sidestepping those fundamental shortcomings? Time to meet the Brainwriting technique [17].

As in traditional brainstorming, in Brainwriting, everyone sits at a table together to simultaneously tackle a problem. The difference is in Brainwriting, each participant thinks and records ideas individually, without any verbal interaction. As we'll see, this small change results in a fundamental difference in the idea-generation effectiveness.

Brainwriting has an interesting premise: group members interact by writing and reading rather than speaking and listening. In this, an individual writes his or her ideas and then passes them on to another, who uses them as a trigger for their own ideas. This can be done in groups where the instructions may be to have six or more people write three ideas each in five minutes. At the end of five minutes, each person is instructed to pass their ideas to the person on their right. A review of the published literature finds several variants of this in use.

Paulus and Yang found this leads to enhanced group performance in small groups. In their studies, they found this leads to a 41 percent increase in ideas generated over that of brainstorming. They suggest the success of this method is that it overcomes production blocking [18]—that is, a loss of productivity as a result of group members being required to wait for their turns to present ideas in which the waiting is hypothesized to interfere with the cognitive processes of idea generation.

I will, with caution, state the jury is still out on Brainwriting and its variants because the ideas being generated may be little more than variants of the original ideas or examples—that is, how the problem is presented, which is subject to the phenomena of fixation. But, as stated earlier, this would be a problem with all forms of brainstorming. Hypothetically speaking, if Brainwriting eliminated the need to reach a majority opinion, it would remove thinking from the singular perspective of the majority, remove the tendency to focus on only the majority perspective, and remove the tendency to move toward the majority, be it right or wrong. It could (emphasis on could) bring into perspective alternatives and alternative objectives, contingencies, and divergent thinking.

Note: this is only the briefest of synopses. For a more in-depth review, I suggest reading *Group Performance and Interaction* by Parks and Sanna [19].

Section 3: Channeling the Solution

Chapter 22: Constructive Dissent: The Right and Obligation to Disagree

Taking constructive dissent—informed alternative views—seriously is essential both to healthy institutions and effective policy. This means consistently promoting and nurturing a corporate culture that publicly values creative, vigorous challenges to conventional wisdom, and is not satisfied with only the form, rather than the substance, of dissent.

—Susan R. Johnson [1]

The Importance of Constructive Dissent:

Make no mistake about it. We are predictive. For as much as we value our individual selves, we are all part of a great patterned and predictive collective. So predictive that consumer marketers count on us behaving in a predictive manner. Not individually, but in aggregate.

Individually, we are little more than random variables, but in aggregate, our randomness takes on patterns. This is why companies spend millions on compiling databases of consumer behavior to predict the associative buying habits of segments of their customer base.

Consider the online retail giant Amazon. If you have ever purchased something from them, you may have noticed that following the description of the item there is an additional list of items that says: "*Customers have also shopped for.*"

Retailers who do this are involved in something called associative mining—that is, data mining for discovering relationships between items in a sales transaction. For instance, in a supermarket, what is the probability when customers buy a bag of potato chips, they will also buy soft drinks? Is this greater or less than the probability of buying Brussels sprouts when purchasing potato chips? This is the probability of association, and supermarkets take advantage of it. Have you ever wondered why grocery stores do not necessarily place entry doors on the left? Generally, it is on the right or, less commonly, the middle. It is because research has shown people like to shop counterclockwise. Even if the door is on the left, the layout of the front of the store will direct you to the right [2].

Now, with no prior knowledge, a person cannot be accurately predicted to prefer shopping counterclockwise when entering a grocery store. But in aggregate, it is an entirely different story. Merchants know this and position products to take advantage of this behavior. No, they do not position their most popular items to take advantage of this. Rather, this is where they position the "must move" and "psychological impression" items. What are those? Think produce or bakery items. Produce doesn't have the luxury of sitting around like bottled water or canned goods. Neither do freshly baked goods. Both have a short shelf life and need to move off the shelves quickly.

So, what is placed in front of the consumer as they enter the store? Fresh heads of lettuce glistening with water droplets and misted carrots, parsley, and cilantro all connoting freshness and cleanliness, which is the impression the merchant wants you to have of their entire store. Along with this are freshly baked specialty bread, cakes, and pies. The merchant takes advantage of our aggregate behavior, and while we as individuals may exhibit randomness in our shopping behavior, on the large scale we are predictable. So are our thought patterns, and while merchants may take advantage of the aggregate predictability, this works to the disadvantage of innovation and iconoclastic momentum.

Take groupthink, for example, i.e., our tendency to make decisions everyone can agree on. Why do we do this? Because our minds pay more attention to things that confirm existing dogma and less to non-confirming information. Groupthink is an energy saving tactic based on the flawed premise that consensus is always good. Much of industry is based on models similar to that of the grocery store—that is, the channeling of employees, similar to the channeling of customers, to take advantage of the quick gain, to avoid the expense of carrying for long periods the perishable commodity, or the idea that may not work out. Groupthink has the unfortunate tendency to regress toward the lowest common denominators of safety, obviousness, and the inconsequential—the major exception being the Bay of Pigs invasion discussed earlier.

Peter Drucker is often quoted as saying, "*All the first-rate decision-makers I've observed had a very simple rule, if you have quick consensus on an important matter, don't make the decision. Acclamation means nobody has done the homework*" [3].

But what is a good decision-maker? It is common in business to recognize the decisive, quick-to-the-right-answer manager as a successful manager. After all, speed to market relies on the push to singularity and the avoidance of ambiguity, and in many business practices, this works quite well. The solution is quickly found and implemented, and the issue is relegated to the past. The difficulty in this is the solution can be very shortsighted if the problem is simply considered representative of past dilemmas and solutions, little more than patterns of the past—the usual algorithmic approach to problem-solving.

On the other hand, the iconoclastic solution may not be quick and decisive. Why? Because the iconoclastic solution will necessitate the luxury of considering the multi-faceted reasons why the problem exists. Only then can the questions be asked of what can be done to fix it. In this is the dilemma managers have been trained to avoid, i.e., dwelling in uncertainty (why the problem exists). Staying within uncertainty is career threatening, but quickly moving from uncertainty means moving away from the issues surrounding the question.

It is not uncommon to find business environments in which dwelling on the issues (the question) is considered a character flaw. As a result, and it should not come as a surprise to anyone, the quick-to-answer manager's solution is generally a solution of sufficiency. As an example, a broken weld joining two pieces of metal calls for a solution.

The sufficient solution requires a rewelding of the parts. The iconoclastic solution requires not only discovering the reasons the weld broke, but also whether the weld, or the part, is even necessary.

Again, consider the Internet retail giant Amazon. The desire to increase profitability would be, to many, a call for more aggressive marketing campaigns. Instead, Amazon realized the time from purchase to putting the product in the hands of the consumer was key to increasing sales. They decided to lower shipping costs or remove them completely, as with Amazon Prime, and increase the speed of shipping by investing in the building of what it calls fulfillment centers (shipping centers) around the world. A big investment on Amazon's part, and with a fixed cost business model, it was something many would consider inherently risky. Nevertheless, the company took the stance that focusing on the propensity for instant (or very quick) consumer gratification was the right direction to move forward.

Of course, the key to all of this is customer experience. With Amazon, the customer experience is the driving force. Satisfied customers are repeat customers, and they are word-of-mouth advertisers who in turn attract more sellers to Amazon, ensuring product choice. The net effect is a lower price point and increased selection. Amazon's strategy was not one of sufficiency; rather, it was iconoclastic, and as of this writing (2020), it has moved Amazon into the position of the largest company in the world by market value (reported by CNBC) [4], [5].

But this is Amazon, and suffice it to say, not all businesses have the courage to take the risks they do. As an example, Amazon CEO Jeff Bezos, in his 1997 letter to shareholders, states, "*One area where I think we are especially distinctive is failure. I believe we are the best place in the world to fail (we have plenty of practice!), and failure and invention are inseparable twins… Most large organizations embrace the idea of invention, but are not willing to suffer the string of failed experiments necessary to get there. Outsized returns often come from betting against conventional wisdom, and conventional wisdom is usually right. Given a ten percent chance of a 100 times payoff, you should take that bet every time*" [6].

In other words, as Taleb stated, "*Big events don't come from big parents*" [7]. It is fair to say most CEOs would not take this bet at a 50 percent chance no matter what the payout.

So, assuming one has a greater risk-averse corporate mentality than Amazon, how do they move from a culture of sufficiency toward a more innovative environment? The answer, while not necessarily simple to put in place, may not be that difficult to realize. By consciously exploring counterintuitive or alternate information, which is the view from another perspective. By incorporating the zero-gravity thinker responsibility. By doubting conventional wisdom or accepted truths. By offering plausible or even non-plausible alternatives. By avoiding generalizations and commonalities and instead exploring the exceptions. Remember, the exceptions exist in the tails of the distribution, and this is where the big events happen. By incorporating constructive dissent.

From the roots of conflict come the fruits of innovation [8].
—Shari Caudron, *Keeping Team Conflict Alive*

Here are some questions I will put to you. How many meetings have you walked into where you knew the meeting leader, perhaps a higher-level manager or senior-level executive, already had the answer they were looking for? How many meetings have you been in where those at the table simply nodded in agreement with the meeting leader? Where the meeting leader had a quick defensive response to everything and anything contrary? Where discussions amounted to little more than confirmation? Where constructive dissent was not just rejected by the leader, but swatted down as quickly as a bug on a wall?

Leaders, such as described above in the questions, are leaders rejecting the fact that conflict in the form of constructive dissent can be a good thing. Perhaps they are simply conflict avoiders, believing conflict is only a destructive mechanism moving all toward failure. So, taking advantage of their leadership position, they actively avoid it, push it off the table. Such leaders fail to understand one very important thing: conflict in the form of constructive dissent is a necessary part of the solution process.

Chapter 23: The Problem

Too many years ago to matter, but remembering it anyway, the chairman of my graduate program said—upon assigning me to a project he had a special interest in—"*Don't give me anything that I won't believe.*" Certainly not the most liberating phrasing of how to chase a research problem.

Properly stating the problem may be the single most important item in the search for solutions. Einstein, in speaking of Galileo formulating the problem for determining the speed of light, said, "*The formulation of the problem is often more essential than its solution, which may be merely a matter of mathematical or experimental skill*" [1]. But, as we have discussed, or alluded to, this is not necessarily recognized by people seeking solutions. Whether the solutions are sufficient, creative, or innovative is derived from the context in which the problem is stated.

It should be well understood that creative or innovative solutions are not the result of algorithmic linear processes, but rather from how opportunity is positioned within inefficiency. The definition of the problem should be a statement of potential: here is the deficit in our knowledge; here are the opportunities awaiting the reduction in the deficit. In fairness, we may not know, let alone understand, the opportunities—the potential. But that shouldn't limit the problem statement. Consider our discussion from Chapter 3 regarding the parking problem. If the problem is stated as too few parking spots, the solution becomes one of sufficiency; expand the parking structure. But if the problem is stated as one of the idle cars, we move our thinking away from solving for limits toward the opportunities that arise from a lack of use.

But let's take this even further. What if problems were not discussed at all? What if only the gaps in the knowledge were discussed? Think of a meeting where people clustered around a conference table said, "*We don't know this*," and then began to speculate on what knowledge would bring. *If we knew this it might... If we knew this, we would... If we knew this, we could...* Hmmm. Discussing gaps in knowledge as if they were assets to be exploited? A novel concept? Not necessarily.

Steven Brown and Marion Walter, in their book *The Art of Problem Posing*, 2005, present the formula $x^2 + y^2 = z^2$, which some of you may recall has something to do with right triangles or Pythagorean Triplets [2]. They have, according to their own words, asked students and colleagues over the years to provide answers, and the answers they received are somewhat predictable because the students and colleagues have accepted the given, i.e., the formula begs to be solved. They then ask a different phrasing of the question; rather than asking their students and colleagues to provide answers, they ask, what are the questions (a new perspective). In this, they find not only the predictable, but also questions regarding the manipulation of the formula (what if the right triangle is replaced by a sixty-degree triangle) and what are the applications for it (is there a three-dimensional analog). As they state, this is challenging the given: "*Turned inside out or upside down, or even only slightly altered, do we gain a better understanding or the implicit assumptions the context and significance of what is given*" [2, p18].

In the finite parking space problem, the given may be that when faced with more cars than parking spaces, the sufficient solution comes from increasing the available parking spaces, while the creative solution may come from making use of idle cars. However, another perspective could come from restating the problem to the extent of discovering and understanding why people choose to park in this location. Perhaps understanding this would lead us to discover commuters would prefer public transportation (a solution in waiting), not requiring the inconvenience of finding a parking space. Conversely, perhaps understanding this would lead us to discover why commuters dislike public transportation and prefer the trade-off in the inconvenience of finding a parking space. Both tracks strategically define the performance of a system that is "not good enough," thus representing the potential for opportunity.

It may be that this is not a parking space problem at all, but rather the lack of available space calls our attention to an "other" problem—that of inefficiency in the ability of the district to handle high-volume, intermittent traffic patterns. In this, we now find multiple opportunities positioned within the inefficiency. Think of our previous discussions on communication. The problem of communicating over long distances did not exist in the lack of speed of communication; this was only a result. The problem existed in a rapidly advancing world in which slowing down was not a solution.

In the finite parking space problem, a solution other than one of sufficiency must consider whether there are related events such as traffic congestion, an increase in fender benders, or the need for designated pedestrian walkways. Is the problem persistent and growing, and will a sufficient solution relieve the problem (and for how long)? Viewing the problem this way allows for a discussion of weaknesses as if they were strength potentials in which the problem will voice itself; think of the first three words in the SWOT acronym, i.e., strengths, weaknesses, and opportunities.

There is one other perspective I would like to take. In posing this problem, the perspectives under discussion all are based on the premise that a problem exists. What if, in Brown and Walter's terms, the problem was *turned inside out or upside down*? Suppose this was approached from the perspective of "in this district of the city, there are no parking problems." What are the possible reasons for this? The list of potential reasons may include efficient public transportation; no or minimal curb restrictions; all new construction has incorporated a minimum number of parking spaces; residents have been issued special low-fee curb permits, making it less costly for them to park on the street and not in a limited space parking structure; the area is a carpool-only area; etc. The reasons now provide numerous solutions without directing the problem. We have moved from the perspective of "here's a problem, find the solution" to no problem exists, what are the reasons, and in doing so, discover solutions to the parking dilemma.

Note: Brown and Walter recognized that the formula they presented to students was neither a problem nor a question, but rather a statement (as equations are), and that a correct response by a student should have been "what is the question?". By interpreting statements, such as the formula above, as problems, there is a natural tendency to limit inquiry into the context and significance of the statement.

In this, we have moved away from the classic view of solution finding—that is, state the given, determine the goal, and find the means in which to achieve it. Instead, by turning upside down or inside out, we state the problem does not exist, discover the reasons for this, and transfer this to our current situation.

This is similar to the position Dee Hock took when attempting to turn around the multitude of problems facing the credit card industry in the late 1960s [3], [4]. Hock, an iconoclast, may rightfully claim membership in the elite club of original American thinkers. Basically, self-educated, a passionate reader, and with little tolerance for orthodoxy, he somehow wound up as a mid-level manager of a Seattle bank. As the bank was a licensee of Bank of America, deep into credit card chaos, he attended a meeting in 1968 in Columbus, Ohio. A meeting organized to find a way out of the dilemmas facing the industry. At a low point in the meeting, Hock suggested a committee be formed to study the problem, which seemed far more reasonable than continuing with the acrimonious environment the meeting had regressed into. As usual, those with the suggestion, by a vote of apathy, were assigned the responsibility. Hock accepted and went about the process of selecting people he trusted to help in this endeavor.

In 1969, squirreled away in a week-long meeting in a hotel in Sausalito, California, Hock's committee undertook what must have seemed an insurmountable task—deciding how to best resolve the issues of a troubled credit card industry. But this meeting had an unusual premise; they would not talk about the problems that existed. A rule was put on the table to not discuss the problems at hand, but rather to talk only of principles. The logic in that was, if the principles were sound, the solutions would be self-evident.

This takes the notion of "the problem doesn't exist," which we discussed earlier, one step further. Hock, instead of asking what the organization would look like if no problems existed, asked what the ideal situation would be. In Hock's words, "*Set aside all thoughts of the problem and address a single question; if anything imaginable was possible, if there were no constraints whatever, what would be the nature of an ideal organization to create the world's premier system for the exchange of value*?" To cut to the chase, the result was the Visa credit card association, Visa Inc., which is now the largest electronic payment network in the world with over 124.3 billion transactions for the calendar year 2018 [5].

Hock intentionally moved his team away from the perspective that a problem existed. Whether he knew at the time that focusing on the situation, as a problem, would result in time ill spent on attempting a solution where others had previously failed, we can only surmise. Whether he knew retrieving from memory sufficient solutions from past dilemmas would result in no more than a quick fix, a bandage, to the current dilemma, we also can only surmise. These apparently were pathways he did want to follow. His methods tend to make us believe he was aware that generating conventional ideas to solve the problem ran the risk of sufficiency at best. A result he did not want. Therefore, his approach did not require a solution to a problem because he had removed the problem. Rather, he required a creative and innovative approach to building a new environment for the credit card industry. He required his team to remove constraints, open all possibilities, and create an environment for an ideal organization.

Let me pose this to you. What if meetings about problems started with the premise that nothing was wrong? Instead, following Hock's example, put forth the issue of principles and the questions of what an ideal organization would look like and what would allow an ideal organization, product, application, or service to exist. And as mentioned in Chapter 6, the word "no" would be banished from discussions. Could we then eliminate problems due to fixation, errors of confirmation, or inattentional blindness, perhaps move away from sufficiency due to linearity of thought?

We would have one advantage in doing this; we would not be governed by the expectation of finding a solution.

Chapter 24: It's Like This

"*A spate of bumpy uncertain trading has knocked the Dow Jones Industrial Average down 5.3 percent.*" This quote is from a February 2014 issue of the *Wall Street Journal* [1]. The question is: why didn't the author simply say the Dow was down 5.3 percent? The answer is there is a requirement to know why the Dow was down to come to an understanding. But a complete understanding would involve a lengthy discussion of market volatility, which is dependent on the socio-politico economics of world order. Perhaps involving more time on one topic than the average reader wants to spend or more words than the average editor wants to pay for.

So, instead the author speaks of a "spate" and "bumpy uncertainty" "knocking" the DJIA. In doing so, the author is attempting to convey a message of complexity that hopefully will emerge in the mind of the reader in a manner similar to the intent of the message. The author has invoked his right of metaphor—that is, giving the thing a name that belongs to something else. The thing, in this case, is the market volatility.

Consider the following short phrase taken from a back issue of *Health Affairs*: "*Members of the jail-involved population…*" [2]. Taken out of context, which it is, the phrase could direct one's thoughts toward prison officials and staff. Thoughts could also go towards an appointed group of citizens (members) involved with the rehabilitation success of penal institutions (jail involved)—that is, a social activist group. But this is not the case.

The word "members" refers to those with a criminal background who have been or are currently sentenced to incarceration. Their incarceration, with all its societal implications to include recidivism, is referred to as jail-involved, but the text does not convey this. The text superimposes an image that moves the reader away from the reality of murderers and rapists, drug pushers and armed robbers, and other evildoers by substituting the term "members" with the hope the reader will emerge with a different perspective, or at least consider a different perspective of this community. Note: the word "community" in this context is a metaphor for those sentenced in a court of law to be removed from society.

In cancer, therapy drugs such as interleukin-2 are talked about as firing up the immune system and making it more likely to recognize and attack cancer cells. The phrase "firing up" evokes mental images of turning on something, stoking a boiler, or creating energy. Immune systems do not recognize and attack. These are instead biochemical reactionary processes evolved for a biological benefit. But invoking the metaphor brings the military sense of a process that identifies, seeks, and destroys.

Combining the phrases, we get an interpretation of an immune system with an active and heightened sense of urgency and resolve. The idea that the immune system is defending the body is conveyed. However, one scientist communicating this to another would be just as likely to phrase this as: *binding to cells and mediating the T cell proliferative response, supporting the conclusion that binding site detection is on the receptor through which the biological effects are initiated.* Not nearly as imagination evoking as "recognize and attack" or as likely to convey the sense of an active protective immune system; nor as likely to promote a discussion on what this means with the layperson. Nor is it likely to promote understanding from a different perspective.

This is the strength of metaphor, i.e., the ability to promote discussion in an understandable way between experts and nonexperts. In doing this, the expert must assess his or her knowledge and the layperson must utilize "other perspective" probing for understanding to come to some sense of commonality on the subject. But hopefully it is not an identical understanding. This is where the "but ifs" and the "it's like this" come into focus. The "but ifs" challenge while the "it's like this" answers the challenge. If the answer to the challenge is not satisfactory, the discussion continues until the connection is made. "It's like watching paint dry" is a metaphor for a very boring act or event. The person describing such an act or event has already come to this conclusion in their own mind but must convey this to the listener.

The metaphor is the thread that connects the experience of the describer (paint drying is equated with slow, dull, devoid of context or content) to the imagination of the listener. In other words, when a message is difficult to convey or express in proper terminology, the metaphor conveys or expresses the meaning through patterns of relations or associations. Linguistic experts refer to this as carrying across, juxtaposing different things resulting in the emergence of unanticipated similarities.

Frank Lloyd Wright, early in his career, verbalized his contempt for homes of the day when he described floor plans as "*boxes besides boxes*" or "*inside boxes*" and the whole being "*inside a complicated outside boxing*" [3].

Wright's metaphoric denouncement of houses of the day suggested an emerging philosophy of the spiritual unity of form and function, a continuity—not the independence of function devoid of form. This continuity of form and function he metaphorically described as plasticity, and based on his emerging philosophy, he describes his ideal for houses of a new age in terms of a "*spiritual principle*" and "*vistas of inevitable simplicity and ineffable harmony*." Incidentally, the concept of form following function was put to words by Wright's mentor Lewis Sullivan, whom he referred to as Master. Sullivan, in an 1896 essay for *Lippincott's Magazine*, wrote:

> *Whether it be the sweeping eagle in his flight, or the open apple-blossom, the toiling work-horse, the blithe swan, the branching oak, the winding stream at its base, the drifting clouds, over all the coursing sun,* ***form ever follows function****, and this is the law. Where function does not change, form does not change.*

> *It is the pervading law of all things organic and inorganic... **that form ever follows function.** This is the law.* [4]

The author, Alan Lightman, in his magical *Einstein's Dreams* [5], metaphorically conveys the message of a world without time as a simple series of mental images: "*a child on a bicycle...sunlight in long angles...a broken bottle...a bead of water...a great stone bridge.*"

If time moves forward, then a world without time is a frozen world. The mental images do not do anything. There is no movement, no prior action to tell how the image came about, no forward momentum to tell the future story. The child remains in place without moving the pedals of the bike, the angles of the sunlight do not lengthen as the day ends, the bead of water does not evaporate or reconstitute itself as water vapor. To the external observer, someone not of the timeless world, there is only the current state to be seen independent of the paths that may have brought it to this situation. There is no mechanical work or heat of process because there is no transition. To the other than a casual observer of this timeless world, Lightman, through metaphor, has engaged his reader not only with a dialogue of a world without time, but also inserted the perspective of entropy into the discussion.

Niels Bohr once said, "*When it comes to atoms, language can be used only as in poetry. The poet, too, is not nearly so concerned with describing facts as with creating images*" [6].

Bohr understood that complex subjects are often more aptly described in verbal imagery. That the ability to convey form and function of a complicated subject is not to be found in technical language alone.

The interesting thing about metaphors and their relationship to innovation and iconoclastic momentum is that they have the ability to make the strange familiar, and the familiar strange. The philosophy and process of Synectics [7], as developed by William J. J. Gordon—inventor and psychologist (1919–2003)—over fifty years ago delves deeply into this. As Gordon explained, the term Synectics comes from the Greek, meaning the joining together of different and apparently irrelevant elements. In practice, it is the integration of diversity into problem stating and problem-solving. Synectics holds that creative efficiency can be increased and in the creative process, the irrational is more important than the rational.

The Synectic process is first about team building and group dynamics. To build a group dynamic and move it to the point of problem stating and problem-solving, the Synectics process takes great pains in candidate selection; who's on the team? Among the attributes considered vital in the candidate selection process is the ability to create analogies (direct, fantasy, or otherwise) and to speak metaphorically. Gordon states a candidate's ability to do this offers insight into the conscious process of achieving a "new look" at a familiar world, achieving a dis-familiarity.

***

We have already discussed the need for properly understanding the problem at hand and the fact that in the process this may change the problem. In our discussions to this point, we have come to understand that our view of what is, is probabilistic—that is, based upon a similar or repeatable sequence of past events providing a semblance of order and a degree of certainty. In other words, an interactive working model of the world peculiar to ourselves.

When faced with the new or strange, our mind forces what we observe into a familiar space constructed of similarities with past events. In other words, our mind attempts to make the strange familiar. But there is a stumbling block in this. In doing so, the mind is moving toward a sufficiency of solution and away from innovation. Away from looking at the world anew, as Einstein suggested [8], or to paraphrase: looking at the problem anew.

It is rare to have a totally unique problem. Most problems have analogies somewhere in the experience of the solution seeker. But if something other than sufficiency is required, the challenge is not to dredge up an analogy, but rather to view from a different perspective.

How? Gordon states this is done by distorting, inverting, or transposing our propensity to "*render the world a secure and familiar place*," and instead pursue the strangeness. Consider painting a tree. You could paint the trunk followed by the branches and then the leaves. This would be a common method of visually portraying a tree. But what if you did not paint the tree? Rather, you painted the sky around the tree, and then the sky and the sunlight peering through the gaps in the branches and leaves. Would you then not have a tree in much the same way that Kanizsa's triangle is portrayed? All viewing your painting would see the tree even though it is not there; merely suggested by gaps and voids.

Gordon takes this further by inserting a sculptor into the scenario, chiseling voids and holes within a solid block of air. If moments earlier I had asked you to visualize a tree in your mind, you no doubt would have quickly pictured a tree, perhaps a lone oak or a pine, silhouetted against a sky. Would there have been anything new in your solution to my request? But now, having turned this inside out, where the air is solid and the solid are gaps and holes, do you have the same picture, or have you made the familiar strange?

Consider Cubist sculptures such as Picasso's *Bouteille et Guitare*, in which shapes are represented by forms in reverse such as a hole represented by a circular projection, voids replaced by solids, and solids replaced by voids. Now, consider the statement of a problem. Should one describe the problem and point out the gaps in knowledge, or should one describe the gaps in knowledge and let the listener perceive the problem?

Making the Familiar Strange

Consider common business models that attempt to predict the wants and needs of the consumer to realize a profit and increase market share. Now, consider a world where 3D printers and laser scanners (cell phone laser apps) are as inexpensive and as common place in the home as an iPhone or Android. In this world, all bets are off on the predictability of consumer trends because the consumer now has the potential to become a micro-competitor.

A few years ago, I was asked to participate in an innovation group. A series of off-site meetings were scheduled, and people from various branches of the sponsoring company, from the United States and Europe, were assembled. There were clinicians, engineers, marketers, chemists, production people, as well as quality assurance personnel represented. Those gathered ran the professional gamut from VPs to grunts. They all had two things in common. They were intimately familiar with the current product portfolio, and all spoke the same product language.

The group leader was not a corporate associate and therefore freed from the constraints of worrying about offending the wrong person. On day one of the meetings, the groundwork was established—to bring to the table innovative product offerings within the product portfolio. On day two of the meetings, the walls of the meeting room began to fill with the accumulated knowledge of the personnel in attendance. Large sheets of paper were hung on the walls, and sticky notes directed toward the issues surrounding current product offerings were placed in matrices of categories and levels. Everyone had a voice, and all voices were listened to.

On day three, the sticky note matrices were analyzed, summarized, and agreed upon. At the end of the meeting, everyone in the room had a fair idea of the current state of products and why they were designed in that particular fashion. The meeting ended with an agreement to adjourn for a period of months (an incubation period), and then meet again to decide the next course of action—which would be to first build on what was known, now common knowledge to all, and then go beyond what was known. To make a long story short, nothing came of this except more meetings. After a long period, it was decided to dissolve the group. Why?

I have three problems with the meeting just described. The first is everyone spoke the same product language. The second is everyone understood the product portfolio. The third, and perhaps most important, is everyone saw the same picture, as established by the directive to stay within the product portfolio, therefore increasing the potential for fixation on what is known. Everything we have discussed to this point says commonality on this level works against innovation. The familiar was made even more familiar, the perspective even more narrowed.

Have you heard the old joke about the drunk who lost his house keys and was searching for them under a lamppost? His friend, equally as intoxicated, asked, “Is this where you lost them?”

“No,” he replied. “I lost them in the alley.”

"Then why are you looking here?"

"The light is better."

Earlier, we discussed the need for diversity in problem-solving meetings or innovation meetings, but the meeting just described clearly had a diversity of profession. People from various backgrounds within the company were chosen. A good thing. So, what was missing? The answer is the diversity of strange. Instead, there was a conscious attempt to familiarize in an environment where the "message" was already easily conveyed or expressed. There was no attempt to turn the world upside down, to invert or pervert ideas, concepts, and perceptions; much as Gordon's sculptor would see a tree as a series of holes and gaps in a block of air.

In other words, we were metaphorically missing the boat through familiarity, which did not express meanings through patterns of relations or associations. Thus, diversity is not only the diversity of background; that just sets the stage. It must also encompass the diversity of strange.

If our view of what is, is based upon similar or repeatable personal sequences of past events, then what is the view of someone else? This is the value in diversity, the ability to see the world from other perspectives, which individually are products of different concepts, and in turn, utilize this. The placing of a new or different concept into a familiar context is to move from the known to the unknown, making the familiar strange—that is, a new way of viewing the world or a different perspective on a problem by distorting or misrepresenting the "usual" perception and expectation of what is.

How is this done?

For those of you who may have written a dissertation during your college years, you no doubt had to reject the accepted—that is, the taken for granted knowledge or assumed logic of words or phrases such as "it's normal," "generally," "as a rule," or "naturally." In other words, you had to defamiliarize yourself with what is taken for granted. Instead, in the construction of the thesis, there was not just an investigation of the known, but rather a personal interrogation. You had to question yourself as to what this meant. In doing so, you were making the familiar strange.

Consider the run-of-the-mill house cat. Most children learn to recognize a cat from a dog early in life. By the time they start uttering single word expressions, they can correctly identify kitties from doggies. At some point, early on in their young lives, they can correctly identify cats from dogs at great distances, as we all can, without error. Yet if we were asked to visually describe a cat from its appearance as it might look from a short distance—say outside our living room window—and to describe it so a person could correctly identify it from a dog, this would be near impossible. No, the difference does not exist in whisker length or pointy ears. If we were skilled, we could draw a picture showing the difference, but could we verbally describe the difference? Try it and make the familiar strange.

The above example emphasizes the point: it is our very awareness of the thing, our cumulative experience, that makes the thing strange. Not our ability to describe what we already know, but rather to discover the unidentified, the heretofore unrecognized gaps, the latent factors that lead us down the previously undisclosed path. The problem with knowledge of the familiar—whether it be knowledge of how to do something effectively, knowledge of similar situations, or knowledge of the way things are supposed to be—is it has the potential to stifle creativity.

In the above example, if instead a person was told to identify the type of animal, dog or cat, by listening to someone describe the behavior of the animal in the presence of a person walking with the animal, they may not have a problem at all. Dogs behave differently than cats do, and in the presence of us, even more so. This is associative behavior and as such it provides a different perspective on the identity of the animal. Much in the way Gordon's sculptor chiseled gaps in a solid block of air to visualize a tree, that which surrounds the "thing" adds an element of relational knowledge to our holistic view, i.e., a multiplicity of perspective.

Try this simple exercise. Describe to yourself a social event, familiar or not, that you would like to take part in. Describe the event holistically. Describe the important components of the event in excruciatingly painful detail. Leave out nothing vital. Ask two or three of your friends to do the same.

Now, having done so, answer this: In your description, have you described the air you are breathing? The inhalation and exhalation that allows you to survive and function in the event? No? Why not? You cannot take part in the event without the air you must breathe. This is crucial for survival. Is it that the air is so commonplace, so well-known to you, such a part of who you are that you have dismissed its importance? While this may be an overemphasis of the point, it is one of the problems with familiarity—that is, the penchant to dismiss the intimately familiar. I suspect even if I had challenged you to describe a social event on Mars, air would still not be part of your description. Again, the strength of the zero-gravity thinker is to make us look inward, to challenge what we take for granted, or bring to light that which we have dismissed so the commonplace—the familiar or intimate—can be made strange through new perspectives of its importance.

Air, like all things familiar, is more than the price of entry to the thought process; it is also the unrecognized factors and relationships waiting for discovery. How many discoveries are there in describing or viewing air? I don't know. But, as an example of the complexity of metaphor in all of this, consider the word "regulate" and what it can connote. The word "limit" may have come to mind. Now, let's borrow an idea from James Geary [9], author and deputy curator of the Nieman Foundation for Journalism at Harvard. Think of the way the word "limit" can be used. Stick it in front of the phrase, "Twelve per customer," that is, "Limit, twelve per customer." We can now associate limit with value and scarcity.

Similarly, the word "air" used in conjunction with phrases such as "___ filled the sails," "up in the___," or "___ captured in a balloon" moves past the idea of a necessity for life by provoking thoughts of transportation, a place to be or ambiguity, and containment and portability.

Try the word "kick," which connotes an activity done with the foot, but if inserted into various phrases such as "I get a kick out of you," "They're going to kick me out," or I felt the "furnace kick in," we find fond amusement, anticipating being terminated, and heat.

In metaphor, we find the unique ability to take the personal and familiar—with the aid of imagination—to suggest a larger, more multidimensional world than previously thought—a world of inner mechanisms, broad-connected perspectives, and processes of various scope and scale. Again, making the familiar strange.

Chapter 25: Conclusions

In our discussion of the innovative process, it should be clear by now that innovation is not an independent or spontaneous event, but rather an evolving, continuous process, albeit disorganized and complex. It is not a random series of unrelated events, but rather a "dynamic" waiting, the sorting and ordering by time. New ideas are not generated from nothingness, but rather pieced together from what is known, challenging why they are known and exploring what is not known. It is a recombinant process requiring other perspectives to move away from sufficiency. It is linked in time to past events and discoveries, often with no apparent relevance or economic value. It is both the pragmatic and visionary application of creativity, and as mentioned in the beginning of this text, both creativity and innovation are not for the faint of heart as both can be forces of immeasurable energy. Neither creativity nor innovation exists in the averages, only in the necessity of the future, the forward tail of a moving distribution.

Creativity is a function of the preparedness of the individual, or group, to respond to the chance appearance of appropriate insight or information. For creativity to occur, there must be an interest in discovery, there must be motivation, a sense of exploration coupled with the ability to fantasize.

Where creativity is about the generation of ideas, alternatives, and possibilities, innovation is the measurable construct of those factors. It is application, action, and the process of change. More importantly, innovation challenges and proves false the fundamental belief in a predictable destiny resulting from the singular perspective or in-the-box thinking.

Innovation is disruptive and destructive. It is groundbreaking and revolutionary, creating new markets and values through the often-catastrophic replacement of established technologies. For companies looking into the future, it is a survival skill to be mastered because it is often a customer expectation and always a competitor option. Because innovation abhors sufficiency, it is the differentiator between leading and following.

The question that must be asked at this point is: how does a company, institution, or organization establish itself as creative or innovative? It is not as simple as putting a group of like individuals in a room with the marching orders to come up with something new, although there are those who would believe this.

If we start with the belief that the singular perspective is an obstacle to creativity and innovation, as has been the premise of this text, then championing a multiplicity of perspectives must become ingrained in the managerial culture. This means conflicts of interest, often thought to be obstacles to innovation by managers—and to be avoided—are an inevitable and necessary part of the process because there is value in searching past the single answer: that importance, i.e., value, exists on different planes at different depths.

The problem with the singular perspective is uniformity. It is conventional wisdoms, traditional views, accepted knowledge, and the confirmation of the reasons for being. In other words, it is in-the-box thinking. It is a probabilistic view of the future based upon a similar or repeatable sequence of past events providing a semblance of order. Order, as we now know, while making experiences possible, also excludes; preventing new experiences. It is wagering the averages, allocating productive resources to current enterprises, and getting little out of this than what is already in hand. This is mandating conformance to accepted norms and the current perspective of the long-range goal identified with historically profitable competencies. It is not a future vision.

So, if a key to innovation is a multiplicity of perspectives, how does the successful future-oriented company or organization arrive at this? The answer first is in diversity. Embracing and championing diversity. Building a diverse team, cultural and professional, complete with its inherent conflicts and abrasiveness, and with Rabe's zero-gravity thinker to promote comprehension. When we comprehend, we subsume information and integrate it into our body of knowledge. This, in turn, is integrated into our personal internal and interactive working model of the world around us, allowing us to realize far more than we have been taught.

We often do this through the use of metaphor, a rhetorical device invaluable to the diverse team. Metaphors are a functional basis for understanding complex subjects or competing paradigms. Terms used within competing paradigms do not necessarily have the same meaning; therefore, the metaphor moves understanding to a common ground. It expands the range of a limiting language, such as the specialty languages of science or engineering. It provides a common ground for the diverse team and its many perspectives, such as the perspectives of the customer or engineering, technology, sales, and marketing professionals—and even social and ethnic cultures. A diverse team is a team that embraces variance—that is, breaking away from experience-dependent categories through the continual exposure to new experiences. However, a diverse team is only one piece of the overall picture.

It should be remembered that the task of finding a solution is not the sole responsibility of those assigned to the task, but of equal responsibility to those presenting the challenge.

As pointed out, cues being given that describe the problem can also be cues that hint at a solution, and this can be a problem in itself. Evidence from studies have shown those who give such cues will not recognize solutions outside the constraints of the cue. Those who are given such cues are prone to think along the lines of the cue and not go beyond this.

The successful manager or team leader must present the dilemma—situation or problem—to the team in a manner that does not define limitations. If solutions rest on the statement of the problem, the discovery of the problem is often more crucial than the discovery of the solution; yet very few teams ever spend time on the discovery of the problem. By discovery, I mean the environment within, around, and of the problem. The holistic view of the problem with all its knowledge gaps and perceptions of why it exists. This includes viewing the problem with an element of curiosity. To this end, the successful manager may take one of two paths.

Path one: He or she may place the team in an environment where sufficient cursory information is given, which provides fundamental knowledge of the situation. The successful manager or team leader then points out gaps in the knowledge, allows novel questions to be put forth, and promotes imagination—balancing what is known with what is not known to tip the scale in favor of curiosity and the potential for a solution.

Successful managers and team leaders must recognize curiosity is an attitude of wanting to know, and they should actively foster it. It is an attribute, and as an attribute, it can be heightened. Curiosity leads to discovery; new knowledge, in turn, leads to the freedom to adapt, create, and innovate. Curiosity is best aroused when some level of familiarity is in place for one to develop a sense of discovery. This is often predicated on the inclusion of novel or imaginative questions and complex ideas into the level of familiarity. Add in an unsolved problem and the environment of curiosity is created.

The interesting thing about the curious mind is that it is not a passive observer. It does not sit by idly as information passes in front of it. It is an active participant engaged in the multidimensional resolution of tasks at hand while simultaneously storing gained knowledge for yet undiscovered tasks. The curious mind has expectations of discovery and success that take it far from sufficiency, to realize the potential momentum to move toward innovativeness.

In all of this, the successful manager avoids rules. Rules are often unwittingly devised to maintain the problem. Rules such as stay within the current portfolio, stay within the price structure, stay within the demographics of the average or current customer, etc. It must be understood that such rules are often why the problem or dilemma currently exists. Such rules have little or nothing to do with solvability and are actually impediments. Rules become boundaries and imposed—often self-imposed—limitations: much like the frame of a canvas on which the artist must limit the length of the brushstroke. Managers and team leaders must understand if the team is to provide a solution, then the team is allowed to think beyond the real and self-imposed constraints and be given the freedom to change their perspective as a team and individually.

Path two: The successful manager may ask of the team, "*What would this particular world look like if the problem did not exist*?" In other words, turn the problem upside down. In this, the team moves away from the usual view of solution finding, where there is a statement of the dilemma and the goal, and the challenge to find the means in which to achieve it. By allowing the team to create a world in which the problem does not exist, the problem is turned upside down, or inside out, and the team is free to discover a multitude of reasons why the problem would not exist—and thereby discover the reasons for this. This, in turn, allows the transfer of this knowledge to the current situation, resulting in multiple perspectives for a solution. Perhaps more importantly, in this world in which the problem does not exist, would be to challenge the team to now create the problem and discover the resultant factors required for the problem to exist. From this, the team can determine whether this is applicable to their dilemma.

In both paths, the team must welcome other opinions and perspectives to fill in gaps, bridge voids, and build on existing idea structures, each according to how they perceive the problem. This is not just multiple perspectives, but also an enrichment of perspectives. Some perspectives, taken at face value, may not seem to have value, immediate or otherwise, but it must be remembered the process of moving to an innovative solution is an irrational process. Innovative solutions in themselves are rational, but the process of moving to the solution is not. Innovation does not start at the discovery of the solution, but rather at the discovery of the problem or discovery of gaps and voids within the knowledge base.

Managers and team leaders must also be aware when engaged in an attention-demanding task that the team runs the risk of selective attention, also known as sustained inattentional blindness. This is the failure to notice the unexpected and can be the result of how the problem is framed—that is, the cues being given that describe the problem. It may be both the manager/team leader and the problem-solvers need to become irrational thinkers, viewing the problem from a multiplicity of perspectives to bring forth opportunities for solutions. To not do so runs the risk of erringly confirming the problem either has no solution or at least not a satisfactory solution. The successful manager, team, or team leader must guard against this and push aside the negative confirmations and perspective that make it possible.

One method of doing so is to focus on the falsification—that is, the perspective that makes a negative confirmation a refutable position. Guarding against embracing the "nonsolution" as irrefutable means it can be questioned. This, in turn, opens the mind to the existence of other perspectives. Conscious problem finding is integral to iconoclastic momentum, but teams must be careful they do not stop with the first "right" discovery and subsequent "right" answer. Problems will have as many unique solutions as there are perspectives of the stakeholders. In other words, there is no such thing as one right answer to a true problem. It must be remembered that iconoclastic momentum does not necessarily recognize right discoveries and answers, but its nemesis sufficiency does. Whether solutions are sufficient, creative, or innovative is derived from the context in which the problem is stated.

In business, there is a tendency to tie successes together with strings of like thinking and central themes. To adhere to canonical regimes, rules and conventions comply with dominant corporate values. In such companies, innovation can be a frightening thing because of its potentially destructive nature. But companies, particularly large companies, should not resist change. Large companies are in the best position to be the source of change—having the financial ability to invest in ideas that seem more imagination than substance; more extraordinary than ordinary; more nonaligned with the current product portfolio; and the potential to pay huge dividends in the long run.

However, understanding the wherewithal to change and acting on this—that is, innovate and render profitable products obsolete as a survival technique—is a difficult thing to do. So difficult it makes in-the-box thinking an attractive but failure-oriented option consisting of standard operating procedures in place to direct forward momentum. For many, success in a stable organization is built on the status quo, not the momentum of change. For these, gain, in the face of crisis, is not just disruptive; it is destructive, provoking discontinuity inducing turmoil in organizational identity and in the market. Such companies have what could be called current portfolio inertia.

Organizations, finding they have too much current portfolio inertia, have great difficulty acquiring or adopting new technologies. They are at risk of losing dominance in their market. For such companies, wagering the averages while ignoring the tails of the distribution—that is, ignoring what is on the event horizon simply because it is less probable in the moment—can be their demise. Neither creativity nor innovation exists in the averages, only in the necessity of the future, the forward tail of a moving distribution. It is difficult to invent or even recognize the future when vision is turned to the present based on past accomplishments. Failing to recognize the future puts emphasis on maintaining tradition, and as stated previously, tradition is an innovation killer.

To this end, it is recognized the creative process will generate alternative solutions, whereas routine problem-solving, an algorithmic deductive process, generates solutions that tend to suffice. In this, I encourage creative and innovative people, and teams, to move away from a culture of sufficiency; to consciously explore counterintuitive or alternate information. To view from another perspective; to incorporate the zero-gravity thinker; to doubt conventional wisdom or accepted truths. To offer plausible or even non-plausible alternatives; to avoid generalizations and commonalities and instead explore the exceptions; and to incorporate constructive dissent.

I end this dialogue with a quote from the comedian, actor, and musician Steve Martin, a wild and crazy guy. A quote that is not just an appropriate summary of our discussion, but perhaps a roadmap for those who seek creative and innovative pathways.

> *I was seeking (sic) originality, and fame fell on me as a byproduct. The course was more plodding than heroic: I did not strive valiantly against doubters but took incremental steps studded with a few intuitive leaps. I was not naturally talented—though working around this minor detail made me inventive. [1]*

Food for Thought:

- Avoid the tendency to believe "what is" is what it should be. (Chapter 1)
- Innovation abhors sufficiency. (Chapter 1)
- Revolution is not brought about by rational plans, but by conflicts of interests. (Chapter 1, Karl Popper)
- Iconoclastic momentum does not necessarily recognize right discoveries and answers, but its nemesis sufficiency does. (Chapter 5)
- Convergent thinking results not in creative solutions, but rather in solutions of sufficiency. (Chapter 20)
- Those who would believe in a perennial lull do not understand the perennial gale of creative destruction. (Chapter 1, Joseph Schumpeter)
- The space around the object is equal to the object itself. (Chapter 2)
- Order, while making experiences possible, also prevents experience, excluding as it includes. (Chapter 3)
- We need a multiplicity of visions, dreams, and prophecies—images of potential tomorrows. (Chapter 3, Alvin Toffler)

- Without multiple visions, or multiple perspectives, we tend to fixate on a solution within the constraints of the dilemma. (Chapter 3)
- If solutions rest on the statement of the problem, it may be fair to say the discovery of the problem is more crucial than the discovery of the solution. (Chapter 3)
- If asked to provide a solution to a problem that is considered unsolvable, then think beyond the real and self-imposed constraints. Think outside the box (outside of the dimensions given) and have the freedom to change your perspective. (Chapter 4)
- An unsolvable problem will remain unsolvable when the solution is sought within the constraints of the problem. (Chapter 4)
- If asked to solve an unsolvable problem, the constraints of the problem are no longer valid. (Chapter 4)
- The irrefutability of an unsolvable problem is not established by solutions not being known. (Chapter 4)
- What observers actually experience in response to any visual stimulus is its accumulated statistical meaning, i.e., what the stimulus has turned out to signify in the past. (Chapter 4, Purves and Lotto)
- There is no faster method of walking away from a problem than to listen to an "expert" state it is unsolvable. (Chapter 4)
- It ain't so much the things we don't know that get us into trouble. It's the things we know that just ain't so. (Chapter 4, Artemus Ward)
- Big events don't come from big parents. (Chapter 5, Taleb N.N.)
- To see things differently than others requires "*bombarding the brain with things it has never encountered before.*" (Gregory Berns, Chapter 5 [16])
- The word "no" has the ability to confine a problem or the search for a solution to a single perspective. It is a word used to move toward sufficiency and to support in-the-box thinking. (Chapter 20)
- Where innovation is to be fostered, curiosity must be managed. (Chapter 6)
- Chance may favor the prepared mind, but curiosity is the medium, the environment that chance takes its random walks in. (Chapter 6)
- Repetition of success is the momentum of the company, and it is indeed risky to challenge it. But it is also risky not to. (Chapter 8)

- Social vision is not just how the company perceives itself in a competitive environment, but rather the ability to perceive itself or its product offerings in a similar manner as their customers. (Chapter 8)
- Defining a product is more than seeing its physical dimensions and understanding its primary function. It is defining the attributes according to the customer's perspective. (Chapter 8)
- The essence of spirit is the experience of diversity. (Chapter 9)
- "*A leader's role is not to control people or stay on top of things, but rather to guide, energize, and excite.*" (Jack Welch, Chapter 9 [9])
- Catering to the non-consumer is a hallmark of disruptive technology. (Chapter 10)
- Disruptive technologies, in part, are tangents off existing technologies that exploit the non-consumer of the existing technology. (Chapter 10)
- "*The temptation in the existing business is always to feed yesterday and to starve tomorrow.*" (Peter Drucker, Chapter 11 [3]–[5])
- If team leaders recognize conflict is not a competition, but rather a necessary merging of perspectives for the common good, then the potential for one of the greatest mistakes found in science or in business is avoided—that is, solving the wrong problem. (Chapter 11)
- The serendipitous nature of discovery is an ardent effort, coming from being highly motivated in the search for the new and valuable. It favors the prepared mind. (Chapter 12)
- "*A new scientific truth does not triumph by convincing its opponents and making them see the light, but rather because its opponents eventually die, and a new generation grows up that is familiar with it.*" (Max Planck, Chapter 13 [6])
- Say it loud enough and often enough, and eventually it will become someone else's good idea. (Chapter 13)
- Progress is not a random series of unrelated events, but rather a "dynamic" waiting—the sorting and ordering by time. New ideas are not generated from nothingness, but rather pieced together from what is known, challenging why they are known, and exploring what is not known. Thus, challenge becomes a recombinant process. (Chapter 14)

- Inefficiency breeds opportunity. (Chapter 15)
- If inefficiency sponsors opportunity, then crisis sponsors novelty. (Chapter 16)
- Problems will have as many unique solutions as there are perspectives of the stakeholders. (Chapter 16)
- Groupthink has the unfortunate tendency to regress toward the lowest common denominators of safety, obviousness, and the inconsequential. (Chapter 21)
- Whether the solutions are sufficient, creative, or innovative, they are derived from the context in which the problem is stated. (Chapter 22)
- The problem with knowledge of the familiar, whether it be knowledge of how to do something effectively, knowledge of similar situations, or knowledge of the way things are supposed to be, is it has the potential to stifle creativity. (Chapter 23)
- Make the familiar strange. (Chapter 23)

References

Chapter 1: References

[1] J. Suchet, *Mozart: A Man Revealed*. New York: Pegasus Books, 2017.

[2] P. Dimond, *A Mozart Diary, A Chronological Reconstruction of the Composer's Life*. West Port, Connecticut, London: Greenwood Press, 1997.

Chapter 2: References

[1] "Iconoclast" Merriam-Webster. [Online]. Available: https://www.merriam-webster.com/dictionary/iconoclast. [Accessed: Aug. 20, 2020].

[2] A. Einstein, "On Solving Problems." [Online]. Available: http://www.gurteen.com/gurteen/gurteen.nsf/id/X00063A06/. [Accessed: June 12, 2019].

[3] P. Senge, *The Fifth Discipline: The Art and Practice of the Learning Organization*. New York: Currency Doubleday, 1990, p. 192.

[4] B. Morris, "5 Quotes by General Patton That Transfer to the Business World." Dec. 26, 2013. [Online]. Available: https://www.business2community.com/leadership/5-quotes-general-patton-transfer-business-world-0725423. [Accessed: June 12, 2019.]

[5] R. Friedenthal, *Letters of the Great Artists—From Blake to Pollock* translation: Daphne Woodward, London: Thames and Hudson, 1963, p. 264.

[6] K. Popper, *The Poverty of Historicism*. London & New York: Routledge Classics, 2002, p. 124.

[7] K. Popper, *The Poverty of Historicism*, 1957, p. 42.

[8] J. Schumpeter, *Can Capitalism Survive? Creative Destruction and the Future of the Global Economy*. New York: Harper Perennial ModernThought, 2009, p. 43.

Chapter 3: References

[1] A. Danchev, *Cézanne: A Life*. New York: Pantheon Books, 2012.

[2] L. Venturi, *Four Steps toward Modern Art: Giorgione, Caravaggio, Manet, Cézanne*. New York: Columbia University Press, 1956.

[3] J. Huneker, Ivory, Apes, and Peacocks: Joseph Conrad, Walt Whitman, Jules Laforgue, Dostoievsky and Tolstoy, Schoenberg, Wedekind, Moussorgsky, Cézanne, Vermeer, Matisse, Van Gogh, Gauguin, Italian Futurists, Various Latter-Day Poets, Painters, Composers, and Dramatists. New York: Charles Scribner's Sons, 1915.

[4] A. Danchev, *Georges Braque: A Life*. New York: Arcade Publishing, 2005.

[5] D.P. Tryphonopoulus, and S.J. Adams, Eds., *The Ezra Pound Encyclopedia*. Westport, CT: Greenwood Press, 2005, p. 124.

[6] T.L. Gaillard, Jr., "Hemingway's Debt to Cézanne: New Perspectives," *Twentieth Century Literature*, Vol. 45, No. 1, pp. 65–78, Spring 1999.

[7] E. Hemingway, *In Our Time:* "The Three-Day Blow." New York: Boni & Liveright, 1925.

[8] R. Berman, *Modernity and Progress: Fitzgerald, Hemingway, Orwell*. Tuscaloosa, AL: University of Alabama Press, 2005, p. 75.

[9] A. Baker, *Ernest Hemingway: A Life Story*. New York: Scribner's, 1969.

[10] M. Secrest, *Frank Lloyd Wright*. New York: Alfred A. Knopf, 1992.

Chapter 4: References

[1] B. Waldenfels, *Order in the Twilight*. Athens: Ohio University Press, 1996, p. 110.

[2] D. Sobel, *A More Perfect Heaven: How Copernicus Revolutionized the Cosmos*. New York: Bloomsbury, Kindle Edition, 2011.

[3] B.T. Moran, "The Universe of Philip Melanchthon: Criticism and Use of the Copernican Theory," *Comitatus: A Journal of Medieval and Renaissance Studies*, Vol. 4, No. 1, pp. 1–23, 1973.

[4] A.I. Miller, *Einstein, Picasso: Space, Time and the Beauty That Causes Havoc*. New York: Basic Books, 2001, p. 130.

[5] A. Toffler, *Future Shock*. New York: Bantam Books, 1971, p. 463.

[6] J. E. Davidson, and R. J. Sternberg, Eds., *The Psychology of Problem Solving*. Cambridge, England: Cambridge University Press, 2003, p. 20.

[7] J. E. Davidson, *The Nature of Insight*, R. J. Sternberg and J. E. Davidson (Eds.). Cambridge, MA: MIT Press, 1995, p. 191.

[8] D. Kahneman, *Thinking: Fast and Slow*. New York: Farrar, Straus and Giroux, 2011.

[9] M. Michalko, *Thinkertoys: A Handbook of Creative Techniques*. New York: Ten Speed Press, 2006.

[10] T.M. Kubiak, and D.W. Benbow, *The Certified Six Sigma Black Belt Handbook*, 2nd ed. Milwaukee: ASQ Quality Press, 2009, p. 427.

[11] "Zipcar Reports 2012 Third Quarter Results," 2012. [Online]. Available: https://www.zipcar.com/press/releases/zipcar-reports-2012-third-quarter-results. [Accessed: Feb. 6, 2016].

[12] R. Martin, "Carsharing Services Will Surpass 12 Million Members Worldwide by 2020." Navigant Consulting. Aug. 22, 2013, [Online]. Available: https://en.wikipedia.org/wiki/Carsharing. [Accessed: April 11, 2020].

[13] Navigant Research, "Navigant Forecasts Global Carsharing Services to Grow to $6.2B by 2020." Green Car Congress. Aug. 22, 2013. [Online]. Available: https://www.greencarcongress.com/2013/08/20130822-navigant.html. [Accessed: Feb. 6, 2016].

[14] M.D. Mumford, M.I. Mobley, C.E. Uhlman, R. Reiter-Palmon, and L.M. Doares, "Process Analytic Models of Creative Capacities," *Creativity Research Journal*, Vol. 4, No. 2, pp. 91–122, 1991.

Chapter 5: References

[1] Martin Gardner, *The Scientific American book of Mathematical Puzzles and Diversions, New York: Simon and Schuster,* (1959)

[2] R.S. Calinger, *Leonhard Euler: Mathematical Genius in the Enlightenment*. Princeton, NJ: Princeton University Press, 2016.

[3] *Zeno's Paradoxes*, Stanford Encyclopedia of Philosophy. [Online]. Available: https://plato.stanford.edu/entries/paradox-zeno/. [Accessed: June 18, 2019].

[4] Pablo Picasso, Still Life With Fruit and Glass, Museum of Modern Art, Manhattan, https://www.moma.org/collection/works/79380.

[5] Pablo Picasso, Still Life With Fish and Bottles, Metropolitan Museum of Art, New York, [Online] https://arthive.com/pablopicasso/works/376122~Still_life_with_fish_and_bottles.

[6] Pablo Picasso, Fruit Dish, Museum of Modern Art, Manhattan, https://www.moma.org/collection/works/79322.

[7] R. Rosenblum, *Cubism and Twentieth Century Art*, Revised ed. New York: Harry N. Abrams, 1966, p. 93.

[8] K. Wilkin, *Georges Braque.* New York: Abbeville Press Inc., 1991, pp. 51–52.

[9] G. Kanizsa, "Margini quasi-percettivi in campi con stimolazione omogenea," *Rivista di Psicologia,* Vol. 49, No. 1, pp. 7–30, 1955.

[10] G. Kanizsa, "Subjective Contours," *Scientific American,* Vol. 234, No. 4, pp. 48–53, 1976. [Online] Available: http://www.jstor.org/stable/24950327.

[11] R. Luccio, and W. Gerbino, "Gaetano Kanizsa (1913–1993)—Things and Perceptions," *Review of Psychology,* Vol. 2, No. 1–2, pp. 71–80, 1995.

[12] E.H. Adelson, "Perceptual Organization and the Judgment of Brightness," *Science,* Vol. 262, pp. 2042–2044, 1993.

[13] E. H. Adelson, *The New Cognitive Neurosciences*, M. Gazzaniga, Ed., 2nd ed. Cambridge, MA: MIT Press, 2000, pp. 339–351.

[14] D. Purves, and R. B. Lotto, *Why We See What We Do: An Empirical Theory of Vision*. Sunderland, MA: Sinauer Associates Inc., 2003.

[15] F. Smith, *Understanding Reading: A Psycholinguistic Analysis of Reading and Learning to Read*, 5th ed. Hillsdale, NJ: Lawrence Erlbaum Associates, 1994, p. 8.

[16] L. Carroll, *Through the Looking Glass*. Macmillan and Co, London (1948).

[17] M. Gardner, *The Annotated Alice: The Definitive Edition*. New York: W. W. Norton and Company, 1999.

[18] I. Laka, Jabberwocky, or the poetry of function words, Mapping Ignorance. Dec. 2013. [Online]. Available: https://mappingignorance.org/2013/12/13/jabberwocky-or-the-poetry-of-function-words/. [Accessed: Aug. 20, 2020].

[19] What is Language, Linguistics 105*Words and Sounds, Lecture Number Two. [Online]. Available: https://www.departments.bucknell.edu/linguistics/lectures/05lect02.html. [Accessed: Aug. 20, 2020].

[20] Chuck Berry, Brown-Eyed Handsome Man, , Label: Chess , Producer(s): Leonard Chess, Phil Chess. Chicago, Recorded: April 16, 1956.

[21] D. Kahneman, *Thinking: Fast and Slow*. New York: Farrar, Straus and Giroux, 2011.

[22] K.E. Standovich, and R.F. West, "Individual Differences in Reasoning: Implications for the Rationality Debate," *Behavior and Brain Sciences,* Vol. 23, pp. 645–665, 2000.

[23] R. Cottle, E. Johnson, and R. Wets, "George B. Dantzig (1914–2005)," *Notices of the AMS,* Vol. 54, No. 3, pp. 344–362, 2007. [Online]. Available: https://www.ams.org/notices/200703/fea-cottle.pdf. [Accessed: June 14, 2019].

[24] W.I.B. Beveridge, *The Art of Scientific Investigation*. New York: W.W. Norton and Company, p. 2, 1957.

[25] https://quotefancy.com/quote/763424/Albert-Einstein-We-must-learn-to-see-the-world-anew, accessed July 12, 2021.

[26] T. Vitale, *Armory Show That Shocked America in 1913, Celebrates 100*. Feb. 17, 2013. [Online]. Available: https://www.npr.org/2013/02/17/172002686/armory-show-that-shocked-america-in-1913-celebrates-100.

[27] D.K. Simonton, *Greatness: Who Makes History and Why*. New York: Guilford Press, 1994, p. 256.

[28] E.T. Bell, *Mathematics: Queen and Servant of Science*. Washington, DC: Mathematical Association of America, 1951.

[29] D.K. Simonton, "Niles Bohr to Wolfang Pauli on His Presentation of a Theory of Elementary Particles," in *Greatness: Who Makes History and Why*. New York: Guilford Press, 1994, p. 101.

[30] J. Cohen, *Science Friction*. July 13, 2008. [Online] Available: https://www.latimes.com/archives/la-xpm-2008-jul-13-bk-susskind13-story.html. [Accessed: Apr. 11, 2020].

[31] C.F. Browne (AKA Artemus Ward), The Complete Works of Artemus Ward, EBook #6946, Aug. 4, 2012,

https://www.gutenberg.org/files/6946/6946-h/6946-h.htm. [Accessed: Aug. 20, 2020].

[32] Bee Movie. DreamWorks Animation, 2007.

[33] https://www.brainyquote.com/quotes/mary_kay_ash_101496. [Accessed 26 July 2021].

[34] https://www.theguardian.com/world/2007/dec/06/uselections2008.suzannegoldenberg1. [Accessed 26 July 2021].

[35] Wendy's 4 for $4 TV Commercial, "UnBEElievable!" [Online]. Available: https://www.ispot.tv/ad/Ambw/wendys-4-for-4-unbeelievable#.

Chapter 6: References

[1] G.A. Kimble, and M.C. Wertheimer, Eds., *Portraits of Pioneers in Psychology*, Vol. 3. Washington, DC: American Psychological Association, 1998, p. 162.

[2] K. Duncker, "On Problem Solving," *Psychological Monographs,* Vol. 58, pp. i-113, 1945.

[3] R.E. Adamson, Functional Fixedness as related to problem solving: A repetition of three experiments. Journal of Experimental Psychology, 44, 288-291, 1952.

[4] The Inattentional Blindness Collection, Viscog Productions, Inc. 3001 Weeping Cherry Drive, Champaign, IL 61822, USA, 2008.

[5] D.J. Simons, and C.F. Chabris, "Gorillas in Our Midst: Sustained Inattentional Blindness for Dynamic Events," *Perception,* Vol. 28, pp. 1059–1074, 1999.

[6] K. Popper, *Conjectures and Refutations*. London: Routledge and Keagan Paul, pp. 33–39, 1963.

[7] N.N. Taleb, *The Black Swan: The Impact of the Highly Improbable*. New York: Random House Publishing Group, 2010.

[8] B. Russell, *The Problems of Philosophy*. Project Gutenberg, , Release date 2009, EBook 5827, [Online] https://www.gutenberg.org/files/5827/5827-h/5827-h.htm. [Accessed Feb 10, 2021].

[9] A. Kirtzman, *Betrayal: The Life and Lies of Bernie Madoff*. New York: Harper Collins, 2009.

[10] J. Colombo, Iceland's Post-2009 Housing Bubble. [Online]. Available: http://www.thebubblebubble.com/iceland-housing-bubble/. [Accessed: June 21, 2019].

[11] H. Fountain, "Trial over Earthquake in Italy Puts Focus on Probability and Panic," *New York Times*. Oct. 3, 2011. [Online]. Available: https://www.nytimes.com/2011/10/04/science/04quake.html?src=rechp.

[12] S.Y. Tan, and Y. Tatsumura, "Alexander Fleming (1881–1955): Discoverer of Penicillin," *Singapore Medical Journal,* Vol. 56, No. 7, pp. 366–367, 2015.

[13] M. Sklar, *Dream It Do It: My Half Century Creating Disney's Magic Kingdoms*. Santa Clarita, CA: Disney Editions, 2013, p. 36.

[14] J. Mulholland, The Language of Negotiation: A Handbook of Practical Strategies for Improving Communication. New York: Routledge, 1991, p. 177.

[15] Neurodope, http://neurodope.com/http:/neurodope.com/category/share-dope. [Accessed July 27, 2021].

[16] G. Berns, *Iconoclast: A Neuroscientist Reveals How to Think Differently*. Brighton, MA: Harvard Business School Publishing Corporation, 2008.

[17] F. Johansson, *The Medici Effect*. Boston: Harvard Business School Press, 2004.

[18] D.T. Campbell, and D.W. Fiske, "Convergent and Discriminant Validation by the Multitrait-multimethod Matrix," *Psychological Bulletin,* Vol. 56, No. 2 , pp. 81–105, 1959.

[19] *Gallo, The Innovation Secrets of Steve Jobs: Insanely Different Principles for Breakthrough Success. New York: McGraw Hill, 2010.*

[20] da Vinci, Leonardo, *Leonardo's Notebooks*. London: The Folio Society, 1883.

[21] D.A. Brown, *Leonardo Da Vinci: Origins of a Genius*. London: Yale University Press, 1998.

[22] H.W. Brands, *The First American: The Life and Times of Benjamin Franklin*. New York: Anchor Books, 2000.

[23] R.P. Feynman, The Pleasure of Finding Things Out: The Best Short Works of Richard P. Feynman. Cambridge, MA: Helix Books, 2000, p. 243.

Chapter 7: References

[1] J. Pinkowski, *6 Priceless Documents that Reveal Key Moments Early in Einstein's Career*, Mental Floss. Dec. 27, 2017. [Online]. Available: https://www.mentalfloss.com/article/518759/6-priceless-documents-reveal-key-moments-early-einsteins-career. [Accessed: Feb 10, 2021].

[2] Walt Disney Archives, Walt's Quotes. [Online]. Available: https://d23.com/section/walt-disney-archives/walts-quotes/. [Accessed: June 25, 2019].

[3] P.E. Shah, H.M. Weeks, B. Richards Blair, N. Kaciroti, Early Childhood Curiosity and Kindergarten Reading and Math Academic Achievement, Pediatr Res Sep;84(3):380-386.

[4] R.E. Kay, "Let's Stop Teaching and Let Our Children Learn," Social Policy, Vol. 22, pp. 1–4, Summer 1991.

[5] F.L. Wright, Frank Lloyd Wright: An Autobiography. San Francisco, CA: Pomegranate Communications, 2005.

[6] 30 Frank Lloyd Wright Quotes On Mother Nature, Space, God, And Architecture. [Online]. Available: https://blog.miragestudio7.com/frank-lloyd-wright-quotes/6560/. Jan 30, 2020. [Accessed: Feb 10, 2021].

[7] C. Howett, "Modernism and American Landscape Architecture," in Marc Treib, Ed., Modern Landscape Architecture: A Critical Review. Cambridge, MA: MIT Press, 1992, p. 25.

[8] F.L. Wright, and B.B. Pfeiffer, Frank Lloyd Wright, the Guggenheim Correspondence. Fresno, CA: Press at California State University, 1986, p. 4.

[9] D. Cole, "The Science of the Yellow Brick Road: Why the Risks of Curiosity Make Our Lives Better," Science & Spirit, Vol. 18, No. 2, p 47+, May–June 2007.

[10] H. Day, "The Measurement of Specific Curiosity," in H. Day, D. Berlyne, and D. Hunt, Eds., Intrinsic Motivation: A New Direction in Education, Toronto: Holt, Rinehart, and Winston, 1971, pp. 99–112.

[11] G. Garrison, M. Harvey, and N. Napier, "Global Decision-Making: The Role of Managerial Curiosity in Assessing Potentially Disruptive Information Technologies," Multinational Business Review, Vol. 16, No. 1, p. 21, Winter 2008.

[12] D. E. Berlyne, "A Theory of Human Curiosity," *British Journal of Psychology*, Vol. 45, No. 3, p. 180, Aug. 1954.

[13] D. E. Berlyne, *Conflict, Arousal, and Curiosity*. New York: McGraw-Hill, 1960.

[14] G. Loewenstein, "The Psychology of Curiosity: A Review and Interpretation," *Psychological Bulletin,* Vol. 116, pp. 75–98, 1994.

[15] J.A. Litman, T.L. Hutchins, and R.K. Russon, "Epistemic Curiosity, Feeling of Knowing, and Exploratory Behavior," *Cognition and Emotion*, Vol. 19, No. 4, pp. 559–582, 2005.

[16] J. Metcalfe, B. Schwartz, and P. Bloom, "The Tip-of-the-Tongue State and Curiosity," *Cognitive Research: Principles and Implications*, Vol. 2, p. 31, 2017.

[17] J.W. Gentry, A.C. Burns, J.R. Dickinson, S. Putrevu, S. Chun, Y. Hongyan, L. Williams, T. Bare, and R.A. Gentry, "Managing the Curiosity Gap Does Matter: What Do We Need To Do About It?", *Developments in Business Simulation and Experiential Learning*, Vol. 29, pp. 67–73, 2002.

[18] D.A. Levinthal, and J.G. March, "A Model of Adaptive Organizational Search," *Journal of Economic Behavior and Organization*, Vol. 2, pp. 307–333, 1981.

[19] M.L. Tushman, and P. Anderson, "Technological Discontinuities and Organizational Environments," *Administrative Science Quarterly,* Vol. 31, pp. 439–465, 1986.

[20] D.A. Levinthal, and J.G. March, "The Myopia of Learning," *Strategic Management Journal*, Vol. 14, pp. 95–112, 1993.

[21] D. Koranda, and K.B. Sheehan, "Teaching Curiosity: An Essential Advertising Skill?" Journal of Advertising Education, Vol. 18, No. 1, p. 14+, Spring 2014.

[22] E. Bierbaum, "A Paradigm for the '90s," *American Libraries*, Vol. 21, No. 1, p. 18, 1990.

[23] G.K. Zipf, *Human Behavior and the Principle of Least Effort*. Cambridge, MA: Addison-Wesley Press, 1949.

[24] D. Kahneman, *Thinking Fast and Slow*, Farrar. New York: Strauss and Giroux, 2011.

[25] Humphreys, S. Saraiya, W. Belenky, and J. Dworkin, "Nasal Packing with Strips of Cured Pork as a Treatment for Uncontrollable Epistaxis in a Patient with Glanzmann Thrombasthenia," *Annals of Otology, Rhinology and Laryngology*, Vol. 120, No. 11, pp. 732–736, 2011.

[26] S. McDonough, *Curiosity Credited for Great Inventions*, Associated Press, Oct. 20, 2002. [Online]. https://www.deseretnews.com/article/943905/Curiosity-credited-for-great-inventions.html. [Accessed: June 26, 2019].

Chapter 8: References

[1] J.S. Antrobus, "Toward a Neurocognitive Processing Model of Imaginal Thought," in J.A. Singer and P. Salovey, Eds., *At Play in the Fields of Consciousness: Essays in Honor of Jerome L. Singer*. Mahwah, NJ: Lawrence Erlbaum Associates, 1999, p. 4.

[2] E. Klinger, "Thought Flow: Properties and Mechanisms Underlying Shifts in Content," in At Play in the Fields of

Consciousness: Essays in Honor of Jerome L. Singer, Mahwah, NJ: Lawrence Erlbaum Associates, 1999, p. 46.

[3] E. Klinger, "Daydreaming and Fantasizing: Thought Flow and Motivation," in *Handbook of Imagination and Mental Simulation*, New York: Psychology Press, pp. 225–239, 2009.

[4] B. Soper, "A Comparison of Daydream and Dream Perspectives," College Student Journal, Vol. 33, No. 2, p. 217, June 1999.

[5] M.E. Raichle, "The Brain's Dark Energy," *Scientific American,* Vol. 302, No. 3, pp. 44–49, March 2010.

[6] M.E. Raichle, A.M. MacLeod, A.Z. Snyder, W.J. Powers, D.A. Gusnar, and G.L. Shulman, "A Default Mode of Brain Function," *Proceedings of the National Academy of Sciences,* Vol. 98, pp. 676–682, 2001.

[7] B. Kaczmarek, K. Markiewicz, Current and Traditional Views on the Brain Works, Acta Neuropsychologica, 16(2): 201-212, May, 2018, [Online]. Available: https://www.researchgate.net/publication/328045226_Current_and_traditional_views_on_the_brain_works.

[8] Psychologies, What your daydreams reveal about you, March 3, 2018, https://www.psychologies.co.uk/self/what-your-daydreams-reveal-about-you.html. [Accessed July28, 2021].

[9] Colino Stacy, The Upside of Daydreaming, What you can learn about yourself from your daytime reveries. U.S.News, Oct. 31, 2018, https://health.usnews.com/wellness/mind/articles/2018-10-31/the-upside-of-daydreaming, accessed July 28, 2021

Chapter 9: References

[1] E. Sadun, "Apple Announces iPod Touch: iPhone Without the Phone," *TUAW*. [Online]. [Accessed: Sept. 5, 2007].

[2] J. Dunn, "The Rise and Fall of Apple's iPod in One Chart," *The Business Insider*, July 28, 2017.

[3] J.A. Schumpeter, *Capitalism, Socialism, and Democracy.* New York: Harper & Brothers, 1942.

[4] J.A. Schumpeter, *Essays: On Entrepreneurs, Innovations, Business Cycles, and the Evolution of Capitalism*, Classics in Economics Collection, New Brunswick: Transaction Publishers, 1951, pp. xviii-xix.

[5] H.C. Lucas, *The Search for Survival: Lessons from Disruptive Technologies*. New York: ABC-CLIO, 2012, p. 16.

[6] "The Last Kodak Moment?" *The Economist*, 14, Jan. 2012. [Online]. Available: https://www.economist.com/business/2012/01/14/the-last-kodak-moment. [Accessed: Apr. 11, 2020].

[7] The Rediff Interview/Steven J. Sasson, inventor of the digital camera, Rediff.com India Limited. 7, Aug. 2006. [Online]. Available: https://www.rediff.com/money/2006/aug/07kodak.htm. [Accessed: Sept. 22, 2011].

[8] "History of the Digital Camera and Digital Imaging," Digital Camera Museum. [Online]. Available: https://www.digitalkameramuseum.de/en/history, [Accessed: July 2, 2019].

[9] J. Estrin, "Kodak's First Digital Moment." *New York Times*, Aug. 12, 2015.

[10] Quinn Renee C., Meet the Medal Recipients, Plus President Obama's Remarks, Nov. 18, 2010, IPWatchdog, [Online]. Available: https://www.ipwatchdog.com/2010/11/18/meet-the-medal-recipients-plus-president-obamas-remarks/id=13392/. [Accessed Jan 29, 2021].

[11] List of Countries by Number of Mobile Phones in Use. https://en.wikipedia.org/wiki/List_of_countries_by_number_of_mobile_phones_in_use. [Accessed July 28, 2021].

[12] *History of Polaroid and Edwin Land.* Boston: New York Times Company, 2012. [Online]. Available: Boston.com, https://www.boston.com/uncategorized/noprimarytagmatch/2012/10/03/history-of-polaroid-and-edwin-land. [Accessed: Jan. 31, 2015].

[13] "Polaroid Quits Instant Film," *Sun Journal,* Lewiston. Maine: Associated Press, Feb. 9, 2008, pp. B8, B7.

[14] CASE 18: Polaroid and the Family-Imaging Market. [Online]. Available: https://nscpolteksby.ac.id/ebook/files/Ebook/Business%20Administration/Marketing-Planning%20and%20Strategy%20(2010)/36.pdf.

[15] "The Vindication of Edwin Land," *Forbes Magazine,* Vol. 139, p. 83, May 4, 1987.

[16] O. Kmia, "Why Kodak Died and Fujifilm Thrived: A Tale of Two Film Companies," Oct. 19, 2018. [Online]. Available: https://petapixel.com/2018/10/19/why-kodak-died-and-fujifilm-thrived-a-tale-of-two-film-companies/. [Accessed June 28, 2019].

[17] J.A. Schumpeter, *Capitalism, Socialism, and Democracy.* London: Routledge, 1994, p. 83.

[18] V.K. McElheny, Insisting on the Impossible: The Life of Edwin Land. Cambridge, MA: Perseus Books, 1998, p. 440.

[19] Cashberry. "Tired Brands: Polaroid." Nov. 3, 2006. [Online]. Available: http://brandfailures.blogspot.com/2006/11/tired-brands-polaroid.html. [Accessed: June 28, 2019].

[20] Griffith Erin, Pinterest Is a Unicorn. It Just Doesn't Act Like One. - The New York Times, - The New York Times, Sept 9, 2018, https://www.nytimes.com/2018/09/09/technology/pinterest-growth.html. [Accessed July 28, 2021].

[21] Constine Josh, Snap shares skyrocket on first earnings beat with revived user growth – TechCrunch.– TechCrunch. techcrunch.com, Feb 6, 2018 https://techcrunch.com/2018/02/06/snap-inc-earnings-q4-2017/, Retrieved April 11, 2018.

[22] Facebook Reports First Quarter 2021 Results, https://investor.fb.com/investor-news/press-release-details/2021/Facebook-Reports-First-Quarter-2021-Results/default.aspx. [Accessed July 28, 2021].

[23] W.C. Coleman, Kansapedia, Kansas Historical Society. 2013. [Online]. Available: https://www.kshs.org/kansapedia/william-coffin-coleman/12018. [Accessed: April 11, 2020].

[24] M. Gershman, *Getting It Right the Second Time*. Reading, MA: Addison-Wesley, 1990, pp. 228–232.

[25] P. Hoehnle, "Foerstner, George Christian," *The Biographical Dictionary of Iowa*. Iowa: University of Iowa Press, 2009.

[26] M. Gershman, *Getting It Right the Second Time*. Reading, MA: Addison-Wesley, 1990, pp. 53–54.

[27] R.D. Hershey, Jr., “George Foerstner, 91, Amana Founder and Advocate of the Microwave Oven,” *New York Times*, Jan. 24, 2000.

[28] W. Hammack, *The Greatest Discovery Since Fire, Invention and Technology Magazine*, Vol. 20, No. 4, Spring 2005. [Online]. Available: http://todayinsci.com/Events/Technology/Microwave%20Oven%20History%20-%20The%20Greatest%20Discover%20Since%20Fire.htm.

[29] C. Harress, “The Sad End of Blockbuster Video: The Onetime $5 Billion Company Is Being Liquidated as Competition from Online Giants Netflix and Hulu Prove All Too Much for the Iconic Brand.” *International Business Times*, Dec. 5, 2013.

[30] E. Griffith, “Will Pinterest Prove a Saner Model, or Wash Out?”, *New York Times*, Sept. 9, 2018, p. B1.

[31] Case 19-80064-TLS Doc 4 Desc Main Document, The United States Bankruptcy Court For The District Of Nebraska In re: Chapter 11)Specialty Retail Shops Holding Corp., et al.,1) Declaration Of Russell L. Steinhorst, Chief Executive Officer, Of Specialty Retail Holdings Corp., In Support of Chapter 11 Petitions And First Day Motions, Filed 01/16/19 Entered 01/16/19 08:27:31, [Online]. Available:

[32] http://www.pszjlaw.com/assets/htmldocuments/Shopko%20first-day%20declaration.pdf. [Accessed April 11, 2020].

[33] L. Adamson, *The History of eCommerce*, March 21, 2016. [Online]. Available: https://www.statementagency.com/blog/2016/03/the-history-of-ecommerce.

[34] M.L. Tushman, and P. Anderson, “Technological Discontinuities and Organizational Environments,” *Administrative Science Quarterly,* Vol. 31, pp. 439–465, 1986.

[35] P. Anderson, and M.L. Tushman, "Technological Discontinuities and Dominant Designs: A Cyclical Model of Technological Change," *Administrative Science Quarterly,* Vol. 35, No. 4, pp. 604–633, Dec. 1990.

[36] M. Kundera, *The Book of Laughter and Forgetting*, Perennial Classics. New York: Harper Collins Publishers, 1999.

Chapter 10: References

[1] J.H. Dyer, H. Gregersen, and C.M. Christensen, "Five Discovery Skills that Distinguish Great Innovators, Business Research for Business Leaders, Research & Ideas," *Harvard Business School*. July 20, 2011. [Online]. Available: https://hbswk.hbs.edu/item/five-discovery-skills-that-distinguish-great-innovators. [Accessed: July 3, 2019].

[2] J.H. Dyer, H. Gregersen, and C.M. Christensen, "The Innovator's DNA," *Harvard Business Review*, Dec. 2009.

[3] R.G. Wesson, *Soviet Communes*. New Brunswick, NJ: Rutgers University Press, 1963, p. 158.

[4] D. Joravsky, *The Lysenko Affair*. Chicago: University of Chicago Press, 1970.

[5] P.R. Josephson, "Soviet Scientists and the State: Politics, Ideology, and Fundamental Research from Stalin to Gorbachev," *Social Research*, Vol. 59, No. 3, pp. 589–614, Fall 1992.

[6] Y. Jiaqi, and G. Gao, *Turbulent Decade: A History of the Cultural Revolution*. Honolulu: University of Hawaii Press, 1996, p. xxiv.

[7] T. B. Mam, *Children of Cambodia's Killing Fields*, "Worms from Our Skin," Memoirs compiled by Dith Pran. New Haven, CT: Yale University, 1997.

[8] J.C. Manzella, *Common Purse, Uncommon Future: The Long, Strange Trip of Communes and Other Intentional Communities*. Santa Barbara, CA: Praeger, 2010, p. 167.

[9] 109 Top Jack Welch Quotes on Winning and Leadership. [Online]. Available: https://quotes.thefamouspeople.com/jack-welch-1713.php.

[10] W. Manchester, *A World Lit Only by Fire*. Boston: Little, Brown and Company, 1992, p. 96.

[11] D. Teresi, *The Ancient Roots of Modern Science-From the Babylonians to the Maya*. New York: Simon Schuster Paperbacks, 2002.

[12] T. Christensen, "Did East Asian Printing Traditions Influence the European Renaissance?" [Online]. Available: http://www.apworldhistory.org/Gutenberg%20and%20the%20Koreans.pdf. [Accessed: Feb. 26, 2019].

Chapter 11: References

[1] J.D. Wolff, *Western Union and the Creation of the American Corporate Order: 1845–1893*. Cambridge: Cambridge University Press, 2013. [Online]. Available.

[2] Laura Chaparro, Antonio Meucci, the Italian Immigrant who couldn't patent the telephone, OpenMind BBVA, Oct. 18, 2017, https://www.bbvaopenmind.com/en/science/leading-figures/antonio-meucci-the-italian-immigrant-who-couldnt-patent-the-telephone/. [Accessed Aug 3, 2021].

[3] "*1984*," Ridley Scott Director. [Online]. Available: https://www.youtube.com/watch?v=vNy-7jv0XSc.

[4] R. Rosenberg, S. Gaul, W. Ford, and O. Tomilova, *Microcredit Interest Rates and Their Determinants, 2004–2011*, Access to

Finance Forum Reports by CGAP and Its Partners, No. 7, June 2013.

[5] N. MacFarquhar, "Banks Making Big Profits From Tiny Loans," *New York Times*, April 4, 2010. [Online]. Available: http://www.nytimes.com/2010/04/14/world/14microfinance.html?pagewanted=all&_r=0. [Accessed: July 5, 2019].

[6] Safaricom, About Us, [Online]. Available: https://www.safaricom.co.ke/about. [Accessed: Feb 10, 2021].

[7] Safaricom, About Us, [Online]. Available: https://www.safaricom.co.ke/about/innovation/social-innovation/m-tiba. [Accessed: Feb 10, 2021].

[8] B. Popper, "Guest editor Bill Gates, Can Mobile Banking Revolutionize the Lives of the Poor?" [Online]. Available: http://www.theverge.com/2015/2/4/7966043/bill-gates-future-of-banking-and-mobile-money. [Accessed: July 5, 2019].

[9] W. Jack, and T. Surit, "The Economics of M-PESA1." Aug. 2010. [Online]. Available: http://faculty.georgetown.edu/wgj/papers/Jack_Suri-Economics-of-M-PESA.pdf.

[10] K. McKemey, N. Scott, D. Souter, T. Afullo, R. Kibombo, and O. Sakyi-Dawson, *Innovative Demand Models for Telecommunications Services*, Final Technical Report Contract Number R8069, Department for International Development (DFID), 2003.

[11] Experience M-Pesa, [Online]. Available: https://www.safaricom.co.ke/personal/m-pesa/getting-started/experience-m-pesa. [Accessed: Jan 29, 2021].

[12] "M-Pesa now ventures abroad to tap into diaspora cash," The East African / Business, Oct 17, 2009, [Online]. Available: https://www.theeastafrican.co.ke/tea/business/m-pesa-now-

ventures-abroad-to-tap-into-diaspora-cash--1296538. [Accessed: Feb 10, 2021].

[13] Online Fintech Definition, Fintech Weekly [Online]. Available: https://www.fintechweekly.com/fintech-definition. [Accessed: July 5, 2019].

[14] EY FinTech Adoption Index 2017: The rapid emergence of FinTech. [Online]. Available: https://www.ey.com/Publication/vwLUAssets/ey-fintech-adoption-index-2017/$FILE/ey-fintech-adoption-index-2017.pdf.

[15] S. Hurst, "Credit Data Giant Experian to Purchase UK Fintech Startup ClearScore For £275 Million," *CrowdFund Insider*. March 15, 2018. [Online]. Available: https://www.crowdfundinsider.com/2018/03/130224-credit-data-giant-experian-purchase-uk-fintech-startup-clearscore-275-million/.

[16] C. Salazar, "NYC Taxis Through the Years: From Horse-Drawn Cabs to Hybrids and Beyond," amnewyork. June 29, 2016. [Online]. Available: https://www.amny.com/transit/nyc-taxis-through-the-years-from-horse-drawn-cabs-to-hybrids-and-beyond-1.10037203. [Accessed: April 4, 2019].

[17] A Legacy of Innovation: Timeline of Motorola History since 1928. [Online]. Available: https://www.motorolasolutions.com/en_us/about/company-overview/history/timeline.html.

[18] D. Blystone, "The Story of Uber," *Investopedia*. June 25, 2019. [Online]. Available: https://www.investopedia.com/articles/personal-finance/111015/story-uber.asp. [Accessed: July 5, 2019].

[19] Winnie Hu, Taxi Medallions, Once a Safe Investment, Now Drag Owners Into Debt, The New York Times, Sept 10, 2017,

https://www.nytimes.com/2017/09/10/nyregion/new-york-taxi-medallions-uber.html?.?mc=aud_dev&ad-keywords=auddevgate&gclid=CjwKCAjwgviIBhBkEiwA10D2jwMJyGMnVC_954-bF2mJS_mNoXFPsyeRkPp7z--mmwANlPqyY4oWaRoC3HAQAvD_BwE&gclsrc=aw.ds.

[20] C.M. Christensen, M.E. Raynor, and R. McDonald, "What Is Disruptive Innovation?" *Harvard Business Review*, Dec. 2015.

[21] H. Bhasin, "Top 7 Uber Competitors," Jan. 24, 2019. [Online]. Available: https://www.marketing91.com/uber-competitors/.

[22] J.A. Schumpeter, Capitalism, Socialism and Democracy. London: Routledge, 1942], pp. 82–83.

[23] G. Eckhardt and F. Bardhi, "The Sharing Economy Isn't About Sharing at All," *Harvard Business Review*, Jan. 28, 2015.

[24] B. Matofska, "What Is the Sharing Economy?" [Online]. Available: https://www.benitamatofska.com/what-is-the-sharing-economy. [Accessed: Aug. 30, 2019].

Chapter 12: References

[1] *Bell Labs Today: The State of US Telecom Industry R&D*. [Online]. Available: http://www.marcus-spectrum.com/Blog/files/BTLshrinkage114.html. [Accessed: Apr. 5, 2019].

[2] M. Bellis, "History of the Fax Machine." *ThoughtCo*, Aug. 28, 2020, [Online]. Available: https://www.thoughtco.com/history-of-the-fax-machine-1991379.

[3] Gertner Jon, Like Building Refrigerators: Bell Labs and the End of Game-Changing Innovation, Time, March 27, 2012. https://business.time.com/2012/03/27/like-building-refrigerators-bell-labs-and-the-end-of-game-changing-innovation/. [Accessed Aug 19, 2021].

[4] P.F. Drucker, *Innovation and Entrepreneurship, Practice and Principles*. New York: HarperCollins Publishers Inc., 1985, p. 149.

[5] P.F. Drucker, *The Atlantic, Beyond the Information Revolution*. Oct. 1999 Issue. [Online]. Available: https://www.theatlantic.com/magazine/archive/1999/10/beyond-the-information-revolution/304658/. [Accessed: Apr. 13, 2020].

[6] L. Buchanan, "The Wisdom of Peter Drucker from A to Z," Editor-at-Large, *Inc. Magazine*, Nov. 19, 2009. [Online]. Available: https://www.inc.com/articles/2009/11/drucker.html. [Accessed: Apr. 13, 2020].

[7] E. Ivanov On Steve Jobs, Henry Ford, and Faster Horses, Innovation Observer. [Online]. Available: https://innovationobserver.com/2020/03/06/on-steve-jobs-henry-ford-and-fast-horses/. [Accessed Jan 30, 2021].

[8] S. Denning, "Why the World's Dumbest Idea Is (Finally) Dying," *Forbes*, June 17, 2014.

[9] R. L. Martin R. The Age of Customer Capitalism, Harvard Business Review, January–February 2010 Issue. [Online]. Available: https://hbr.org/2010/01/the-age-of-customer-capitalism. [Accessed: April 2020].

[10] T.J. Stiles, *The First Tycoon: The Epic Life of Cornelius Vanderbilt*. New York: Vintage Books, 2010.

[11] J. Trout, "Peter Drucker on Marketing," *Forbes*, July 3, 2006.

[12] A.E. Ingram, M.W. Lewis, S. Barton, and W.B. Gartner, "Paradoxes and Innovation in Family Firms: The Role of Paradoxical Thinking," *Entrepreneurship: Theory and Practice,* Vol. 40, No. 1, pp. 161-176, 2006.

[13] D. Boyd, "A Structured, Facilitated Team Approach to Innovation," *Organization Development Journal*, Vol. 25, No. 3, p. 119+, Fall 2007.

[14] C.B. Rabe, *The Innovation Killer: How What We Know Limits What We Can Imagine—And What Smart Companies Are Doing About It*. New York: American Management Association, 2006, p. 87.

[15] R.I. Sutton, *Weird Ideas That Work*. New York: Free Press, 2007, p. 147.

[16] S.T. Coleridge, *Rime of the Ancient Mariner in Lyrical Ballads*, 1st ed. London: J. & A. Arch, 1798.

[17] B. Gates, *Have You Hugged a Concrete Pillar Today?* June 12, 2014. [Online]. Available: http://www.gatesnotes.com/Books/Making-the-Modern-World. [Accessed: July 8, 2019].

[18] L. Van Dyne, and R. Saavedra, "A Naturalistic Minority Influence Experiment: Effects on Divergent Thinking, Conflict and Originality in Work-Groups," *British Journal of Social Psychology*, Vol. 35, pp. 151–167, 1996.

[19] D.H. Gruenfeld, "Status, Ideology, and Integrative Complexity on the U.S. Supreme Court: Rethinking the Politics of Political Decision Making," *Journal of Personality and Social Psychology*, Vol. 68, pp. 5–20, 1995.

[20] C.K.W. De Dreu, and M.A. West, "Minority Dissent and Team Innovation: The Importance of Participation in Decision Making," *Journal of Applied Psychology*, Vol. 86, pp. 1191–1201, 2001.

[21] C.J. Nemeth, “Differential Contributions of Majority and Minority Influence,” *Psychological Review,* Vol. 93, pp. 23–32, 1986.

[22] P.B. Paulus, and B.A. Nijstad, Eds., *Group Creativity: Innovation through Collaboration*, New York: Oxford University Press, 2003, p. 35.

[23] J. Gertner, *The Idea Factory: Bell Labs and the Great Age of American Innovation*, Reprint edition. New York: Penguin Books, March 15, 2012, pp. 80–81.

[24] J. Hirshberg, *The Creative Priority: Putting Innovation to Work in Your Business*, New York: Harper Business, 1998, p. 19.

[25] J. Hirshberg, *The Creative Priority: Putting Innovation to Work in Your Business*, New York: Harper Business, 1998, p. 15.

[26] F. Johansson, *The Medici Effect*. Boston: Harvard Business School Press, 2004.

[27] P.B. Paulus, and B.A. Nijstad, Eds., *Group Creativity: Innovation through Collaboration*. New York: Oxford University Press, 2003, p. 35.

[28] M. Kenney, and R. Florida, *Beyond Mass Production: The Japanese System and Its Transfer to the U.S.* New York: Oxford University Press, 1993, p. 4.

[29] I.L. Janis, *Groupthink: Psychological Studies of Policy Decisions and Fiascoes*, 2nd ed. Boston: Houghton Mifflin, 1982.

[30] D.A. Statt, *Using Psychology in Management Training: The Psychological Foundations of Management Skills*. London: Routledge, 2000, p. 108.

[31] *Bay of Pigs Invasion*, History.com Editors. [Online]. Available: https://www.history.com/topics/cold-war/bay-of-pigs-invasion. [Accessed: Apr. 22, 2019].

[32] The Imagineers with Melody Malmberg, *Imagineering: A Behind the Dreams Look At Making More Magic Real*, A Welcome Book, Disney Editions, 2010, p. 180.

[33] G. Berns, *Iconoclast: A Neuroscientist Reveals How to Think Differently*. Boston: Harvard Business School Publishing Corporation, 2008, p. 157.

Chapter 13: References

[1] "Serendipity." *Merriam-Webster.com Dictionary*, Merriam-Webster, https://www.merriam-webster.com/dictionary/serendipity. [Accessed: 1 Feb. 2021].

[2] T.G. Remer, Ed., *Serendipity and the Three Princes of Serendip; From the Peregrinaggio of 1557*. Norman: University of Oklahoma Press, 1965.

[3] de Saint-Victor, Niepce, "Mémoire sur une nouvelle action de la lumière (On a New Action of Light)," *Comptes Rendus*, Vol. 45, pp. 811–815, 1857.

[4] A. Lim, *Henri Becquerel and the Serendipitous Discovery of Radioactivity*. Dec. 3, 2018 [Online]. Available: https://www.thoughtco.com/henri-becquerel-radioactivity-4570960. [Accessed: Mar. 11, 2019].

[5] APS News, This Month in Physics History, November 8, 1895: Roentgen's Discovery of X-Rays, APS News, Vol. 10, No. 10, Nov. 2001. [Online]. Available: https://www.aps.org/publications/apsnews/200111/upload/nov01.pdf. [Accessed: May 1, 2019].

[6] T.L. Walden, Jr., "The First Radiation Accident in America: A Centennial Account of the X-ray Photograph Made in 1890," Radiology, Vol. 181, No. 3, pp. 635–639, 1991.

[7] E.A. Poe, "The Philosophy of Composition," *Graham's Magazine*, Vol. XXVIII, No. 4, pp. 163–167, April 1846.

Chapter 14: References

[1] R.P. Feynman, *The Pleasure of Finding Things Out: The Best Short Works of Richard P. Feynman*. Cambridge MA: Perseus Publishing, 2000, p. 3.

[2] T. Pipes, *Learning from the Feynman Technique*, July 21, 2017. [Online]. Available: https://medium.com/taking-note/learning-from-the-feynman-technique-5373014ad230. [Accessed: Nov 7, 2019].

[3] "Atoms in Motion," *The Feynman Lectures on Physics*, Vol. I, Chapter 1. [Online]. Available: http://www.feynmanlectures.caltech.edu/I_01.html. [Accessed: July 10, 2019].

[4] J. Mehra, *The Beat of a Different Drum: The Life and Science of Richard Feynman*. Oxford: Clarendon Press, 1994, p. 270.

[5] A. Semmelweis, *The Etiology, Concept, and Prophylaxis of Childbed Fever*, Translated by K. Codell Carter. Madison: The University of Wisconsin Press, 1983.

[6] P. Coy, *Science Advances One Funeral at a Time. The Latest Nobel Proves It*, Bloomberg Businessweek. Oct. 10, 2017. [Online]. Available: https://www.bloomberg.com/news/articles/2017-10-10/science-advances-one-funeral-at-a-time-the-latest-nobel-proves-it. [Accessed: July 10, 2019].

[7] D.K. Simonton, *Greatness, Who Makes History and Why.* London: The Guildford Press, 1994, p. 200.

[8] S. Crotty, *Ahead of the Curve: David Baltimore's Life in Science.* Berkeley, CA: University of California Press, 2001, p. 1.

[9] R.P. Feynman, *The Pleasure of Finding Things Out: The Best Short Works of Richard P. Feynman.* Cambridge, MA: Perseus Publishing, 2000, p. 187.

[10] G.B. Shaw, Goodreads, [Online]. Available: https://www.goodreads.com/quotes/536961-the-reasonable-man-adapts-himself-to-the-world-the-unreasonable. [Accessed Feb 2, 2021].

Chapter 15: References

[1] R.I. Sutton, *Weird Ideas That Work.* New York: Free Press, 2007.

[2] Y. Noguchi, *Why Borders Failed While Barnes & Noble Survived, All Things Considered,* National Public Radio, July 19, 2011.

[3] A. Lowrey, Readers Without Borders: What Killed the Big-Box Retailer? Hint: It Wasn't the Internet. July 20, 2011. [Online]. Available: https://slate.com/business/2011/07/borders-bankruptcy-done-in-by-its-own-stupidity-not-the-internet.html. [Accessed: April 13, 2020].

[4] G. Rifkin, Marvin Minsky, Pioneer in Artificial Intelligence, Dies at 88, The New York Times, Jan 26, 2016, [Online]. Available: https://www.nytimes.com/2016/01/26/business/marvin-minsky-pioneer-in-artificial-intelligence-dies-at-88.html. [Accessed Feb 10, 2021].

[5] Corrine Ruff, Deep Dive, Inside the final days of Borders' bankruptcy-and what Mike Edwards learned as its last CEO, Retail Dive, Nov 1, 2016, https://www.retaildive.com/news/borders-bankruptcy-mike-edwards-ceo/428173/. [Accessed Aug 23, 2021].

[6] M.A. Lemley The Myth of the Sole Inventor, Michigan Law Review, V110, Issue 5, pp 709- 760, 2012.

[7] T. Ricci, Biography: Jethro Tull, The American Society of Mechanical Engineers, June 25, 2012, [Online]. Available: https://www.asme.org/topics-resources/content/jethro-tull. [Accessed Feb 3, 2021].

[8] The Book of Jubilees: Chapter 11, http://www.pseudepigrapha.com/jubilees/11.htm. [Accessed July 19, 2021].

[9] J. Bendick, *Galen and the Gateway to Medicine*. Bathgate, ND: Bethlehem Books, Ignatius Press, 2002.

[10] S.P. Mattern, *Prince of Medicine: Galen in the Roman Empire*. New York: Oxford University Press, 2013.

[11] Center for Internal Change. Center for Internal Change, "DISC History." [Online]. Available: https://www.onlinediscprofile.com/what-is-disc/disc-history/. [Accessed: Mar. 19, 2019].

[12] A. Vesalio, *De humani corporis fabrica libri septem*. Basileae: per Ioannem Oporinum, 1543.

[13] W. Harvey, *On the Motion of the Heart and Blood in Animals*, Robert Willis, Trans. Amherst, NY: Prometheus Books, 1993.

[14] P. Prioreschi, "Anatomy In Medieval Islam," *Journal of the International Society for the History of Islamic Medicine*, Vol.

5, No. 10, 2006. [Online]. Available: https://www.ishim.net/ishimj/910/vol5%20No10.htm. [Accessed: July 12, 2019].

[15] D. Teresi, *The Ancient Roots of Modern Science-from the Babylonians to the Maya*. New York: Simon & Schuster Paperbacks, 2002.

[16] S., Dudzianka, *"Oblicza polskiego feminizmu* (Faces of Polish feminism)*, Deon.pl*. Zofia Nałkowska, 'Organizacja erotyzmu'," *Wiadomości Literackie,* Vol. 9, No. 25, p. 7, June 19, 1932. [Online]. Available: https://www.zmescience.com/science/flying-universities-poland/. [Accessed Mar. 11, 2019].

[17] F. Zampieri, A. Zanatta, M. Elmaghawry, , and G. Thiene, "Origin and Development of Modern Medicine at the University of Padua and the Role of the 'Serenissima' Republic of Venice," *Global Cardiology Science and Practice,* Vol. 2013, No. 2, pp. 149–162, 2013.

[18] S. Thieling, "Elena Lucrezia Cornaro Piscopia, Biographies of Women Mathematicians." [Online]. Available: https://www.agnesscott.edu/lriddle/women/piscopia.htm. [Accessed: Mar. 4, 2019].

[19] M. Akmal, M. Zulkifle, and A.H. Ansari, "Ibn Nafis—A Forgotten Genius in the Discovery of Pulmonary Blood Circulation," *Heart Views,* Vol. 11, No. 1, pp. 26-30, March-May 2010.

[20] F.J. Ragep, "Copernicus and His Islamic Predecessors: Some Historical Remarks," *History of Science,* Vol. 45, pp. 65–81, 2007.

[21] E. Masood, *Science and Islam: A History*. London: Icon Books, 2009.

[22] The Newton Project Canada, History of Science and Technology, University of King's College, Nova Scotia, "The General Scholium to Isaac Newton's Principia Mathematica." [Online]. Available: https://web.archive.org/web/20100524103006/http://www.isaacnewton.ca/gen_scholium/scholium.htm. [Accessed, July 12, 2019].

[23] G. Smith, *Isaac Newton, The Stanford Encyclopedia of Philosophy*, Edward N. Zalta, Ed., Fall 2008 Edition. [Online]. Available: https://plato.stanford.edu/archives/fall2008/entries/newton/. [Accessed July 12, 2019].

[24] K. Smith, *Descartes' Life and Works*, The Stanford Encyclopedia of Philosophy, Edward N. Zalta, Ed., Winter 2014 Edition. [Online]. Available: http://plato.stanford.edu/archives/win2014/entries/descartes-works/.

[25] J. Bennett, "Space and Subtle Matter in Descartes's Metaphysics," in R. Gennaro and C. Heunemann, Eds., *New Essays on the Rationalists.* Oxford: Oxford University Press, 1999, pp. 3–25.

[26] K. Smith, "Descartes' Life and Works," *The Stanford Encyclopedia of Philosophy* (Winter 2018 Edition), Edward N. Zalta (ed.), [Online]. Available: https://plato.stanford.edu/archives/win2018/entries/descartes-works/. [Accessed Feb 2, 2021].

[27] N. Tesla, *My Inventions and Other Writings. Part VI, The Art of Telautomatics*. New York: Penguin Books, 2011, p. 79.

Chapter 16: References

[1] K. Silverman, *Lightning Man: The Accursed Life of Samuel B. Morse*. New York: Da Capo Press, 2005.

[2] S.F.B. Morse, *Samuel F.B. Morse, His Letters and Journals—In Two Volumes*, Vol. I, Edward Lind Morse, Ed., Filiquarian Publishing, LLC/Qontro, 1914, p. 223. [Online]. Available: www.qontro.com.

[3] B. Baigrie, *Electricity and Magnetism: A Historical Perspective*. Westport, CT: Greenwood Press, 2007, pp. 7–8.

[4] J. Stewart, *Intermediate Electromagnetic Theory*. Singapore: World Scientific, 2001, p. 50.

[5] J. Mullaly, "The laying of the cable, or the ocean telegraph; being a complete and authentic narrative of the attempt to lay the cable across the entrance to the gulf of St. Lawrence in 1855, and of the three Atlantic telegraph expeditions of 1857 and 1858: with a detailed account of the mechanical and scientific part of the work, as well as biographical sketches of Messrs. Cyrus W. Field, William E. Everett, and other prominent persons connected with the enterprise," Making of America Books, pp. 34–35. [Online]. Available: https://quod.lib.umich.edu/m/moa/AGX3847.0001.001?rgn=main;view=fulltext.

[6] S.F.B. Morse, Samuel F.B. Morse, His Letters and Journals—In Two Volumes, Vol. II, Edward Lind Morse, Ed. Filiquarian Publishing, LLC/Qontro, 1914. [Online]. Available: www.qontro.com.

[7] M. Kuehn, and H. Klemme, Eds., "Samuel Thomas von Soemmerring (1755–1830), The Dictionary of Eighteenth-Century German Philosophers." *Continuum*. 2010. [Online]. Available: https://www.gproxx.com/https://users.manchester.edu/FacStaff/SSNaragon/Kant/bio/FullBio/SoemmerringST.html. [Accessed: May 5, 2012].

[8] Electrical Telegraph, Wikipedia. [Online]. Available: https://en.wikipedia.org/wiki/Electrical_telegraph. [Accessed: Apr. 13, 2020].

[9] A.P. Yuste, Universidad Politécnica de Madrid, Madrid, Spain. [Online]. Available: http://oa.upm.es/8539/2/INVE_MEM_2010_83801.pdf. [Accessed: July 18, 2019].

[10] R.H. Kargon, *Science in Victorian Manchester: Enterprise and Expertise*. Baltimore: Johns Hopkins University Press, 1977.

[11] "A-M. Ampère." Famous Scientists, Oct. 1, 2015. [Online]. Available: www.famousscientists.org/andre-marie-ampere/. [Accessed: Feb. 3, 2021].

[12] R. De Andrade Martins, "Resistance to the Discovery of Electromagnetism: Ørsted and the Symmetry of the Magnetic Field." [Online]. Available: http://ppp.unipv.it/Collana/Pages/Libri/Saggi/Volta%20and%20the%20History%20of%20Electricity/V&H%20Sect3/V&H%20245-265.pdf. [Accessed: July 18, 2019].

[13] W.K. Towers, *Masters of Space*. New York: Harper & Brothers Publishers, 1917.

[14] Benjamin Franklin, *Experiments and Observations of Electricity, Made at Philadelphia in America, by Benjamin Franklin*, and Communicated in Several Letters to Mr. P. Collinson, of London, F.R.S. London: Printed and fold by E. Cave, at St. John Gate, 1751.

[15] A letter from Mons. Du Fay, F. R. S. and of the Royal Academy of Sciences at Paris, to his Grace Charles Duke of Richmond and Lenox, concerning electricity. Translated from the French by T. S. M D, Vol 38, Issue 431, The Philosophical Transactions of the Royal Society, Dec 1733, pp. 258-266.

[16] *Letter from Mr. Benj. Franklin, in Philadelphia to Mr. Peter Collinson, F.R.S.* London: S.I. Ry, Sept. 1, 1747.

[17] N.H. de V. Heathcote, "Guericke's Sulphur Globe," *Annals of Science*, Vol. 6, pp. 293–305, 1950. [Online]. Available: https://www.tandfonline.com/doi/abs/10.1080/00033795000201981. [Accessed: July 18, 2019].

[18] M.B. Schiffer, Draw the Lightning Down: Benjamin Franklin and Electrical Technology in the Age of Enlightenment. Los Angeles, CA: University of California Press, 2003, pp. 18–19.

[19] D.H. Clark, and S.H.P. Clark, *Newton's Tyranny: The Suppressed Scientific Discoveries of Stephen Gray and John Flamsteed*, W. H. Freeman. New York: Macmillan Publishers, 2001.

[20] B. Park, *A History of Electricity (the Intellectual Rise in Electricity) from Antiquity to the Days of Benjamin Franklin.* New York: John Wiley & Sons, 1898, pp. 470–73.

[21] F. Ronalds, *Descriptions of an Electrical Telegraph, and of some other Electrical Apparatus*. London: R Hunter/Charles Wood, 1823.

[22] "Foreign Telegraphic Notes," *The Telegrapher, A Journal of Electrical Progress*, Vol. VI, No. 35, Whole No. 197, p. 279, Apr. 23, 1870.

[23] J. Henry, *Scientific Writings of Joseph Henry, Volume II, Part II, Statement in Relation to the History of the ElectroMagentic Telegraph.* Washington: The Smithsonian Institute, 1886, p. 434.

[24] H. Schellen, "Der Elektromagnetische Telegraph in den Haupstadien seiner Entwickelung und in seiner gegenwartigen Ausbildung und Anwendung, nebst einem Anhange uber den

Betrieb der elktrischen Uhren," *Ein Handbuch*, Druck und Verlag von Friedrich Vieweg und Sohn, 1867, p. 298.

[25] W.F. Cooke, *The Electric Telegraph: Was It Invented by Professor Wheatstone?* London W.H. Smith and Son, 1854.

[26] K. Silverman, *Lightening Man, The Accursed Life of Samuel F.B. Morse*. Boston: DaCapo Press, 2004.

[27] J.D. Reid, *The Telegraph in America: Its Founders, Promoters, and Noted Men.* New York: Derby Brothers, 1879. [Online]. Available: https://babel.hathitrust.org/cgi/pt?id=chi.15605299&view=1up&seq=1.

[28] Samuel F.B. Morse, His Letters and Journals in Two Volumes. Edward Lind Morse, Ed. Filiquarian Publishing, Minneapolis, Vol II, 1914 p. 39.

[29] "Early History of the Electro-Magnetic Telegraph," from *Letters and Journals of Alfred Vail*, arranged by J. Cummings Vail. New York: Hine Brothers, 1914.

[30] J.D. Reid, *The Telegraph in America, Its Founders Promoters and Noted Men*. First published in 1879, reprinted New York: Arno Press, 1974, pp. 67–68.

[31] R. Dahm, "Discovering DNA: Friedrich Miescher and the Early Years of Nucleic Acid Research," *Human Genetics*, Vol. 122, No. 6, pp. 565–581, 2008.

[32] M.E. Jones, "Albrecht Kossel, A Biographical Sketch," *Yale Journal of Biology and Medicine*, National Center for Biotechnology Information, Vol. 26, No. 1, pp. 80–97, 1953.

[33] Science History Institute "James Watson, Francis Crick, Maurice Wilkins, and Rosalind Franklin." [Online]. Available: https://www.sciencehistory.org/historical-profile/james-

watson-francis-crick-maurice-wilkins-and-rosalind-franklin. [Accessed: July 17, 2019].

[34] P. Israel Thomas Edison's Places of Invention, March 1, 2010, [Online]. Available: https://invention.si.edu/thomas-edisons-places-invention. [Accessed: Feb. 3, 2021].

[35] D.R. Headrick, *The Tentacles of Progress: Technology Transfer in the Age of Imperialism, 1850–1940.* New York: Oxford University Press, 1988, p. 98.

[36] Samuel F.B. Morse, His Letters and Journals in Two Volumes. Edward Lind Morse, Ed. Filiquarian Publishing, Minneapolis, Vol II, 1914 p. 238.

[37] Wireless Communication Reference Website, © Jean-Paul M.G. Linnartz, Ed. [Online] Available: http://www.wirelesscommunication.nl/reference/chaptr07/history.htm. [Accessed: May 3, 2019].

[38] D. Hughes, *Encyclopædia Britannica Online*, Encyclopædia Britannica Inc., 2014. [Online] Available: https://www.britannica.com/biography/David-Hughes. [Accessed: Sept. 2, 2019].

[39] T.K. Sarkar, Mailloux, Robert, and Oliner, Arthur A., History of Wireless. New York: John Wiley & Sons, 2006, pp. 260–261.

[40] M.J. Seifer, *The Life and Times of Nikola Tesla*. New York: Citadel Press and Kensington Publishing, p. 185.

[41] Marconi Wireless Tel. Co. v United States, 320 U.S. 1 (1943), Justia US Supreme Court, [Online]. Available: https://supreme.justia.com/cases/federal/us/320/1/. [Accessed: Feb 4, 2021].

[42] W.A. Atherton, "John Ambrose Fleming (1849–1945)," [Online]. Available: http://www.r-type.org/articles/art-092a.htm. [Accessed: Feb 4, 2021].

[43] A.T. Anderson, "Changes at the BBC World Service: Documenting the World Service's Move From Shortwave to Web Radio in North America, Australia, and New Zealand," *Journal of Radio Studies,* Vol. 12, No. 2, pp. 286–304, 2005.

[44] J. Careless, "The Evolution of Shortwave Radio," *Radio World*, NewBay Media. [Online]. Available: https://www.radioworld.com/news-and-business/the-evolution-of-shortwave-radio/338422. [Accessed: May 6, 2019].

Chapter 17: References

[1] I.I. Mitroff, Why Some Companies Emerge Stronger and Better from a Crisis: 7 Essential Lessons for Surviving Disaster. New York: American Management Association, 2005, p. 75.

[2] Experts Name the Top 19 Solutions to the Global Freshwater Crisis. [Online]. Available: https://www.circleofblue.org/2010/world/experts-name-the-top-19-solutions-to-the-global-freshwater-crisis/. [Accessed: July 22, 2019].

[3] E. Klinenberg, *Heat Wave: A Social Autopsy of Disaster in Chicago*. Chicago: Chicago University Press, 2002.

[4] Lean About Heat Islands, United States Environmental Protection Agency, https://www.epa.gov/heatislands/learn-about-heat-islands. [Accessed July 29, 2021].

[5] I.I. Mitroff, Why Some Companies Emerge Stronger and Better from a Crisis: 7 Essential Lessons for Surviving

Disaster. New York: American Management Association, 2005, p. 81.

[6] Junior Woodchucks, https://en.wikipedia.org/wiki/Junior_Woodchucks#Junior_Woodchucks%27_Guidebook. [Accessed Mar 2, 2021].

[7] Crowdfunding, https://en.wikipedia.org/wiki/Crowdfunding. [Accessed July 29, 2021].

[8] J. Pulitzer, "Pulitzer-in Depth." [Online]. Available: https://www.nps.gov/stli/learn/historyculture/pulitzer-in-depth.htm. [Accessed: May 7, 2019].

[9] The History of Crowdfunding. [Online]. Available: https://www.fundable.com/crowdfunding101/history-of-crowdfunding. [Accessed: May 7, 2019].

[10] V. Mather, "How the NBA 3-Point Shot Went from Gimmick to Game Changer," *New York Times*, Jan. 21, 2016.

[11] D. McCall, *Monty Python: A Chronology, 1969-2012*, 2nd ed. Jefferson, NC: McFarland, 2013, p. 18.

[12] R.J. Plunkett, "Science History Institute." [Online]. Available: https://www.sciencehistory.org/historical-profile/roy-j-plunkett. [Accessed: July 22, 2019].

[13] P. Raccuglia, K. C. Elbert, P.D.F. Adler, C. Falk, M.B. Wenny, A. Mollo, M. Zeller, S.A. Friedler, , J. Schrier, and A.J. Norquist, "Machine-Learning-Assisted Materials Discovery Using Failed Experiments," *Nature,* Vol. 533, pp. 73–76, May 5, 2016.

Chapter 18: References

[1] N. Tesla, "The Future of the Wireless Art," in Walter W. Massie and Charles R. Underhill, Eds., *Wireless Telegraphy & Telephony*. New York: D. Van Nostrand, 1908, pp. 67–72.

[2] J.B. Kennedy, "When Woman is Boss, An Interview with Nikola Tesla," *Collier's*, New York & Springfield. OH: P.F. Collier & Son Company, Jan. 30, 1926. [Online]. Available: http://www.tfcbooks.com/tesla/1926-01-30.htm. [Accessed: Feb. 18, 2021].

[3] J.J. Astor, *A Journey in Other Worlds: A Romance of the Future*, D. Appleton and Company, New York 1894, [Online]. Available: https://publicdomainreview.org/collection/a-journey-in-other-worlds-a-romance-of-the-future-1894. [Accessed: Feb. 4, 2021].

[4] M.J. Seifer, *Wizard: The Life and Times of Nikola Tesla, Biography of a Genius*. New York: Citadel Press, 1998, pp. 220–229.

[5] N. Tesla, *My Inventions and Other Writings*. New York: Penguin Classics, 2011, p. 166.

[6] A.F. Osborn, *Applied Imagination: Principles and Procedures of Creative Problem Solving*, 3rd rev. ed. New York: Charles Scribner's Sons, 1963.

[7] R.C. Litchfield, "Brainstorming Reconsidered: A Goal-Based View," *The Academy of Management Review*, Vol. 33, No. 3, pp. 649–668, 2008.

[8] "A Way to Harness Free Electric Currents Discovered by Nikola Tesla," *The World Sunday Magazine*, March 8, 1896, Twenty-First Century Books, Breckenridge, CO. [Online]. Available: http://www.tfcbooks.com/tesla/1896-03-08.htm. [Accessed: Feb. 4, 2021].

[9] A. Hargadon, *How Breakthroughs Happen: The Surprising Truth about How Companies Innovate*. Boston: Harvard Business School Publishing Corporation, 2003, p. 34.

[10] APS News, "This Month in Physics History, December 20, 1900: Nature Reports on William Dudde's Musical Arcs," *APS News*, Vol. 19, No. 11. Dec. 10, 2010. [Online]. Available: https://www.aps.org/publications/apsnews/201012/physicshistory.cfm. [Accessed: July 22, 2019].

[11] Engineering and Technology History WIKI, "Early Light Bulbs." [Online]. Available: https://ethw.org/Early_Light_Bulbs. [Accessed: July 22, 2019].

[12] NNDB, Soylent Communications, "Moses Farmer." [Online]. Available: http://www.nndb.com/people/236/000160753/. [Accessed: July 23, 2019].

[13] Light Bulb, "Joseph Wilson Swan 1878, British Inventions Discoveries Creations and Innovations, MUIB." [Online] Available: http://madeupinbritain.uk/Light_Bulb. [Accessed: July 22, 2019].

[14] Lighting a Revolution, "Lamp Inventors 1880–1940: Carbon Filament Incandescent." [Online]. Available: http://americanhistory.si.edu/lighting/bios/swan.htm. [Accessed: July 23, 2019].

[15] Britannica, The Editors of Encyclopaedia. "Joseph Swan". *Encyclopedia Britannica*, 27 Oct. 2020, [Online]. Available: https://www.britannica.com/biography/Joseph-Wilson-Swan. [Accessed: Feb. 11, 2021].

[16] G. Gooday, and S. Arapostathis, *Patently Contestable: Electrical Technologies and Inventor Identities on Trial in Britain*. Cambridge, MA: The MIT Press, 2013, Chapter 7.

[17] C.D. Wrege, "J.W. Starr: Cincinnati's Forgotten Genius," *Cincinnati Historical Society Bulletin*, Vol. 34, pp. 102–120, Summer 1976.

[18] K. Mainzer, *Thinking in Complexity: The Computational Dynamics of Matter, Mind, and Mankind*, 5th ed. New York: Springer, 2007, p. 405.

[19] R.B. Gallupe, W.H. Cooper, M-L. Grise, and L.M. Bastianutti, "Blocking Electronic Brainstorms," *Journal of Applied Psychology*, Vol. 79, No. 2, pp. 77–86, 1994.

[20] T. Chamorro-Premuzic, "Why Brainstorming Works Better Online," *Harvard Business Review*. April 2, 2015. [Online] Available: https://hbr.org/2015/04/why-brainstorming-works-better-online. [Accessed: Sept. 4, 2019].

[21] T. Gowers, "Is Massively Collaborative Mathematics Possible?" *Gowers' weblog*. [Online] Available: https://gowers.wordpress.com/2009/01/27/is-massively-collaborative-mathematics-possible/. [Accessed: Mar. 30, 2009].

[22] A.W. Hales, and R.I. Jewett, "Regularity and Positional Games," *Transactions of the American Mathematical Society*, Vol. 106, No. 2, pp. 222–229, 1963.

[23] American Chemical Society National Historic Chemical Landmarks, "Edwin Land and Polaroid Photography." [Online]. Available: http://www.acs.org/content/acs/en/education/whatischemistry/landmarks/land-instant-photography.html. [Accessed: July 23, 2019].

[24] P. Buse, *The Camera Does the Rest: How Polaroid Changed Photography*. Chicago: University of Chicago Press, May 27, 2016, p. 129.

[25] L. Ward, "Electric Vehicles." Huntington Beach, CA: Smithsonian Institution, 2019.

[26] Automostory, "First Cars in History." San Bernadino, CA: AutomoStory. [Online]. Available: http://www.automostory.com/first-electric-car.htm. [Accessed: July 23, 2019].

[27] Biography.com, "Ferdinand Porsche Biography." [Online]. Available: https://www.biography.com/people/ferdinand-porsche-9542414. [Accessed: Jan. 4, 2019].

[28] Ferdinand Porsche. [Online]. Available: https://www.automotivehalloffame.org/honoree/ferdinand-porsche/. [Accessed: July 23, 2109].

[29] S. Moore, and J.L. Simon, *It's Getting Better All the Time: 100 Greatest Trends of the Last 100 Years*. Washington, DC: Cato Institute, 2000, p. 146.

[30] V. Bush, "As We May Think: A Top U.S. Scientist Foresees a Possible Future World in Which Man-Made Machines Will Start to Think," *Atlantic Monthly*, July 1945.

Chapter 19: References

[1] M. Barney, and T. McCarty, Eds., *The New Six Sigma: A Leaders Guide to Achieving Rapid Business Improvement and Sustainable Results*. Upper Saddle River, NJ: Prentice Hall PTR, 2003.

[2] W.A. Shewhart, *Statistical Method from the Viewpoint of Quality Control*. New York: Dove Publication, 1939, p. 4.

[3] C.F. Gauss, Theoria, *Motus Corporum Coelestium in Sectionibus ConicisSolem Ambientium*. Crawley, United Kingdom: ABC Books, Lowfield Heath, 1809.

[4] J.N. Shurkin, *Broken Genius: The Rise and Fall of William Shockley, Creator of the Electronic Age.* New York: Palgrave MacMillan, 2008.

[5] M. O'Mara, *The Code: Silicon Valley and the Remaking of America.* New York: Penguin Press, 2019.

[6] L. Berlin, The Man Behind the Microchip: Robert Noyce and the Invention of Silicon Valley. New York: Oxford University Press, 2005, p. 66.

[7] California Legislative Information https://leginfo.legislature.ca.gov/faces/codes_displayText.xhtml?lawCode=BPC&division=7.&title=&part=2.&chapter=1.&article. [Accessed July 30, 2021].

[8] L. Berlin and H.Casey Jr., Robert Noyce and the Tunnel Diode: A 50 year old notebook reveals the seed of a great invention, IEEE Spectrum, May 2, 2005, https://spectrum.ieee.org/robert-noyce-and-the-tunnel-diode. [Accessed Aug13, 2021].

[9] Shockley, William, NNDB. [Online]. Available: http://www.nndb.com/people/106/000026028/. [Accessed: July 24, 2019].

Chapter 20: References

[1] S.P. Gaskin, A. Griffin, J.R. Hauser, G.M. Katz, and R.L. Klein, "Voice of the Customer." [Online]. Available: https://www.mit.edu/~hauser/Papers/Gaskin_Griffin_Hauser_et_al%20VOC%20Encyclopedia%202011.pdf. [Accessed: Jan. 5, 2019].

[2] M. Linderman, "The Story of Polaroid Inventor Edwin Land, One of Steve Jobs' Biggest Heroes," *Signal v. Noise*, Nov. 18, 2010.

[3] H. Wouk, *Aurora Dawn, Michael Wilde's Oration*. New York: Simon & Schuster, 1947, p. 144.

Chapter 21: References

[1] S.M. Smith, *The Constraining Effects of Initial Ideas*. Sept. 2003. [Online]. Available: https://pdfs.semanticscholar.org/a8ae/5213bccd4d0f1a2e2bc5853e178183c36186.pdf, [Accessed: Nov. 19, 2019].

[2] S.M. Smith, T.B. Ward, and J.S. Schumacher, "Constraining Effects of Examples in a Creative Generation Task," *M*emory & Cognition, Vol. 21, No. 6, pp. 837–845, Nov. 1993.

[3] D.G. Jansson, and S.M. Smith, "Design Fixation," Design Studies, Vol. 12, No. 1, pp. 3–11, Jan. 1991.

[4] E.G. Chrysikou, and R.W. Weisberg, "Following the Wrong Footsteps: Fixation Effects of Pictorial Examples in a Design Problem-Solving Task," *Journal of Experimental Psychology, Learning, Memory, and Cognition*, Vol. 31, No. 5, pp. 1134–1148, 2005.

[5] P. Shrestha, "Convergent Vs Divergent Thinking," *Psychestudy*. Nov. 17, 2017. [Online]. Available: https://www.psychestudy.com/cognitive/thinking/convergent-vs-divergent. [Accessed: July 29, 2019].

[6] A.F. Osborn, *Applied Imagination: Principles and Procedures of Creative Thinking*, Rev. ed. New York: Charles Scribner's Sons, 1957.

[7] W. Stroebe, and M. Diehl, "Why Groups Are Less Effective than Their Members: On Productivity Losses in Idea-Generating Groups," *European Review of Social Psychology*, Vol. 5, pp. 271–303, 1994.

[8] M. Diehl, and W. Strebe, "Productivity Loss in Brainstorming Groups: Toward the Solution of a Riddle," *Journal of Personality and Social Psychology*, Vol. 53, No. 3, pp. 497–509, 1987.

[9] J. Hirshberg, *The Creative Priority: Putting Innovation to Work in Your Business*. New York: Harper Business, 1998, p. 83.

[10] J. Jaynes, *The Origin of Consciousness in the Breakdown of the Bicameral Mind*, First Mariner Books edition, New York, 2000.

[11] A. Rothenberg, *Creativity and Madness: New Findings and Old Stereotypes*. Baltimore: Johns Hopkins University Press, 1990, p. 55.

[12] A. Rothenberg, *The Emerging Goddess: The Creative Process in Art, Science, and Other Fields*. Chicago: University of Chicago Press, 1979, p. 130.

[13] P.B. Paulus, T.S. Larey, V.L. Putman, K.L. Leggett, and E.J. Roland, "Social Influence Processes in Computer Brainstorming," *Basic and Applied Social Psychology*, Vol. I8, No. 1, pp. 3–14, 1996.

[14] J.A. Silver, and J.C. Thompson Jr., "Understanding Customer Needs: A Systematic Approach to the 'Voice of the Customer,'" *Master's Thesis*. Cambridge, MA: Sloan School of Management, MIT, 1191.

[15] A. Griffin, and J.R. Hause, "The Voice of the Customer," *Marketing Science* Vol. 12, No. 1, pp. 1–27, Winter 1993.

[16] B.A. Nijstad, M. Diehl, and W. Stroebe, "Cognitive Stimulation and Interference, in Idea-Generating Groups," in Paul B. Paulus and Bernard A. Nijstad, Eds., *Group Creativity:*

Innovation through Collaboration. New York: Oxford University Press, 2003, pp. 146–147.

[17] P.B. Paulus, and H-C.Yang, "Idea Generation in Groups: A Basis for Creativity in Organizations," Organizational Behavior and Human Decision Processes, Vol. 82, No. 1, pp. 76–87, May 2000.

[18] B.A. Niistad, W. Stroeb, and H.F.M. Lodewiikx, "Production Blocking and Idea Generation: Does Blocking Interfere with Cognitive Processes?" Journal of Experimental Social Psychology, Vol. 39, No. 6, pp. 531–548, Nov. 2003.

[19] C.D. Parks, and L.J. Sanna, *Group Performance and Interaction*. Boulder, CO: Westview Press, 1999, p. 47.

Chapter 22: References

[1] S.R. Johnson, "Making Dissent Meaningful Again," *Foreign Service Journal*, Vol. 87, p. 5, Feb. 2010.

[2] G. Anderson, *Counter-Clockwise Traffic Good for Sales*, RetailWire. Jan. 22, 2003. [Online]. Available: https://retailwire.com/discussion/counter-clockwise-traffic-good-for-sales/. [Accessed: Apr. 2020].

[3] P.F. Drucker, J. Collins, P. Kotler, J. Kouzes, J. Rodin, V.K. Rangan, and F. Hesselbein, *The Five Most Important Questions You Will Ever Ask About Your Organization*. San Francisco, CA: Leader to Leader Institute Jossey-Bass, 2008, p 4.

[4] B. Ladd, "These Tools Are Why Amazon Is Successful," *Forbes*. Aug. 27, 2018.

[5] Mirakl, Secrets of Amazon's Winning Marketplace Strategy: The Virtuous Cycle. Sept. 21, 2016. [Online]. Available:

https://www.mirakl.com/secrets-amazons-winning-marketplace-strategy/.

[6] Amazon.com, *Letter to Shareholders*. 1997. [Online]. Available: https://www.sec.gov/Archives/edgar/data/1018724/000119312516530910/d168744dex991.htm, [Accessed: July 30, 2019].

[7] N.N. Taleb, *The Black Swan: The Impact of the Highly Improbable*. New York: Random House Publishing Group, 2010.

[8] S. Caudron, "Keeping Team Conflict Alive," *Public Management*, Vol. 82, No. 2, p. 5, Feb. 2020.

Chapter 23: References

[1] D.K. Simonton, *Greatness: Who Makes History and Why*. New York: The Guilford Press, 1994, p. 92.

[2] S.I. Brown, and M.I. Walter, *The Art of Problem Posing*, 3rd ed. Mahwah, NJ: Lawrence Erlbaum Associates, 2005, p. 12 and 18.

[3] J. Nocera, *Piece of the Action: How the Middle Class Joined the Money Class*. New York: Simon and Schuster, 2013.

[4] D. Hock, *One from Many: Visa and the Rise of Chaordic Organization*. San Francisco, CA: Berrett Koehler Publishers, 2005.

[5] Annual Report 2018: Visa. [Online]. Available: https://s1.q4cdn.com/050606653/files/doc_financials/annual/2018/Visa-2018-Annual-Report-FINAL.pdf. [Accessed: Feb. 5, 2021].

Chapter 24: References

[1] Browning E.S., Most Expect Stock Turmoil to Pass, The Wall Street Journal, Feb. 2, 2014, https://www.wsj.com/articles/BL-MBB-15778. [Accessed Aug. 3, 2021].

[2] S.A. Somers, E. Nicolella, A. Hamblin, S.M. McMahon, C. Heiss, and B.W. Brockmann, "Medicaid Expansion: Considerations For States Regarding Newly Eligible Jail-Involved Individuals," Health Affairs, Vol. 33, No. 3, pp. 455–461, Mar. 2014.

[3] F.L. Wright, *Frank Lloyd Wright: An Autobiography*. San Francisco, CA: Pomegranate Communications, 2005, p. 142.

[4] L.H. Sullivan, "The Tall Office Building Artistically Considered," *Lippincott's Magazine*, Vol. 339, pp. 403–409, Mar. 1896.

[5] Lightman, *Einstein's Dreams*. New York: Warner Books Edition, 1994.

[6] Niels Bohr, [Online]. Available: https://www.goodreads.com/quotes/945437-about-describing-atomic-models-in-the-language-of-classical-physics. [Accessed: Ap. 20, 2020].

[7] W.J.J. Gordon, *Synectics: An Exciting New Method for Developing Creative Solutions to the Problems of Business, Science, the Arts, and Education*. New York: Collier Books, 1971.

[8] Albert Einstein. (n.d.). AZQuotes.com. [Online]. Available: https://www.azquotes.com/quote/1400309. [Accessed: Feb. 5, 2021].

[9] J. Geary, *I Is an Other*, New York: HarperCollins Publishers, 2011.

Chapter 25

[1] Steve Martin, *Born Standing Up: A Comic's Life* [Online]. Available: http://onlinelibrary.wiley.com/journal/10.1111/(ISSN)1467-8691/homepage/ForAuthors.html.

Index

AUTHOR BIO

Thom Nichols, MS, MBA, is a recently retired research fellow in biostatistics and heath economics for a major U.S. manufacturer of medical devices. Additionally, he held the position of adjunct professor of research methods and has been published extensively in peer-reviewed journals.

He spent a career in research; both in academics and industry. Much of this has been a rewarding pursuit of scientific knowledge and industrial application. However, by his own admission, not all has been success. There have been periods of fruitless endeavor on his part and on the part of others he witnessed—knowledgeable people well respected in their chosen professions. In this, he came to question why some efforts are successful, why some are successful but destructive, and why some fail.

In his search for quantifiable answers to these questions, more questions were generated. Why are some companies or organizations creative but fail to capitalize on creativity? Why do some companies or organizations fear innovation? Why does innovation often fail to be a commercial success? What does a successful creative and innovative organizational team look like and how is it managed? What is an innovative corporate vision?

In his search, he looked at the roots of these questions to determine not what creativity and innovation are, for these are well defined, but rather their origins within the individual, the team, the corporate environment, and historically.

www.ingramcontent.com/pod-product-compliance
Lightning Source LLC
Chambersburg PA
CBHW022110210326
41521CB00028B/181
* 9 7 8 1 9 5 6 9 3 2 0 4 1 *